Binswanger and Existential Analysis

FOUCAULT'S EARLY LECTURES AND MANUSCRIPTS

FOUCAULT'S EARLY LECTURES AND MANUSCRIPTS

ENGLISH SERIES EDITOR: BERNARD E. HARCOURT
GENERAL EDITOR: FRANÇOIS EWALD

The philosopher and social critic Michel Foucault began lecturing in the early 1950s on key topics that later gave rise to his major publications, including *The Order of Things*, *Discipline and Punish*, and *The History of Sexuality*. These early lectures and related manuscripts explore central themes ranging from sexuality, existentialism, and phenomenology to anthropology and philosophical discourse, in conversation with key interlocutors including Nietzsche, Husserl, Descartes, and Binswanger. Delivered at universities around the world—from Tunis and São Paulo to Montreal, Buffalo, Paris, Lille, and Clermont-Ferrand—these early lectures and manuscripts shed a whole new light on Foucault's lifelong critical project. Collected in this official edition, these works are presented here for the first time in English.

Sexuality: The 1964 Clermont-Ferrand and 1969 Vincennes Lectures, edited by Claude Olivier Doron, translated by Graham Burchell

MICHEL FOUCAULT

Binswanger and Existential Analysis

Edited by **ELISABETTA BASSO**

General Editor:
FRANÇOIS EWALD

English Series Editor:
BERNARD E. HARCOURT

Translated by **MARIE SATYA McDONOUGH**

Foreword by **BERNARD E. HARCOURT**

Columbia University Press   *New York*

Columbia University Press
Publishers Since 1893
New York   Chichester, West Sussex

First published in French as
Binswanger et l'analyse existentielle
© 2021 Seuil/Gallimard

English translation copyright © 2025 Columbia University Press
All rights reserved

Library of Congress Cataloging-in-Publication Data
Names: Foucault, Michel, 1926–1984 author | Basso, Elisabetta editor | McDonough, Marie Satya translator
Title: Binswanger and existential analysis / Michel Foucault, Elisabetta Basso, Marie Satya McDonough.
Other titles: Binswanger et l'analyse existentielle. English
Description: New York : Columbia University Press, [2025] | Series: Foucault's early lectures and manuscripts | First published in French as: Binswanger et l'analyse existentielle.
Identifiers: LCCN 2024051610 | ISBN 9780231195003 hardback | ISBN 9780231195010 trade paperback | ISBN 9780231551137 ebook
Subjects: LCSH: Psychoanalysis | Psychoanalysis and anthropology | Psychiatry | Binswanger, Ludwig, 1881–1966
Classification: LCC BF173 .F61355 2025 | DDC 150.19/5—dc23/eng/20250605

Cover photo: Michel Foucault giving a lecture at the University of California, Berkeley © Randolph Badler
Cover design: Chang Jae Lee

GPSR Authorized Representative: Easy Access System Europe, Mustamäe tee 50, 10621 Tallinn, Estonia, gpsr.requests@easproject.com

CONTENTS

A Preface to Experience by Bernard E. Harcourt   vii
Foreword to the French Edition by François Ewald   xlix
Rules for Editing the Text by Elisabetta Basso   li
Translator's Note by Marie Satya McDonough   liii

Binswanger and Existential Analysis

Introduction   3

Chapter 1
The Ellen West Case   45

Chapter 2
Space   83

Chapter 3
Time   103

Chapter 4
The Experience of the Other   135

Chapter 5
Existential Anthropology   169

Manuscript Context

The Research Projects of the 1950s: Between Philosophy and Psychology, by Elisabetta Basso   227

Detailed Contents   261
Index of Notions   265
Index of Names   275

A PREFACE TO EXPERIENCE

BERNARD E. HARCOURT

"An experience is something you come out of changed."
—Michel Foucault, *Remarks on Marx* (1978)

An historical account of how people said they experienced life in earlier times can transform the way readers today experience their own lives. It can unsettle how they live their present. It can change their conception of self. This may be one of Michel Foucault's most penetrating philosophical insights. It certainly is one of the most salient. Foucault developed this insight into an historical-experiential method that he used to study madness, punishment, and sexuality. By historicizing how reality was experienced, across domains, across time, Foucault challenged his readers and shifted their experience of the present and their sense of self in a process that he often referred to as "de-subjectification."[1]

In the realm of sexual practices, Foucault detailed the ways in which people claimed to experience intimacy at different historical periods—through the lens of sin and confession in early Christianity, of ethical practices of self-care in late antiquity, of a science of sexuality beginning in the nineteenth century.

By historically documenting how people experienced sexual relations at those different times, Foucault's work challenged how we approach sexuality today—the term "sexuality" itself being of recent vintage. Reading *The History of Sexuality* can shake and unsettle our own experiences of ourselves today. It can rattle our sense of self.

Similarly, reading *Discipline and Punish*—an historical account of punishment practices in France from the ancien régime to 1840—can transform the way someone experiences life in Western liberal democracies today. It can reveal disciplinary mechanisms that one had previously never felt. It can unsettle one's conception of self. This was, on one reading, the central contribution of Foucault's philosophical praxis: to destabilize his own and his readers' experience of self through close historical, archival analyses of experiences of reality. It is the work he did first in *The History of Madness*.

The seed for this historical-experiential method can be found in an early, unpublished manuscript from 1953 that we are now publishing for the first time in English under the title *Binswanger and Existential Analysis*—brilliantly edited by Elisabetta Basso, the world's leading expert on the relationship between Foucault and Binswanger and the author of *Young Foucault*, and expertly translated by Marie Satya McDonough.[2] The kernel of Foucault's unique approach can be located in his early encounter with existential psychiatry and the method of existential analysis, or what was called *Daseinsanalyse* in German. Developed by the Swiss psychiatrist Ludwig Binswanger, existential analysis drew on the phenomenological writings of Edmund Husserl and Martin Heidegger, in active conversation with Sigmund Freud. *Daseinsanalyse* represented for Foucault, at a certain period in the early 1950s, the most promising way forward for critical thought, more so than psychoanalysis or Marxism. *Daseinsanalyse* put

Foucault on the path toward a historicized philosophy of experience that would ground his later philosophical writings.

Foucault's encounter with Binswanger and *Daseinsanalyse* was one of the first steps in his intellectual journey and would shape his later work. Foucault acknowledged this in a preface he penned for the English translation of the second volume of *The History of Sexuality* at the end of his life in 1984. In reference to his final books, Foucault wrote: "To study forms of experience in this way—in their history—is an idea that originated with an earlier project, in which I made use of the methods of existential analysis in the field of psychiatry and in the domain of 'mental illness.'"[3] This manuscript documents Foucault's discovery of that formative insight and novel method.

The manuscript *Binswanger and Existential Analysis* also reveals what Foucault found lacking in existential psychiatry and where he would head next. In the manuscript—in contrast to the lengthy introduction to the French translation of Binswanger's *Dream and Existence* that he published in 1954—Foucault felt more free to criticize *Daseinsanalyse* and does so, at times, severely.[4] In the end, Foucault argues that Binswanger went astray, recreating a metaphysics or ontology around the notion of love (parallel but in opposition to Heidegger's concept of care, or *Sorge*). For Foucault, that represented a missed opportunity to better understand the notion of experience itself and the coherence of the experiences of the patient being analyzed. As Foucault would later write, in the 1984 preface mentioned earlier, his work on Binswanger left him "unsatisfied" for two related reasons: "its theoretical weakness in elaborating the notion of experience, and its ambiguous link with a psychiatric practice which it simultaneously ignored and took for granted."[5]

This dissatisfaction would push Foucault back, first, to Edmund Husserl's phenomenological approach to philosophy, and then, to the question of the anthropological turn in philosophy—as evidenced by the two sets of manuscripts and lectures Foucault wrote and delivered next, *Phénoménologie et psychologie. 1953–1954* (Phenomenology and Psychology: 1953–1954) and *La question anthropologique. Cours, 1954–1955* (The Anthropological Question in Philosophy: Lectures 1954–1955). This sequence of writings reflects Foucault's trajectory in the early 1950s: a series of attempts and failures, and ultimately disappointments, with existential psychiatry, with phenomenology, with the anthropological turn in philosophy and its demise with Nietzsche—before Foucault sharpened the historical-experiential method and deployed it publicly, for the first time, in *The History of Madness* to study, in his words, "the very historicity of forms of experience."[6]

As Foucault saw it, ultimately, phenomenological approaches to experience collapse into ontological propositions about being—in the case of Heidegger, into propositions about human caring; in the case of Binswanger, about human love. But for Foucault, drawing especially on the writings of Nietzsche, Maurice Blanchot, and Georges Bataille, the historical analysis of experience could lead rather to "the task of 'tearing' the subject from itself in such a way that it is no longer the subject as such, or that it is completely 'other' than itself so that it may arrive at its annihilation, its dissociation."[7]

This was the central task for Foucault: to trace experiences through history as a way to destabilize our conceptions of self. And it is in this manuscript, *Binswanger and Existential Analysis*, that Foucault first began to explore this challenge. At the same time, the writing of the manuscript itself served as an experience that changed Foucault, beginning a long journey toward his unique historical-experiential method of philosophical analysis. This manuscript, one could say, transformed Foucault. As Foucault reminded himself toward the end of his life, "it would probably not be worth the trouble of making books if they failed to teach the author something he hadn't known before, if they didn't lead to unforeseen places, and if they didn't disperse one toward a strange and new relation with himself. The pain and pleasure of the book is to be an experience."[8]

FOUCAULT IN THE EARLY 1950s

By the early 1950s, in his mid-twenties, the young Foucault is steeped in the writings of Hegel, Heidegger, Husserl, Marx, Nietzsche, and Freud. Other promising young philosophers in his circle, such as Tran Duc Thao or Jean-Toussaint Desanti, are using Marx to resolve problems raised by phenomenology and developing a strand of Husserlo-Marxism.[9] Foucault, on the other hand, turns instead to Husserl, Binswanger, and phenomenological methods to resolve problems raised by Marxism and to explore alternative groundings for a materialist approach that might help change society rather than just interpret its hidden meanings. Foucault turns to existential psychiatry as a possible way forward—more precisely, Foucault turns to the phenomenological writings of Heidegger and Husserl first before then turning in 1953 to the method of existential analysis, or what was known in German as *Daseinsanalyse*.[10] His turn to *Daseinsanalyse* is a novel alternative to the mysteries of psychoanalysis, but also a way to ground a materialist philosophy of reality as an alternative to Marxism. At the same time, and along a parallel track, Foucault is also immersed reading, annotating, and writing on Nietzsche.[11]

In the spring of 1953, then, Foucault gives a lecture course on the topic of Ludwig Binswanger and existential analysis. At the time, he is an assistant professor teaching psychology at the

Faculty of Letters at the University of Lille in northern France, and directs the Institute of Psychology at Lille; he is also a tutor of psychology at his alma mater, the École normale supérieure (ENS) at the rue d'Ulm in Paris.[12] The manuscript we are publishing here undoubtedly served both as his lecture notes in support of his teaching and the compilation of his thoughts and writings associated with this teaching.[13] As Elisabetta Basso notes in her remarkable course context, the manuscript represents the best existing archive and record of his public instruction on Binswanger and, more generally, on the relation between psychiatry and existential analysis.

Some English-language readers will be astonished at how psychological these materials are—as are all of Foucault's first publications, including his first monograph, *Maladie mentale et personnalité* (Mental Illness and Personality, first published in English in 2008 using Foucault's revised 1962 text *Mental Illness and Psychology*) and his lengthy introduction to the French translation of Binswanger's *Dream and Existence* (both published in 1954); and his first two published articles in 1957.[14] There are several interlocking reasons for this, and it is crucial to unpack the place of psychology in the academy in mid-twentieth-century France, especially for the reader of this English edition, and Foucault's disciplinary training and location in the French academy. Three points are of particular importance.

First, in mid-twentieth-century France, the field of psychology was still a branch of philosophy. The academic disciplines were organized differently than they are today. At the time in France—and this has changed since—psychology was not part of the social sciences as it is predominantly now in English-speaking academic institutions; it was instead a subfield of philosophy, in the same way that the study of politics in France at the time was a subfield of law, rather than understood (today, as political science) as part of the social sciences.[15] So, for example, a thinker like Maurice Merleau-Ponty, understood to be a philosopher, taught psychology. He was a professor of psychology at the University of Paris at the Sorbonne (1949–1952), before holding the chair in philosophy at the Collège de France (1952–1961).

Second, the discipline of philosophy in mid-twentieth-century France was immersed not only in phenomenology, with leading philosophers such as Jean-Paul Sartre and Maurice Merleau-Ponty developing existentialist forms of phenomenology, but also more directly in existential psychology. In 1940, three years before his philosophical tome *Being and Nothingness*, Sartre had authored a book-length treatment of the imagination in existential psychology, published in English under the titles *The Imaginary: A Phenomenological Psychology of the Imagination* and *The Psychology of the Imagination*. He also treated existential psychiatry at length in *Being and Nothingness*.[16] Merleau-Ponty taught and wrote about existential psychology, especially during his time teaching at the Sorbonne.[17] So French philosophy at mid-century was steeped not just in psychology, but more specifically in existential psychology.

Third, Foucault himself specialized in psychology during and after his student years at the ENS and considered a career in the field of psychiatry.[18] His home institution, the ENS, had a peculiarity, and still does: This august institution, at the pinnacle of French university education, did not confer a cognizable degree in any recognized discipline. Instead, it prepared college-level students for the *agrégation* (a civil service competitive examination for positions teaching in France's public educational system, leading in effect to a state teaching certificate) in disciplines such as philosophy.[19] The ENS did so primarily by means of teacher-researcher tutors in those different disciplines, called *agrégé répétiteurs* or simply *répétiteurs*, also known as *caïmans* (caymans, a crocodilian species) in student slang. Starting in 1949, Althusser was famously the *répétiteur* in philosophy at the ENS; Merleau-Ponty had been *répétiteur* in psychology at the ENS from 1947 to 1949, before being appointed professor of psychology at the Sorbonne.[20] Foucault would become *répétiteur* in psychology at the ENS in October 1951 after passing his *agrégation* in philosophy.[21]

As a result, students at the ENS tended to also, and concurrently with their studies at the ENS, take conventional diplomas at Parisian universities. Foucault did that, studying philosophy and specializing in psychology at the Sorbonne. He obtained a bachelor's degree (*licence*) from the Sorbonne in philosophy in 1948, and then another in psychology in 1949. He passed his *agrégation* in philosophy in August 1951. He then specialized further in psychology, obtaining first a diploma in psychopathology and then a diploma in experimental psychology in June 1953, both from the Institute of Psychology of Paris.

During this period, Foucault was also working in a psychiatric laboratory in a mental hospital. Starting in the fall of 1951, after passing his *agrégation*, he worked in the laboratory of Dr. Georges Verdeaux and Jacqueline Verdeaux. Their lab engaged in electroencephalography research, monitoring brain activity. The next year, in 1952, Foucault began working for Professor Jean Delay, the head of services at the Sainte-Anne psychiatric hospital in Paris. He also worked with Jacqueline Verdeaux at the electroencephalographic lab at the Fresnes Prison south of Paris.[22]

Foucault's first teaching appointments were also in psychology as an assistant professor—first at the University of Lille, from October 1952 to 1955; and then at the University of Clermont-Ferrand, from 1960 to 1966. His first publications were all in psychology. His first monograph, *Maladie mentale et personnalité*, published in 1954, is a guide to contemporary psychology for students. Shortly thereafter, Foucault published an introduction and contributed to Jacqueline Verdeaux's French translation of

Binswanger's *Traum und Existenz* (*Dream and Existence*), which served to introduce *Daseinsanalyse* to the French speaking world. A few years later, he published two articles on the history of psychology, "Psychology from 1850 to 1950" and "Scientific Research and Psychology," both written in 1952–1953 and published in 1957.[23]

Foucault's plans for his doctoral dissertation changed over time but were heavily oriented toward psychology—always with a philosophical and epistemological bent. His first idea was to study the birth of psychology among post-Cartesian philosophers, inspired by a lecture course that Merleau-Ponty taught as *répétiteur* of psychology at the ENS on the union of the soul and body in the work of Nicolas Malebranche, Maine de Biran, and Henri Bergson; at that time, he planned to dedicate his secondary complementary thesis to "Malebranche as psychologist."[24] In 1953, he indicated he had already drafted a secondary thesis on the matter of psychiatry and existential analysis.[25] The following year, Foucault indicated that he planned to write his primary doctoral dissertation on the concept of "world" in phenomenology and its importance for the human sciences, and his complementary thesis on "La psycho-physique du signal et l'interprétation statistique de la perception."[26]

There is no doubt that Foucault's early training and immersion in the fields of psychology and psychiatry—always from a philosophical and epistemological perspective—shaped him into the philosopher he would become in the following decades.

FOUCAULT'S WRITINGS ON EXISTENTIAL PSYCHIATRY

It is through Jacqueline Verdeaux that Foucault encounters Ludwig Binswanger. In March and September 1954, Foucault travels with Jacqueline Verdeaux to Switzerland to visit Binswanger and another psychiatrist, Roland Kuhn. Together, Foucault and Verdeaux work on the translation of Binswanger's 1930 *Dream and Existence*; they also observe the ancient ritual of the carnival of the mad at the Münsterlingen psychiatric hospital that Kuhn headed at the time.[27] According to Stuart Elden, "work on the translation began at the end of 1953, and was completed in February 1954, when a copy was sent to Binswanger."[28] Foucault drafted a preface to the translation, which grew to twice the length of the text, and upon Verdeaux's enthusiastic reception sent it to Binswanger himself at the end of April 1954.[29] The introduction and translation would be published shortly thereafter. As Elden notes, the book "has the publication date of 1954, but printing was delayed, and it did not actually appear until early 1955."[30]

In his lengthy introduction to Binswanger's *Dream and Existence*, Foucault sets out to demonstrate to his French readers, who had not yet been introduced to existential psychiatry, how existential analysis could represent a step forward from both psychoanalysis and phenomenology. At the time, Foucault had the deepest respect for psychoanalysis as a form of human inquiry that centered, rather than excluded, behaviors that had previously been considered deviant, such as homosexuality; he was also immersed in and taken by phenomenology—to which he would return, as we will see. But psychoanalysis had not gone far enough, he suggested. Freud merely hypothesized possible interpretations of dreams and relied on symbolic dualisms and libidinal references that, for Foucault, missed the mark. Freud was not able to tell us, more holistically, about our being. "Psychoanalysis has never succeeded in making images speak," Foucault wrote in his introduction to *Dream and Existence*.[31] Phenomenology represented a step forward. It helped to begin to better understand being, even if it too had some weaknesses. As Foucault wrote,

"Phenomenology has succeeded in making images speak; but it has given no one the possibility of understanding their language."[32] There needed to be a coming-together, an overcoming of psychoanalysis and phenomenology, in order to move understanding forward. "Phenomenology has indeed thrown light on the expressive foundation of all meanings," Foucault maintained in his introduction, "but the need to justify comprehension implies a reintegration of the moment of objective indication on which Freudian analysis had dwelt."[33]

Existential analysis, Foucault believed, offered a more promising way forward: a method of analysis that revealed something deeper about our being. Through certain features of dreams—namely, the recurring themes of upwards ascent and uplifting on the one hand, and of downward fall and descent to the ground on the other, and how these are associated with uplift and freedom versus decline, depression, even death—Binswanger had identified something important about our being-in-the-world. Writing three years after *Being and Time* (1927), in which Heidegger had formalized the notion of *Dasein* as our relationship to and in the world, Binswanger began to explore how and what our dreams may actually tell us about our being-in-the-world. He provided a method to simultaneously actualize phenomenology and concretize Freudian psychoanalysis. As Foucault concluded, "it is thanks to the writings of Binswanger that one can best grasp what the dream-subject might be."[34]

In his introduction to Binswanger's *Dream and Existence*, Foucault promised a forthcoming publication that would situate the place of existential analysis in contemporary thought: "In another work we shall try to situate existential analysis within the development of contemporary reflection on man, and try to show, by observing the inflection of phenomenology toward anthropology, what foundations have been proposed for concrete reflection on man."³⁵ Elsewhere, in an official list of works in progress published in 1953 in the *Annales de l'Université de Lille*, Foucault described a manuscript titled *Psychiatry and Existential Analysis* and said that this manuscript would constitute his complementary or secondary thesis for a doctorate in philosophy.³⁶ Foucault indicated that it had been completed and was in press at Desclée de Brouwer in 1953. That book never followed. It was not published at the time. Foucault also mentioned to Binswanger in correspondence that he intended to publish a study that would constitute a "theoretical and general introduction to *Daseinsanalyse*."³⁷ In his correspondence, Foucault mentioned that his introduction to *Dream and Existence* had only sought to "show the importance of the dream in existential analysis," but that as for the rest, he "intended to pursue it in a broader study of anthropology and ontology."³⁸

As Elisabetta Basso suggests, there is good reason to believe that the manuscript we are publishing now is the book that Foucault was referring to.³⁹ It is likely that Foucault used this manuscript for teaching purposes, but it is also a finished work composed of an introduction and five chapters. It is most probable that Foucault wrote it at the time he delivered his course on Binswanger in the spring of 1953.

FOUCAULT'S CONTEMPORANEOUS WRITINGS IN PSYCHOLOGY

To contextualize the manuscript *Binswanger and Existential Analysis*, it is important to situate the other text that Foucault was working on at the time: his first monograph, *Maladie mentale et personnalité*, published in 1954. It receives little treatment in English-language Foucault studies. The original version from

1954 was never translated into English; only the revised 1962 version was. This has resulted in some recurring misunderstandings about the book in the secondary literature. But that first book is crucial to understand Foucault's intellectual development and his writings in psychology and phenomenology.

As Daniel Defert insisted, *Maladie mentale et personnalité* was written for students, specifically intended for publication in a series of handbooks geared toward students taking their baccalaureates before entering college.[40] The series was published by the Presses universitaires de France (PUF). Louis Althusser, a mentor of Foucault's at the time, recommended to the editors that Foucault author the handbook. According to Defert, this was based on Althusser's interest in Foucault's research on Pavlov. Foucault had presented a paper on materialist psychopathology, focused on Pavlov's work, to a circle of communist students at the ENS in February 1953, at the invitation of Althusser, who wanted to edit that work.[41] It is important to recall here that Foucault, who had joined the French Communist Party (PCF) in 1951, was likely still a member in 1953.[42] As Foucault's close friend Maurice Pinguet recalled, "in 1953, he was still trying to commit his thinking to the Marxism-Leninism of good obedience, and in his first book attempted to apply Pavlov's theories to the problems of psychopathology."[43] Even after leaving the PCF, Foucault continued to search for a materialist philosophical approach, which he sometimes called "Nietzschean communism."[44]

The central theses of *Maladie mentale et personnalité* can be reduced to three key points: first, that mental states, illnesses, and pathologies, are only cognizable as such within a particular cultural and historical context;[45] second, that the principal factor in mental illness traces back to conflicts in social relations and defense mechanisms that surface in the face of those conflicts;[46] and, third, that therapeutic remedies should seek to change social relations, rather than require people to conform to them. Though presented as a student hornbook, the text upends conventional understandings and sets forth a Marxist theory of psychopathology. Foucault severs the traditional link between the study of physical and psychological medicine and stands the modern understanding of psychopathology on its head—in a similar way that Marx's new materialism stood Hegel's idealism on its head. Rather than start from an abnormal condition to understand a set of supposedly pathological traits that would constitute a mental illness, Foucault invites the reader to start from the other end: to start from the diagnosis of mental illness to identify a form of sickness that would spotlight an abnormal social condition.[47]

At the time, Foucault was searching for, in his words, a "rigorously scientific" method for mental health medicine—in the second edition published in 1962, he would redact the term "scientific," though retain the notion of rigor.[48] Foucault proposed to anchor that rigor in the principle that the root of all mental pathologies is to be found in historical reflection on the human condition. The real problems of mental health, Foucault maintained, were due to social conditions of bourgeois capitalist society.

In *Maladie mentale et personnalité*, Foucault first traces the historical development of psychology on the model of a learning process: early nosography of symptoms in the tradition of organic medicine and nineteenth-century psychiatry (chapters 1 and 2); psychoanalysis (chapter 3); and phenomenological approaches and existential analysis (chapter 4). The interiority of the experience of phenomenological psychology opens the path to a more historical approach (chapter 5). The phenomenological method thus plays an important role. It is what upends traditional psychiatry and leads in a more historical and Marxist direction. It asks the readers to place themselves in the shoes of the mentally ill person and to experience what it is like. In fact, it is Binswanger's work and his study of dreams that leads to the historical method.[49] The analysis recounts the way in which, in earlier Christian periods, the mad were thought to be "possessed" by the devil, how the eighteenth century reinterpreted madness as lack of reason, and how the nineteenth century sought to reintegrate—but at the same time effectively excluded—the mad: themes that Foucault would return to in *The History of Madness*.

The historical analysis ultimately demonstrates that madness is the product of social conflict. "The true basis of psychological regressions lies in a conflict of social structures," Foucault writes.[50] The problem is capitalist competition and exploitation—or what Foucault calls "the social relations determined by today's economy, in the forms of competition, exploitation, imperialist wars, and class struggles," and which "offer man an experience of his human environment that is constantly haunted by contradiction."[51] These are sharp words and expressions that lead Foucault ultimately to the conclusion that the real problem of mental illness stems from capitalism and alienation: "Its origin lies, in fact, in the contradiction in social relations."[52]

Foucault is searching for the "real origins" of mental illness.[53] He finds them, at the time, in the notion of "alienation"—but not the technical French concept associated with the "criminally insane"; rather the idea of self-alienation that we know so well from the Young Marx. The double meaning in French is key: "*aliénation*" means both the affirmative defense of insanity in nineteenth-century French criminal procedure and the concept of alienation that Marx would develop in his early philosophical writings in political economy, especially in his Paris manuscripts of 1844. In the conclusion to chapter 6 of *Maladie mentale et personnalité*—which he would expunge in 1962—Foucault writes that mental illness occurs when the individual can no longer master the contradictions in their social milieu and conditions of existence; in other words, when they are alienated "not in the classical sense that they have become a stranger to human nature, as nineteenth-century doctors and jurists put it, but in the sense that the patient cannot recognize themself as a human being in the conditions of existence that humans themselves have constituted."[54] The fundamental problem of mental illness, then, is the alienation that people feel in capitalist society—or as Foucault writes, in "bourgeois society," in pitch-perfect resonance with the Marx of 1844.[55] "Psychological alienation was seen as the ultimate consequence of illness, in order to avoid seeing illness for what it really is: the consequence of the social contradictions in which man has historically alienated himself," Foucault states.[56]

In *Maladie mentale et personnalité*, Foucault is in search of a materialist philosophy—in fact, he writes, he is in search of *"une analyse réellement matérialiste"* (an analysis that is truly materialist).[57] One that does not simply equate social conflict with mental illness, but finds real organic problems as a result. The therapeutic solutions then must be different: not electric shock or lobotomies, nor just psychoanalysis, but rather methods that actually change the person's relationship to their social context. "Instead of the [conventional] kinds of psychotherapies, we should prefer therapies that offer the patient concrete means of overcoming their situation of conflict, modifying their milieu, or responding in a differentiated, i.e. adapted, way to the contradictions of their living conditions," Foucault writes. "There is no healing (*guérison*) possible when we render unreal (*irréalise*) the relations between the individual and their milieu; there is only healing, in fact, that realizes new relations to the milieu."[58] Foucault's book was heavy-handedly Marxist, so much so that a full five years later, in 1959, in a book review of another work that represented in effect the first in-depth engagement with Foucault's writings, the philosopher Robert Misrahi referred to Foucault as *"un philosophe marxiste."*[59]

Foucault later repudiated the Marxism of the two final chapters of the book. He tried to prevent its republication, but unable to do so, he significantly revised the work for a new edition in 1962 under the altered title *Mental Illness and Psychology*. Foucault essentially deleted the last two chapters to erase the Marxism and replaced them with a synopsis of his just-published history of madness, *Folie et déraison*. As Foucault explained later, French Marxism in the period "was imbued with phenomenology and humanism and . . . made the theory of alienation, in a subjectivist key, into the theoretical basis for translating Marx's economic and political analyses into philosophical terms." It was Althusser who had first critiqued this reduction of Marx to alienation. "Althusser reversed this point of view," Foucault goes on. "Returning to Marx's analyses, he asked himself if they themselves manifested that conception of human nature, of the subject, of alienated man, etc., upon which rested the theoretical positions of certain Marxists. . . . We know that his answer was radically negative."[60] Ultimately Foucault's answer would be radically negative too.

English-language readers may not be familiar with the original edition of *Maladie mentale et personnalité* because it has never been translated into English. Only the revised 1962 version has, resulting in several misunderstandings in the English-language literature. Both versions have been sidelined as well in the intellectual history of Foucault in France. Neither the original nor the revised edition were included in the official edition of Foucault's complete works in the Pléiade edition published by Gallimard in 2015.

It is probable that, at the very moment that he published his first book in 1954, Foucault was already beyond it—dissatisfied with his own analysis.[61] Foucault, who had left the French Communist Party by 1953,[62] was in the process of distancing himself from Marxism, while retaining both the desire to understand reality materially and the ambition to change it. According to Defert, Foucault was already working on the concept of the world in Husserl's phenomenology as a way to get beyond Marxism, turning to phenomenology as a way to ground a materialist worldview. That was Foucault's lodestar at the time: to understand our being in the world in a way that avoids the reductionism, as he now saw it, of historical materialism. The movement from Marxism to phenomenology, and his reading of Heidegger, would ultimately lead to his encounter with Nietzsche, which would inaugurate an entirely different body of work on knowledge-power and the genealogical method, reflected in works like *Discipline and Punish* and *The History of Sexuality*—the later Foucault.

FOUCAULT'S 1953 MANUSCRIPT
BINSWANGER AND EXISTENTIAL ANALYSIS

If his introduction to *Dream and Existence* ends respectfully with questions about how to better understand expression, and *Maladie mentale et personnalité* runs aground on the essentialism of alienation, Foucault's 1953 manuscript *Binswanger and Existential Analysis* offers both a more expansive development and a critique of existential psychiatry that highlights the central place of experience to capture reality, to ground a more realistic materialism, and to anchor his philosophical method.

The manuscript is far more expansive than the introduction to *Dream and Existence*. While it includes important discussions of dreams, it is not limited to the interpretation of dreams or to Binswanger's 1930 book. It contains a full chapter on the case of Ellen West, a young woman who became one of Binswanger's most celebrated case studies. It dedicates three full chapters—in a tellingly phenomenological manner—to the concepts of spatiality, temporality, and the relationship to others, or, in other words, to the three key dimensions of reality: space, time, and interpersonal relations. And, perhaps because it remained unpublished, it contains a much sharper critique of Binswanger's approach, especially in the last sections of the manuscript.

Overall, the manuscript reflects a three-step movement: one step back to psychoanalysis, but then two steps forward to existential analysis. Foucault's starting place is Freudian psychoanalysis, as it is so often for him—a landmark that he returned to at different stages of his life. Foucault showed great admiration for the intellectual move that psychoanalysis had operated. Recall, for instance, in his early lectures on sexuality in 1964, published in this series under the title *Sexuality*, how Foucault portrayed psychoanalysis as the foundation or, in his words, the "sovereign" and the "key" to all modern social sciences.[63] Freud, Foucault maintained, had been the first to normalize "perversions" and put them in continuity with "normal" sexuality.[64] His admiration, though, was often tempered by a discerning critique that helped push forward his own thought.

That is precisely the intellectual movement in *Binswanger and Existential Analysis*: one step back to Freudian psychoanalysis and two steps forward, first to phenomenology, and then to existential psychiatry. Throughout the explorations of space, time, and relations, there is this constant three-step pattern. First, an intellectual movement back to the history of psychiatry and psychoanalysis, tied to a critique of psychoanalytic thought drawing on Husserl's phenomenological insights.[65] Then, second, a movement from Husserlian phenomenology to Heidegger's conception of being in the world. And third, the move beyond Heideggerian phenomenology to existential analysis. At each stage, there is a lack, something missing, producing the need to go beyond in order to better understand reality.

The first step is both the development and eventual rejection of a Freudian hermeneutics of suspicion. "The truth for psychoanalysis is always in essence hidden, and its effort to comprehend originates always with a worry of not being duped," Foucault writes. "But, at least in the case of a psychosis, like that of Ellen West, the truth is not of the order of the enigma: the truth is there, in its entirety, present in the sphere of expression of the sick person. Wanting to seek it in the hypothetical domain of an unexpressed, that is to be duped by the worry to not be duped: the truth of the psychosis is right there where it is expressed and nowhere else."[66]

Foucault's central critique of psychoanalysis is that it does not lead to comprehension, but only to disjointed hypotheses regarding conflicting symbolic readings.[67] The problem with psychoanalysis is precisely its constant effort to decipher hidden meaning.[68] Its method fragments the person, pulling apart their conscious from their unconscious, their outward expression from latent or libidinal drives, their instincts towards life and those toward death. Foucault spells this out powerfully and frankly, especially in a note in the margin where he traces it to a fear of being duped: Foucault proposes that in psychoanalysis, the analyst is always worried about being duped by their patient; but in existential psychiatry, the analyst is worried instead about their own self-deception.[69]

To let go of the hermeneutics of suspicion in Freud (and Marx as well), Foucault turns to a phenomenological analysis that privileges the full experience of the person and builds a therapeutic relation on that basis—on the basis of taking, at face value, the experiences of the patient. The phenomenological approach, in contrast to psychoanalysis, takes seriously the conduct and expression of the person, instead of looking beneath it to find the unconscious or hidden pulsion. The quest is to achieve a more comprehensive, coherent, and unified understanding based on the experience of the subjects themselves. It is, in terms of the experience of others, something that resembles coexistence.[70]

The move from Husserl to Heidegger is described well in a passage on spatiality.[71] There, Foucault explores the insufficiency of phenomenological description, first in Husserl's work, but then eventually in Heidegger's as well. Existential analysis provides the way forward. "It is this point the phenomenology had left in the darkness; it is this point that existential analysis gives as itself the task to elucidate."[72] That move from Heidegger's analytics to existential analysis is also described well in the chapter on relations to others.[73] In fact, Foucault suggests there that the break is so deep, and so contingent, that it is almost as if existential analysis could have had a completely independent and different origin.[74] Foucault articulates this as well in terms of a move from understanding the world through the lens of care or concern, Heidegger's "*Sorge*," to understanding it through love, as Binswanger does.[75]

Existential analysis seeks more immediately, and without internal fragmentation, to give meaning to the experience of the person. It seeks to unify the different ways of understanding the subject into one straightforward expression. It takes the patient seriously. It seeks to understand them through their own experience. Rather than looking for hidden meaning, it looks for the coherent expression of self. At the heart of existential psychiatry is the idea of a unity of existence, which means that conduct cannot be separated from what are identified as symptoms or diagnosed as sickness.[76] Rather, behaviors and symptoms—the normal and the abnormal, all of it—have to be understood in a unified way, in a way that does not moralize or judge the behaviors. Rather than interpret the conduct of the patient as reflecting an abnormal existence, the analysis must interpret them as the patient's desire to actually be different than how they are: "The sense of all of this existence, at bottom, has not been the project to be herself, but always the project to not be the self that she is: not herself in her body, nor in her sexuality, nor in her social situation, to not be *here*, in a word, in the world where she is."[77]

Notice how Foucault is flipping on its head the relation between interpretation and the world: one has to understand a person's existence through what they do not want to be, what they find oppressive—not through that being. The result is a reversal of practice: The task is not to make people conform to their oppressive reality, to accept it, but instead to understand the experience of that oppression and change it: notice here, despite the different theoretical register, the continuity from *Maladie mentale et personnalité*. Tragically, for a patient like Ellen West, she only truly found the experience that she was seeking in her suicide. "Her existence—her *Dasein*—becomes authentically herself in the act by means of which she suppresses herself . . . In her suicide, existence finds again its first light."[78]

The central task, then, is to take seriously the world that the patient lives in, not as a deteriorated world vis-à-vis a real world, but as the real world itself. Not to judge the experience of the subject, but to try to understand it fully. In contrast to more traditional psychiatry (by which Foucault is referring to nineteenth-century psychiatrists such as Eugen Bleuler), which tends to interpret the patient's worldview as a discolored or deformed perception of the real world, the task is to see the world authentically through their eyes. To experience it as they do: for *Daseinsanalyse*, "it is not a question of trying to know what alterations of the universe make him schizophrenic, but only in what universe he lives, this person who the psychiatrist designates a schizophrenic."[79]

This is what Foucault refers to as the "capital point," the most important point:[80] the idea that we must understand the person's world on their terms, in their time, in their space, and in their human milieu—thus the three chapters on space, time, and interpersonal relations. One must try to understand the world through the person's experience, not through their purported disease. One must set aside the idea of a deformed space or corrupted time—to understand the experience of a different time and a different space. One must set aside simplistic distinctions between normal and pathological.

Foucault suggests that Binswanger has a completely new way of thinking about therapeutic remedies, one that views experiences as positive developments that create openings for new ways of being, rather than thinking of them as negatives.[81] In this, Foucault identifies a new relationship between theory and practice, one that is in conversation with Max Weber's discussion of the vocation of the scientist.[82] The new orientation is toward the future, "not so much to erase the past," Foucault writes, "but rather to prepare the future."[83] Temporality is key. In fact, the distinction between the psychoanalytic practice and the existential analysis turns on a different relation to time. In psychoanalysis, Foucault suggests, the past (past trauma, for instance) becomes the present reality and as a result, the present takes on the signification of the past: it is a form of reliving the past trauma.[84] By contrast, in existential analysis, the present is oriented toward the future. Treatment is an attempt to make the patient discover—Foucault uses the term "discover" repeatedly in this context—that the past is past, so that, in the present, the patient can reorient themselves towards the future.[85] Temporality is returned to a proper order, with an opening towards the future.[86] In existential analysis, the doctor is the one who opens a possible future for the patient—or as Foucault writes, "The one who can render once again possible the impossible."[87] According to Foucault, Binswanger proposes that, by taking a different approach to the patient, and not being the subject of transference but instead being an actual person who is trying to help, the patient is able to get better because the relationship is not one in which the patient relives old traumas, but instead creates new relations and a new way of being with people.[88]

The movement from phenomenology to existential analysis aims to achieve a better understanding of reality, but it allows for better praxis as well. The deference to the experience and expressions of the sick person calls for a different relationship with the therapist. Not the Freudian relationship, with its codes and rituals of transference and libidinal attachments, nor the use of symbols, but instead a more transparent relationship of concern oriented to helping create a possible future. A doctor who is taking seriously the patient's worldview and associated feelings, without hidden meanings or trickery. The doctor in existential analysis is "a real person, who actually intervenes, who takes risks, so to speak, in the world of the patient, and who on the foundation of the elucidation of existential structures, acts according to the real possibilities of the patient."[89]

Insofar as the project is to comprehend the experience of the person and accept it as fully valid, the therapeutic direction changes. Foucault is trying to comprehend the experience of subjects in order to accept their worldview in a way that is as legitimate, authentic, and justified as possible. This certainly comes through when he discusses the homosexual desires and instincts of patients in different case studies, such as for instance with Ellen West,[90] which he discusses in such a way as to intimate, at the very least, the authenticity of those desires. Here again the point is not to convert the subject, but to recognize the feelings, desires, emotions that lead to forms of alienation. In the end, what Foucault finds in Binswanger—or projects onto him—is a desire to "quite simply restore to the sick person that which is most essentially human in their person."[91]

FOUCAULT'S CRITIQUE OF EXISTENTIAL ANALYSIS

The manuscript, however, is also more critical of existential analysis than Foucault's introduction to *Dream and Existence*. That may be due, in part, to the paradox of the preface. After all, introductions are never elegant when they criticize the text they are introducing. It may also explain why this manuscript did not move to production at the time. There is no indication that Foucault ever sent it to or discussed it with Binswanger, as he had done for the introduction. In any event, for whatever reason, Foucault more clearly identifies his points of departure from Binswanger in this manuscript and, ultimately, levels a harsh critique of Binswanger's existential analysis.[92]

Foucault's critique is that Binswanger's writings devolve into a form of essentialism about being, one that is ultimately tied to the concept of love. For Foucault, Binswanger rightfully displaces Heidegger's concept of "*Sorge*," of care or concern, but mistakenly replaces it with the concept of love. Foucault criticizes that move as a return to mythology and metaphysics. Instead, he argues for a more rigorous study of expression, of language, of experience.[93]

It is not entirely clear whether the critique undermines existential analysis or just Binswanger's version of it. In the manuscript, though, Foucault hints at the broader limits of existential analysis: it has such a radical and extreme ambition, he suggests, that it produces a tension between the ontic and the ontological.[94] This is the distinction between the concrete or physical being on the one hand, and the essence of being on the other. It arises from the fact that, in existential analysis, one must typically start with or at the level of the ontic, but then from that concrete level, one often transcends to the level of the ontological in an attempt to accede to a real comprehension of existence. Too often, existential analysis ends in an ontology, rather than a theory of experience. Years later, in 1984, Foucault would talk about his dissatisfaction with existential analysis in those terms: it was "theoretically insufficient in its elaboration of the notion of experience."[95]

The fact that Foucault did not publish this manuscript, but instead returned to Husserl's phenomenology—and then set off for Uppsala in 1955 to conduct the research that would lead to his thesis and the publication of his first major book, *The History of Madness*—reflects Foucault's philosophical praxis, discussed in my inaugural preface to this new series of lectures and manuscripts.[96] Philosophical work was, for Foucault, a timely, punctual matter that addressed a particular constellation of historico-political facts, a conjuncture, from which he would move on as soon as the philosophical method was no longer productive.

THE PRIMACY OF EXPERIENCE

In this work, Foucault elaborates a theory of experience—here, the experience of the person suffering from mental illness—that would have profound influence on his later work. Foucault takes a phenomenologically-oriented approach to human experience, interpreting it at face value, accepting it as the real experience of the person, in order to help them change their world rather than conform to it. It was an effort to take the worldview of the patient seriously, to inhabit their world and not the world of the normal by contrast to the pathological, to fully understand and comprehend what they were going through, in order to not engage in hidden transference or libidinal exploitation, but instead to develop a caring and genuine relationship oriented toward the future. This approach served to displace Freudian theories of the unconscious and its symbolic interpretation with a surface analysis of the experience of the subject. It also displaced Marxian notions of ideology and alienation with a genuine study and approach to lived experience and human life—as a new way of being materialist.

In this manuscript, Foucault experiments with an experiential method that fails in the end, but that puts Foucault on the track of experience as the key to his philosophical approach. Foucault would explain this best in relation to his own books. Books, Foucault maintained, shape the way we experience our present. They influence the way we experience the world around us. One should not speak about them in terms of truth, even for nonfiction books. Of course, the factual details can be assessed as true or false. But the import of a nonfiction book is not its truth, but the interpretation and experience it offers. Books, especially nonfiction, are interpretations of historical facts, of biographies, of experiences, of reality—and there is never just one experience of reality. There are multiple experiences, such that any book, any work of nonfiction, is creating an experience for the author and for the reader that makes them understand their present differently, experience their present differently, understand their present experiences differently. A different understanding, but also a different emotional experience, with more (or less) apprehension, fear, or optimism. What matters is not the truth of the matter asserted in the book; that is easy and can be factually checked. What matters is the interpretation of a period, or of a phenomenon, and the way it affects our present experience of the world.

For Foucault, it was the encounter with existential analysis that put him on this path to a different way of understanding experience, which was foundational to his work. His work on Binswanger may not have gotten him all the way. It eventually pushed him back to phenomenology and other sources. Nietzsche, as well as Blanchot and Bataille, offered Foucault a different way to understand experience, which would be formative to his work. One can say that existential analysis may have sent him on the path of experience and experiential analysis; but it was its failures—and more generally, the inadequacy of phenomenology—that set him on the path to Nietzsche and the genealogical method. This is why his early writings on Nietzsche in 1953 are so important.[97] But it is crucial to understand the primacy of experience and to see how it begins to develop in this manuscript and will burgeon thereafter. Experiences give a different understanding of the present. This will lead to one of his most important insights and interventions. He explained this in the context of his own experience of writing books:

> *I aim at having an experience myself—by passing through a determinate historical content—an experience of what we are today, of what is not only our past but also our present. And I invite others to share the experience. That is, an experience of our modernity that might permit us to emerge from it transformed. Which means that at the conclusion of the book we can establish new relationships with what was at issue; for instance, madness, its constitution, its history in the modern world.*[98]

A PREFACE TO EXPERIENCE   XXXV

CONTEMPORARY RESONANCES

Foucault's explorations of experience are refracted throughout many current debates in history, literature, and Black studies in the United States. Foucault's position was stark: "an experience is neither true nor false: it is always a fiction, something constructed, which exists only after it has been made, not before; it isn't something that is 'true,' but it has been a reality."[99] Foucault speaks of "this game of truth and fiction—or if you prefer, of evidence and fabrication."[100]

These ideas intersect importantly with the work of Saidiya Hartman and what she calls, in her earlier writings, "critical fabulation."[101] Foucault himself referred to his work, at times, through the framework of "fabrication" to emphasize the way in which accurate historical accounts nevertheless remain interpretations of verifiable historical facts.[102] They may be subject to fact checking and demonstration. One can always confirm or rebut the historical facts. "From this point of view," Foucault explained, "whatever I assert in my writing can be verified or refuted as in any other history book."[103] But the overarching interpretation and resulting experience is not a matter of truth. Any nonfiction book remains an interpretation, whether of a period or of a phenomenon, and what matters is whether we find it convincing and the way in which it affects our experience of the world. Foucault explained:

> *The problem of the truth of what I say is very difficult for me, and it's also the central problem. It's essentially the question which up to now I have never answered.*
>
> *In the course of my works, I utilize methods that are part of the classic repertory: demonstration, proof by means of historical documentation, quoting other texts, referral to authoritative comments, the relationship between ideas and facts, the proposal of explanatory patterns, etc. There's nothing original in that. [. . .].*

Despite that, people who read me, even those who appreciate what I do, often say to me, laughing: "but in the end you realize that the things you say are nothing but fictions!" I always reply: who ever thought he was writing anything but fiction?[104]

This resonates with Hartman's work, especially her book *Wayward Lives, Beautiful Experiments*, which explores the transformation of the lived experience of Black intimate life in New York and Philadelphia in the early twentieth century through an historical analysis that seeks to fill in the gaps of the archives.[105] The debates that *Wayward Lives* has engendered—around the relation between history and literature—are intimately related to the questions of experience that Foucault explored in this manuscript.

As well, the contemporary debate over "surface reading" and hidden meanings, and how to interpret texts, things, and practices, resonates with Foucault's manuscript. At a conference held at Columbia and New York University in 2008, two brilliant scholars assembled a group of critical thinkers to interrogate the paradigm of symptomatic reading in criticism—an approach to reading texts that focuses on the latent meanings hidden under the surface of texts, things, and practices. Born of the hermeneutics of suspicion of nineteenth-century authors like Nietzsche, Marx, and Freud, and refined by critical thinkers such as Fredric Jameson and Louis Althusser in the second half of the twentieth century, symptomatic reading cultivates a deep, penetrating form of interpretation that exposes concealed forms of domination and unearths the dark workings of ideology.

At the conference, the organizers, Stephen Best and Sharon Marcus, proposed that our times no longer call for such subtle hermeneutics. The forms of oppression that surround us today are not masked or veiled. They require little deciphering. They are right there, on the surface, for us to see if we so much as choose to look. "Eight years of the Bush regime may have hammered home the point that not all situations require the subtle ingenuity associated with symptomatic reading," Best and Marcus write. The first four years of Donald Trump and his second mandate may be the final nails in the coffin. Best and Marcus note:

> *Those of us who cut our intellectual teeth on deconstruction, ideology critique, and the hermeneutics of suspicion have often found those demystifying protocols superfluous in an era when images of torture at Abu Ghraib and elsewhere were immediately circulated on the internet; the real-time coverage of Hurricane Katrina showed in ways that required little explication the state's abandonment of its African American citizens; and many people instantly recognized as lies political statements such as "mission accomplished."*[106]

These critics explore new methods of criticism, placing them under the sign of "surface reading," where "surface" is meant to capture "what is evident, perceptible, apprehensible in texts; what is neither hidden nor hiding; what, in the geometrical sense, has length and breadth but no thickness, and therefore covers no depth."[107] They emphasize that their project is not opposed to critique, but rather seeks to breathe new life into it, to get beyond what Bruno Latour decried as the excesses of social construction and ideology critique. Their goal, in the end, is to achieve "a more complete view of reality."[108] They and others reference Michel Foucault's remark that the role of philosophy is not "to reveal what is hidden, but rather to make us see what is seen."[109]

"We find ourselves the heirs of Michel Foucault,"[110] Best and Marcus declare.

Indeed, like Best and Marcus, who pursue "the desire for a more complete view of reality,"[111] Foucault also pursued a closer connection to reality through a more genuine and surface reading of experience.

Conclusion

At the time Foucault was writing and teaching on Binswanger and *Daseinsanalyse*, he was immersed as well in reading Husserl, Heidegger, and Nietzsche, and studying the manuscripts of Husserl that had been entrusted to Merleau-Ponty and Tran Duc Thao at the ENS at the rue d'Ulm.[112] Shortly thereafter, Foucault drafts another lengthy manuscript on Husserl's phenomenology titled *Phenomenology and Psychology*, dated 1953–1954. The manuscript burgeoned in just two months, and in it, Foucault returns to the source, from *Daseinsanalyse* back to Husserl's phenomenological philosophy—the manuscript has now been published in French under the editorial direction of Philippe Sabot.[113] Foucault was also simultaneously drafting manuscripts on Nietzsche, which have also now been published in French.[114] Those experiences would push Foucault forward, again in a three step movement: one step back to Husserl's phenomenology, but then two steps forward to Heidegger and then to Nietzsche and a new genealogical method. As he explained in 1983, "I was divided between existential psychology and phenomenology, and my research was an attempt to discover the extent these could be defined in historical terms. That's when I discovered that the subject would have to be defined in other terms than Marxism or phenomenology."[115]

*

Note: Special thanks to Elisabetta Basso, Stuart Elden, Daniele Lorenzini, and Leonhard Riep for comments on an earlier version of this preface.

NOTES

1. Michel Foucault, *Remarks on Marx: Conversations with Duccio Trombadori*, trans. R. James Goldstein and James Cascaito (Semiotext(e), 1991), 32–34.
2. Michel Foucault, *Binswanger et l'analyse existentielle*, ed. Elisabetta Basso (EHESS/Gallimard/Seuil, 2021); Elisabetta Basso, *Young Foucault: The Lille Manuscripts on Psychopathology, Phenomenology, and Anthropology, 1952–1955*, trans. Marie Satya McDonough (Columbia University Press, 2022).
3. Michel Foucault, "Preface to *The History of Sexuality, Volume II*," in Michel Foucault, *The Foucault Reader*, ed. Paul Rabinow (Vintage, 2010), 334.
4. Michel Foucault, "Introduction," in Ludwig Binswanger, *Le Rêve et l'existence* (Desclée de Brouwer, 1954). As Stuart Elden notes, the book was delayed and actually appeared in early 1955. Stuart Elden, "Foucault as Translator of Binswanger and von Weizsäcker," *Theory, Culture & Society* 40, nos. 1–2 (2020): 91–116, at 91.
5. Foucault, "Preface," 334.
6. Foucault, "Preface," 334.
7. Foucault, *Remarks on Marx*, 31–32.
8. Foucault, "Preface," 339.
9. "Marxism appears to us as the only conceivable solution to problems raised by phenomenology itself," Tran Duc Thao wrote in *Phenomenology and Dialectical Materialism*, published in 1951. Tran Duc Thao, *Phenomenology and Dialectical Materialism*, trans. Daniel J. Herman and Donald V. Morano, ed. Robert S. Cohen (Dordrecht, Holland: D. Reidel, 1986), xxi. Foucault read and took notes on this book by Thao; and Desanti was one of Foucault's instructors at the ENS. See Stuart Elden, *The Early Foucault* (Polity, 2021), 42, 7.
10. On this period of Foucault's intellectual journey, see Philippe Sabot, "Entre philosophie et psychologie: Foucault à Lille, 1952–1955," in *Foucault à Münsterlingen. À l'origine de l'*Histoire de la folie, ed. Jean-François Bert and Elisabetta Basso (EHESS, 2015), 103–26; Elden, *Early Foucault*.
11. Foucault's early writings on Nietzsche from the first half of the 1950s are now published, alongside his course at the Experimental University Center of Vincennes in 1969–70 and other lectures on Nietzsche, in a dedicated volume of Foucault's unpublished writings on Nietzsche titled *Nietzsche: Cours, conférences et travaux*, ed. Bernard E. Harcourt (EHESS/Gallimard/Seuil, 2024).

12. Sabot, "Entre philosophie et psychologie," 108; Daniel Defert, "Chronologie (1926–1967)," xxxv–liv, in *Michel Foucault: Oeuvres*, ed. Frédéric Gros, vol. 1 (Gallimard/Pléiade, 2015), xxxix (October 1951).

13. It is difficult to date with precision the writing of the manuscript. We can ascertain that parts of it postdate November 1952 because of certain pieces of paper used; Basso and Sabot date these sections to 1953–54, which seems right. Basso and Sabot, *Foucault à Münsterlingen*; see also Elden, *Early Foucault*, 36. Elden suggests there is good reason to believe that the manuscript was written before the translation of *Dream and Existence* was completed in 1954; he bases this on the translation of certain common terms used by Foucault in the two works. See Elden, *Early Foucault*, 39.

14. Michel Foucault, *Maladie mentale et personnalité* (Presses Universitaires de France, 1954), only published in English using Foucault's revised second edition from 1962 titled *Maladie mentale et psychologie*; see Michel Foucault, *Mental Illness and Psychology*, trans. Alan Sheridan (Harper & Row, 1976). See also Michel Foucault, "Introduction" to *Rêve et existence* by Ludwig Binswanger, trans. Françoise Dastur (Vrin, 2013); Michel Foucault, "La psychologie de 1850 à 1950" [1957] and "La recherche scientifique et la psychologie" [1957], in Foucault, *Dits et écrits*, vol. 2 (Gallimard, 1994), text 2, 120–37 and text 3, 137–58; regarding the latter two articles, see Philippe Sabot, "Situation," 365–99, in Michel Foucault, *Phénoménologie et psychologie. 1953–1954*, ed. Philippe Sabot (EHESS/Gallimard/Seuil, 2021), 366, 366n5.

15. See Elisabetta Basso, "Situation," in Foucault, *Binswanger et l'analyse existentielle*, 183.

16. Jean-Paul Sartre, *The Imaginary: A Phenomenological Psychology of the Imagination*, trans. Jonathan Webber (Routledge, 2010); Jean-Paul Sartre, *The Psychology of Imagination* (Routledge, 1972). Sartre dedicates a twenty-page section and treatment to existential psychoanalysis in *Being and Nothingness*. See Sartre, *Being and Nothingness: An Essay on Phenomenological Ontology*, trans. Hazel E. Barnes (Philosophical Library, 1956), 557–75. Concerning the young Sartre's interest in psychology, see Grégory Cormann and Gautier Dassonneville, "Traduire la *Psychopathologie générale*: Sartre avec Lagache et Aron, face à Jaspers. Une lecture du mémoire de DES de Sartre sur *L'Image dans la vie psychologique* (1927)," *Revue germanique internationale* 30 (2019): 99–129, available online at https://doi.org/10.4000/rgi.2317.

17. "Maurice Merleau-Ponty," *Stanford Encyclopedia of Philosophy*, accessed January 18, 2022, https://plato.stanford.edu/entries/merleau-ponty/.

18. There are myriad lecture notes and documents in the Fonds Foucault archive at the Bibliothèque nationale de France that reflect Foucault's early interest in psychology. In this regard, it is useful to consult Gautier Dassonneville's article about the young Foucault's notes on psychology: Dassonneville, "Devenir psychologue," Foucault's Reading Notes (Foucault fiches de lecture), accessed December 28, 2024, https://eman-archives.org/Foucault-fiches/exhibits/show/foucault-auditeur-les-ann--es-/devenir_psychologue.

19. The ENS confers a general diploma that allows its matriculating students to refer to themselves as an alumnus/alumna of the ENS (*ancien/ne élève de l'ENS*), which in itself is a great distinction and honor, but does not confer an official academic degree or title.

20. "Maurice Merleau-Ponty," *Stanford Encyclopedia of Philosophy*. "That fall, Merleau-Ponty was appointed to the post of *Maître de conférences* in Psychology at the University of Lyon, where he was promoted to the rank of Professor in the Chair of Psychology in 1948. From 1947 to 1949, he also taught supplementary courses at the École normale supérieure, where his students included the young Michel Foucault."

21. Defert, "Chronologie (1926–1967)," xxxix (October 1951).

22. Elden, *Early Foucault*, 47.

23. See Sabot, "Situation," in Foucault, *Phénoménologie et psychologie*, 366, 366n5.

24. Defert, "Chronologie (1926–1967)," xxxviii (1947) and xxxix (October 1951); Sabot, "Situation," in Foucault, *Phénoménologie et psychologie*, 367n7. Stuart Elden reports an earlier proposal, memorialized by Paul Mazon in about 1951–52, which involved the "problem of the human sciences in the post-Cartesians" and "the notion of culture in contemporary psychology." Elden, *Early Foucault*, 28.

25. In an official document filed in 1953 with the University of Lille in which Foucault was supposed to report his publications and works in progress, Foucault indicated that he had completed a book manuscript titled "Psychiatry and Existential Analysis" and that he intended it to be his complementary doctoral thesis. See Basso, "Situation," F181.

26. Sabot, "Situation," in Foucault, *Phénoménologie et psychologie*, 367n7.

27. Defert, "Chronologie (1926–1967)," xl–xli (Spring 1953).
28. Stuart Elden, "Foucault as Translator," 94.
29. Elden, "Foucault as Translator," 100–101.
30. Elden, "Foucault as Translator," 91.
31. Michel Foucault, introduction to *Dream and Existence*, by Ludwig Binswanger, ed. Keith Hoeller, trans. Forrest Williams, in *Review of Existential Psychology and Psychiatry* 19, no. 1 (1984–1985): 38.
32. Foucault, introduction to *Dream and Existence*, 42.
33. Foucault, introduction to *Dream and Existence*, 42.
34. Foucault, introduction to *Dream and Existence*, 57.
35. Foucault, introduction to *Dream and Existence*, 31.
36. Basso, "Situation," *infra* 181.
37. Correspondence from Foucault to Binswanger, April 27, 1954, in *Foucault à Münsterlingen*, 183.
38. Correspondence from Foucault to Binswanger, April 27, 1954, in *Foucault à Münsterlingen*, 183.
39. As noted by Basso, the manuscript itself does not have a title; in the folder in the archive, there is simply a note in the handwriting of Daniel Defert describing it by the title of "Binswanger et la phénoménologie."
40. Conversation with Daniel Defert, January 1, 2022.
41. Defert, "Chronologie (1926–1967)," xl (February 1953).
42. Didier Éribon, *Michel Foucault: 1926–1984* (Flammarion, 1989), 77 (Foucault was still in the PCF in April 1953); Foucault, *Remarks on Marx*, 51–53 (referring to the "doctors' plot" against Stalin, which occurred in the winter of 1952–53). Defert notes that Foucault had joined the French Communist Party in 1950, in reaction to the French war in Indochina, and suggests that he left it in October 1952 with the approval of Althusser. He had become disaffected with the party as a result of an escalating series of events, climaxing with issues of anti-Semitism and censorship. See Defert, "Chronologie (1926–1967)," xxxviii; *id.* at xl ("According to Gilbert Humbert, he leaves the Communist Party with Louis Althusser's consent. The 'doctor's plot,' a conspiracy that revealed the anti-Semitism of the U.S.S.R., in which Jewish doctors were accused of murdering Soviet leaders, crystallized Foucault's malaise within the P.C.F.").
43. Maurice Pinguet, "Les années d'apprentissage," *Le Débat* 41 (September–November 1986): 127 (my translation); Éribon, *Michel Foucault*, 71–72.

44. Michel Foucault, "Entretien avec Michel Foucault," in *Dits et écrits*, vol. 4 (Gallimard, 1994), 50.

45. Foucault, *Maladie mentale et personnalité*, 71. "La maladie n'a sa réalité et sa valeur de maladie qu'à l'intérieur d'une culture qui la reconnaît comme telle."

46. Foucault, *Maladie mentale*, 108.

47. Foucault, *Maladie mentale*, 103.

48. Foucault, *Maladie mentale*, 2. As Stuart Elden details, this notion of "rigorously scientific" is later edited to read "a new rigor" in the 1962 edition of *Maladie mentale et psychologie*. See Elden, "The Changes Between *Maladie mentale et personnalité* (1954) and *Maladie mentale et psychologie* (1962)," Progressive Geographies, accessed December 30, 2024, https://progressivegeographies.com/resources/foucault-resources/the-changes-between-maladie-mentale-et-personnalite-1954-and-maladie-mentale-et-psychologie-1962/. See also James Bernauer, *Michel Foucault's Force of Flight: Towards an Ethics for Thought* (Prometheus, 1992).

49. Right after discussing Binswanger and the Ellen West case, Foucault writes: "One might be tempted to reduce these analyses to historical analyses, and wonder whether what we call the patient's universe is not merely an arbitrary cross section of their history, or, at the very least, the ultimate state in which their becoming culminates." Foucault, *Maladie mentale*, 67 (my translation).

50. Foucault, *Maladie mentale*, 86.

51. Foucault, *Maladie mentale*, 86–87.

52. Foucault, *Maladie mentale*, 86–87.

53. Foucault, *Maladie mentale*, 89.

54. Foucault, *Maladie mentale*, 102.

55. Foucault, *Maladie mentale*, 104; Karl Marx, *Economic and Philosophical Manuscripts of 1844*, in Karl Marx and Frederick Engels, *Collected Works*, vol. 3 (Marx and Engels 1843–1844), trans. Martin Milligan (International Publishers, 1975).

56. Foucault, *Maladie mentale*, 104.

57. Foucault, *Maladie mentale*, 107. Roland Caillois would specifically object on this point, in his book review of Foucault's work. See Roland Callois, "Michel Foucault, *Maladie mentale et personnalité*," *Critique* 11 (93): 189–90, at 190: "The word materialism is over the top, but that does not

take away from this excellent exposé any of its scientific qualities" (my translation).

58. Foucault, *Maladie mentale*, 109 (my translation). Foucault drops an important footnote here where he develops the point more concretely: "The practical consequences of these ideas are to be found in a structural reform of medical care and psychiatric hospitals. It is a reform of this kind that some doctors are calling for and have already initiated by setting forth their ideas in a remarkable issue of *Esprit* devoted to psychiatry (December 1952)." *Id.* at 109n1; *Esprit* 197, no. 12 (1952): 777–1016. You can read that volume here: https://esprit.presse.fr/tous-les-numeros/misere-de-la-psychiatrie/45.

59. Robert Misrahi, "Le rêve et l'existence: Selon M. Binswanger," *Revue de Métaphysique et de Morale* 64, no. 1 (January–March 1959): 96–106, at 106; for a discussion of the Misrahi review, see Stuart Elden, "Foucault as Translator," 101.

60. Foucault, *Remarks on Marx*, 57–58.

61. Conversation with Daniel Defert, January 1, 2022.

62. See Éribon, *Michel Foucault (1926–1984)*, 77; and note 42 *supra*.

63. Michel Foucault, "Sexuality," in *Sexuality: The 1964 Clermont-Ferrand and 1969 Vincennes Lectures*, ed. Claude-Olivier Doron, trans. Graham Burchell (Columbia University Press, 2021), 16, 31, 43n5.

64. Foucault, "Sexuality," 89–90.

65. The turn to phenomenology in the early 1950s was also influenced by Foucault's work on Hegelian phenomenology, which he completed for his master's degree (*diplôme d'études supérieures*, or DES) in 1949. See Michel Foucault, *La Constitution d'un transcendantal historique dans la* Phénoménologie de l'esprit *de Hegel. Mémoire du diplôme d'études supérieures de philosophie*, ed. Christophe Bouton (Paris: Vrin, 2024); see, generally, Elden, *Early Foucault*, 12–17; Pierre Macherey, "Did Foucault Find a 'Way Out' of Hegel?," *Theory, Culture & Society* 40, nos. 1–2 (2023): 19–36.

66. Foucault, *Binswanger et l'analyse existentielle*, 56.

67. Foucault, *Binswanger*, 54.

68. See, for instance, Foucault's discussion of the case of Lina and the contrast between the psychoanalytic interpretation on page 158 and the existential analysis on page 160.

69. Foucault, *Binswanger*, 56 note a.

70. Foucault, *Binswanger*, 115.

71. Foucault, *Binswanger*, 72.
72. Foucault, *Binswanger*, 72.
73. Foucault, *Binswanger*, 112.
74. Foucault, *Binswanger*, 112.
75. Foucault, *Binswanger*, 133.
76. See generally Foucault, *Binswanger*, 61.
77. Foucault, *Binswanger*, 63.
78. Foucault, *Binswanger*, 63.
79. Foucault, *Binswanger*, 64.
80. Foucault, *Binswanger*, 65.
81. As Stuart Elden reminds us, Binswanger's friend, colleague and promoter, Dr. Roland Kuhn, "underscores that 'Binswanger insisted many times on the fact that *Daseinsanalysis* was above all a method of scientific research and not a method for psychotherapeutic practice.'" Elden, "Foucault as Translator," 93. Despite that, there is a therapeutic dimension to existential analysis, and Foucault spends a considerable amount of time discussing the doctor-patient relationship.
82. Foucault, *Binswanger*, 147.
83. Foucault, *Binswanger*, 149.
84. Foucault, *Binswanger*, 158–59.
85. Foucault, *Binswanger*, 161.
86. Foucault, *Binswanger*, 162. Keith Hoeller, in his preface to Foucault's introduction to *Dream and Existence*, identifies a central unresolved tension in that text, a tension between being and time. Hoeller highlights passages in Foucault's introduction in which he seems to write about being in a somewhat timeless manner—even though, of course, he and everyone else understood the reference to Heidegger's book. Hoeller identifies passages where, writing about Binswanger, Foucault seems to essentialize being and detemporalize it; he suggests that Foucault had Husserl's phenomenology more in mind than Binswanger's work. To be sure, Foucault was focused on Husserl's concept of the world at the time, planned to write his doctoral thesis about it, and did in fact focus on Husserl in his other manuscript *Phenomenology and Psychology*; but this problem does not arise in this manuscript, *Binswanger and Existential Analysis*, which is acutely focused on the question of temporality, with a whole chapter dedicated to it.
87. Foucault, *Binswanger*, 163.

88. Foucault, *Binswanger*, 163.

89. Foucault, *Binswanger*, 164.

90. Foucault, *Binswanger*, 57.

91. Foucault, *Binswanger*, 142.

92. See Foucault, *Binswanger*, 167 and Basso, "Situation," 197; see also Elden, *Early Foucault*, 39.

93. In this sense, Foucault's rejection of the ontological drift in both Heidegger and Binswanger brings him closer to Jean-Paul Sartre's existentialism than is generally recognized. The concept of de-subjectification as the horizon of experience resembles a change in existence rather than essence; the emphasis on experience is close to the Sartrian insistence on being situated (*en situation*). This goes against the grain of most readings of Foucault, which tend to disregard Sartre and his existential phenomenology. Foucault scholars prefer to underscore the way in which Foucault's encounter with Heidegger was formative, especially insofar as it led him to Nietzsche. But what he draws from Nietzsche, importantly, is the notion of "becoming" and "de-subjectification," which depend on a philosophical substratum of existentialism rather than ontology. Foucault always presented as far more of kindred spirit with Heidegger and treated Sartre as an adversary. But that may have been an artifact of Sartre's towering presence in French philosophy at the time. As Althusser notes in his autobiography, philosophical life at the ENS at that time consisted primarily of showing contempt and scorn for Sartre: "la vie philosophique à l'École n'était pas particulièrement intense; la mode était d'affecter de mépriser Sartre." Louis Althusser, *L'avenir dure longtemps* (Stock, 1992), 184. It is almost a pity that Sartre was such a towering figure at the time of Foucault's intellectual development and had to be treated as the foil. For if one thickens the concept of experience with Foucault's own theories of epistemes, knowledge-power, and regimes of truth, the moment of de-subjectification represents precisely a moment of letting go of one's essence, of "*se déprendre de soi*," of self-transformation, that is only possible if our existence precedes our essence.

94. Foucault, *Binswanger*, 65.

95. Basso, "Situation," 203.

96. Bernard E. Harcourt, "A Preface to Philosophical Praxis," in *Sexuality*, ed. Claude-Olivier Doron, trans. Graham Burchell (Columbia University Press, 2021).

97. See, generally, Foucault, *Nietzsche*.

98. Foucault, *Remarks on Marx*, 32–34.

99. Foucault, *Remarks on Marx*, 36.

100. Foucault, *Remarks on Marx*, 37.

101. Saidiya Hartman, "Venus in Two Acts," *Small Axe* 12, no. 2 (June 2008): 1–14.

102. Michel Foucault, *Power/Knowledge*, ed. Colin Gordon (Harvester Press; Random House, 1980), 212.

103. Foucault, *Remarks on Marx*, 33.

104. Foucault, *Remarks on Marx*, 32–33.

105. Saidiya Hartman, *Wayward Lives, Beautiful Experiments: Intimate Histories of Riotous Black Girls, Troublesome Women, and Queer Radicals* (W. W. Norton, 2019).

106. Stephen Best and Sharon Marcus, "Surface Reading: An Introduction," *Representations* 108, no. 1 (Fall 2009): 2.

107. Best and Marcus, "Surface Reading," 9.

108. Best and Marcus, "Surface Reading," 19.

109. Sharon Marcus, Heather Love, and Stephen Best, "Building a Better Description," in "Description Across Disciplines," special issue, *Representations* 135 (Summer 2016): 3. This is citing Anne Orford, "In Praise of Description," *Leiden Journal of International Law* 25, no. 3 (2012): 609.

110. Best and Marcus, "Surface Reading," 2.

111. Best and Marcus, "Surface Reading," 19.

112. Daniel Defert, "Chronologie," 13–64, in Foucault, *Dits et écrits*, vol. 1, *1954–1969* (Gallimard, 1994), 18–19.

113. Foucault, *Phénoménologie et psychologie*.

114. Foucault, *Nietzsche*.

115. Michel Foucault, *Death and the Labyrinth: The World of Raymond Roussel*, trans. Charles Ruas (Doubleday, 1986), 176–77.

FOREWORD TO THE FRENCH EDITION

FRANÇOIS EWALD

From 1952 to 1969, when he was nominated to the chair of the History of Systems of Thought at the Collège de France, Michel Foucault taught in several universities and institutions: psychology at the École normale supérieure (from 1951), Lille (1952–1955), and Clermont-Ferrand (1960–1966); and then philosophy at Tunis (1966–1968) and Vincennes (1968–1970). In addition, in October 1965 he lectured at the University of São Paulo on the subject that is addressed in *The Order of Things: An Archaeology of the Human Sciences* (1966).

Foucault kept only some of the manuscripts of the lectures he delivered during this period. These are deposited in the Foucault collection of the Bibliothèque nationale de France (under NAF 28730). In the same boxes in which the lectures are kept, there are also some texts from the same period, some of which are highly developed. We thought it useful to include them in the volumes that make up this series of "lectures and manuscripts" from the period prior to Foucault's election to the Collège de France.

The volumes are edited according to the following rules:
– The text is based on the manuscripts deposited in the Bibliothèque nationale de France. The transcriptions are as faithful as possible to the manuscripts and have been subject to collective

review within the editorial team. The difficulties that the reading of some words gives rise to are indicated in footnotes. Only minor modifications have been made (the correction of obvious errors, punctuation, and layout) in order to assist the reading and clear understanding of the text. They are always indicated.

– Quotations have been checked, and references to the texts used are indicated. The text is accompanied by a critical apparatus that seeks to elucidate obscure points and clarify critical points.

– To make the text easier to read, each lecture is preceded by a brief summary that indicates its principal articulations.

– As with the editions of the Collège de France lectures, each volume ends with a "context" for which the editor is responsible: it seeks to provide readers with elements of the context needed for them to understand the texts and situate them in Foucault's published work.

The members of the editorial committee responsible for the project are Elisabetta Basso, Daniel Defert, Claude-Olivier Doron, François Ewald, Henri-Paul Fruchaud, Frédéric Gros, Bernard E. Harcourt, Orazio Irrera, Daniele Lorenzini, Philippe Sabot, and Arianna Sforzini.

We would like to extend particular thanks to the Bibliothèque nationale de France for enabling us to consult the manuscripts on which this edition is based.

FRANÇOIS EWALD

RULES FOR EDITING THE TEXT

ELISABETTA BASSO

The manuscript of the text that is the object of the present edition is conserved at the Bibliothèque nationale de France, in the Foucault archives (Fonds Michel Foucault) under the reference NAF 28730, Box 46, folder 1, file 3. It makes up part of a series of texts (lectures, book projects, and various works) dating to the first half of the 1950s, at the time when Michel Foucault was teaching at the University of Lille (1952–1954) and the École normale supérieure.

The manuscript does not bear a title. We have given it that of *Binswanger and Existential Analysis*, which corresponds to its theme. Similarly, to make it easier to read, we have given titles to the chapters based on the indications provided by Foucault himself at the end of the introduction.

The text was edited so as to preserve the page layout and the editing of the manuscript as much as possible. Missing words were restored, problematic constructions were rectified, abbreviations were expanded, and the punctuation was completed when it seemed necessary. The passages in the manuscript that were crossed out by Foucault but that seemed significant are included in the notes. Any intervention on the manuscript not related to spelling or improved formatting is indicated in square brackets.

More broadly, any difficulty that was encountered is mentioned in a footnote. When it seemed appropriate, a critical apparatus clarifying potential obscurities and presenting the broader context was placed in the endnotes.

Foucault did not paginate the manuscript. The page numbers inserted in the margins correspond to the real pagination of the manuscript.

TRANSLATOR'S NOTE

MARIE SATYA McDONOUGH

One of the peculiarities of translating a manuscript is that, by nature of its being unpublished, it must also be seen as essentially unfinished. We cannot know what an author was satisfied with, and what they may have wanted to rework or revisit. Infelicities might be deliberate, or they might reflect thinking in progress. This creates a particular bind for a translator accustomed to rendering an author's thought, already polished and sent out into the world, in another language as elegantly as possible. For the text that we have titled *Binswanger and Existential Analysis*, what we have is Foucault's sentences, and I have translated these as faithfully as possible. Although I am certain many infelicities are mine, I have attempted to preserve Foucault's own style in its rawness—his unexpected tense shifts when he narrates clinical case studies; his very long, winding sentences—and to foreground the immediacy of his encounter with the material. Indeed, this manuscript, and others in this series, give us a glimpse not only of a critical period in Foucault's intellectual trajectory—his encounter with phenomenology and existential psychiatry—but also of his working process. Of course, the text must still be readable in English; where Foucault's sentences were particularly complex, I have occasionally altered the punctuation (for example, by inserting a period where there was a comma).

Like many European writers of this period, Foucault uses *homme*, man, where he means person, and male pronouns in reference to any nonspecific individual. Early on I experimented with inclusive terminology that more accurately renders Foucault's meaning, but I frequently found it unwieldy—introducing confusion into an already-difficult text—and anachronistic. Indeed, Elisabetta Basso's critical apparatus emphasizes the historical intellectual networks to which this text belongs: who Foucault's interlocutors were, and how he read them. I have attempted to preserve this emphasis on *Binswanger and Existential Analysis*'s historical positioning by using the language associated with this body of writing, drawing on other translations of texts by Foucault's interlocutors. Beyond these historical references, though, I have also tried to show how Foucault's manuscript is a rich repository of themes he would continue to develop: experience and truth; psychiatric power; what a meaningful life can look like.

Occasionally, attempts to flag such Foucauldian echoes were overly cumbersome: for example, Foucault uses both *conduite* and *comportement* to describe people's behaviors, especially in his discussions of clinical case studies. My initial attempts to use "behavior" only for *comportement* and "conduct" for *conduite*—in light of the significance that term would take on in Foucault's later work—proved unworkable insofar as Foucault, in the early 1950s, does seem to have meant "behavior" when he wrote *conduite* or *conduites*. However, I did distinguish between *signification*, which stayed "signification," and *sens*, which became "meaning"—or mostly so: the French word *sens* has the great virtue, for phenomenologically-informed work, of conveying both "meaning" and "direction," and Foucault makes use of this ambiguity to great effect. Unfortunately, I had to choose between these, and in each instance I opted for the word whose meaning seemed dominant. I tried to avoid weighing down the text with indications in brackets of corresponding French terms, with one exception: the French noun *visée* and its verb form, *viser*, have a particular meaning in phenomenology, where they are often translated as "meaning" and "mean," respectively (with the conceptual emphasis on the idea of intentionality). In this text, using "meaning" proved to be altogether confusing, and I chose instead to use "aim" and "aim at," indicating the French *visée*, *viser*, and other forms of the term in brackets.

I have many people to thank for their support. Elisabetta Basso patiently answered a mountain of inquiries that ranged from the broad (historical context) to the minute (pronoun referents). Bernard Harcourt offered guidance and advice, helping to adjudicate some of the trickiest translation issues as I revised the text. Trevor Pearce and Walter Hopp stepped in with philosophical expertise and reassurance at key junctures; Hortense de Villers likewise answered thorny French questions. My greatest thanks go to William Huntting Howell and Sean Desilets, who read every word of the manuscript and offered invaluable feedback on style and clarity of meaning; Hunt also kept our household and our children running as I worked on this project. This translation would be significantly worse without their help.

Binswanger and Existential Analysis

Introduction

I. *Psychoanalysis and anthropology of life: 1. The vital and lived experience* [le vital et le vécu]; *2. The return to lived experience: Freud and Husserl. II. Phenomenological psychology as an eidetic science: 1. The return to lived experience in eidetic phenomenology; 2. From the eidetics of lived experience to the genesis of constitutions. III. Phenomenological description and pathological experience: 1. "Lebenswelt"; 2. Negation and contradiction: psychopathology puts the phenomenological model in crisis. IV. The analysis of forms of existence as a radical surpassing of phenomenological analysis.*

In his pamphlet against psychoanalysis, Blondel[1] addresses a strange reproach to Freudian theory, one which is full of meaning when we consider his involuntary homage to Freud's work: he reproaches it for having taken as a point of departure, and as a privileged domain of verification, the classic syndrome of hysteria, which psychiatry, in its later history, would give itself the task of discrediting. According to Blondel, psychoanalysis gave an absolute signification to notions of trauma, of repression, of the unconscious, of symbolism, of conversion, in which it thought it could read the distinguishing mark of hysterical conduct and grasp the unity of its meaning. But by disarticulating the hysterical complex and spreading it across schizophrenic, obsessional, or hypochondriac symptoms, the progress

[1]

of psychiatric analysis rendered the psychoanalytic effort vain and compromised its generalizations forever. As if, in fact, the concept of hysteria had not burst under the pressure of Freudian analysis; as if the meaning of psychoanalysis had not been to dissipate the myth of an illness defined as an organic deficit, without a functional disorder or a lesional origin; as if psychoanalysis had not undertaken the decisive process by which the theme of a miracle illness or a simulated illness,[a] appearing at the borders "of the body and the soul" without entirely belonging either to the organic sequence or to the psychic system, was forever rejected.

By showing that hysterical forgetting had a content, that pithiatic paralysis was another manner of acting and that suggestibility was a weakening of the will only insofar as it marked at the same time an awakening of eros, Freud—and, in part, Janet—raised a problem whose solution could no longer be expected in terms of an opposition between the soul and the body. The unearthing of the meaning of a hysterical symptom made necessary a new scansion of human unity: it became necessary to move the conceptual limit that the metaphysical tradition had traced between the soul-substance and the body-substance; and at the same time, to erase the character of absolute opposition that, by definition, this limit marked. And even if its effort of conceptual renovation did not develop to this point, the direction of Freudian analyses tended toward establishing a new articulation: this cleavage allows us to distinguish and unite at the same time functional disorders (paralysis, unconsciousness, forgetfulness) and the thread of psychological events that made them possible (traumatic event, refusal of the past, negation of the real,

---

a These were one and the same thing for positivist physicians at the end of the nineteenth century.

desire to escape into illness). In other words, if hysteria is a limit-symptom, it is not insofar as this limit separates the soul and the body, but rather insofar as it highlights the articulation between all of the vital functions—the "*Lebensfunktionen*" that encompass those functions considered to be corporeal, such as motor skills or vegetative regulation, and also those functions presumed to be psychic, such as memory, associations, or consciousness—and, on the other side, all of lived history, the "*Lebensgeschichte*" in which all of the experiences whose contents form, in their cohesion, the unity of personal becoming, are collected.² To the old opposition between body and soul, we must ultimately substitute the distinction between the functional and the historical; we would like to say of the biological and of the biographical, if it were possible to restore to these terms the originary richness that the ambiguity of meaning between the *vital* [*le vital*] and *lived experience* [*le vécu*] lent to the word *bios*.

It was enough to clear away the old notion of hysteria, as a nosographical entity in the manner in which Blondel understood it; and there was already enough to assign a new meaning to all of the symptoms of conversion, all of the hysterical signs, all of the psychosomatic aspects in which the historical and the functional perpetually echo back and forth.

But it took a long time to clarify, in its purity, what this substitution implied.ᵇ

[4–5ᶜ]

---

b [The paragraph that follows was crossed out by Foucault: "Psychoanalytic speculation, Janet's psychology, or even the psychiatry inspired by Jackson remained uncomfortably mired in a naturalist anthropology that we find diffused across the evolutionism of the end of the nineteenth century. This anthropology remained halfway between the opposition between soul and body and the distinction between lived experience and the vital. It had grasped the necessity of crossing the distance that metaphysical reflection had established between soul and body, and in this way evolutionism claims to be a more elaborated form of materialism: on one hand, Jackson refuses to draw any separating line between mental activity and sensorimotor activity, accepting for man a functional unity

[4]

[6]   New significations long remained invested in a naturalist anthropology that neutralized them. Every effort to articulate functional disorders to historical significations was enmeshed in the postulate that the truth of man exhausts itself in his

[5] in which the somatic and the psychic are only abstract moments; on the other, he refused any distinction, in substance or principle, between the automatic and the voluntary forms of activity: the only distance separating them is marked by an evolutionary difference, by the less differentiated and more primitive character of the automatic reaction and the more differentiated, more complex, and also more fragile character of voluntary behavior. But if the two terms of the soul-body opposition are thereby reunited, it is only under the false and partial unity of the vital: lived experience returns as its more elaborated and later form, under the aspect of consciousness, ultimate term of evolution, subtle structure of the processes of adaptation; as a result, history and evolution become one and the same thing; genesis becomes conflated with development; and meaning, which must not be understood as lived signification, deploys itself only as a vital orientation. This forgetting of signification, of history, and of lived experience certainly plays a large role in the Freudian theory of the libido, in the hierarchy of tendencies and in the notion of psychic energy in Janet; it is the fundamental character of Jacksonism, even and especially in its "revamped" forms [Footnote: "There is reason to be surprised when certain psychiatrists, from the depths of their neo-Jacksonism, attempt to engage phenomenology; they seem to ignore the essential truth that their starting point is the omission, in favour of the vital, of this lived experience which forms the originary domain of phenomenological thought."] But this anthropology is more than a compromise between an old dualism and the new exigencies of a definition of man in a unitary style. It does not simply make evolution into the truth of man: it constitutes it as a rule and as a norm for him; the truly healthy man is the man who has arrived at the end of this evolutionary path that makes his history possible and fulfills it; but when the individual history does not trace over, in full strokes, the dotted line drawn by the evolution of phylogenesis, the norm is transgressed; the pathological process—disintegration and devolution—is triggered. In this way evolutionism restores, or rather continues to protect, the ethical dualism through which the "healthy man" is distinguished from the sick man, and the former defends himself, as it were, against the latter: the sick man goes in another direction than he does; if his path has already been traced by the becoming of the normal man, his progress is opposed to his, his orientation inversed; his becoming is a fall. We must appreciate that evolutionism was able to overcome the opposition between the somatic and the mental; but we must hold against it the false aspect of the unity it restores, and the ethical dualism that it retains and manages to mask under the theme of organic unity." *In the margin*: "Evolutionism restores the unity of man as a natural being; but it distributes on either side of time the becoming of the normal man and that of the sick man."]

c [The text of pages 4 and 5 was completely crossed out by Foucault (see note b, above).]

natural being and that, consequently, this natural being defines for man the norm of his life and the measure of his history. Between these postulates and the new significations brought to light by analysis, evolutionism maintained a compromise position for a long time. It validated the need for a psychosomatic unity by presenting itself as an elaborated form of materialism; it erased the line along which mental and sensorimotor activity were separated from each other; it highlighted man's functional unity, in which the somatic and psychic aspects form only abstract moments; finally, it rejected any opposition of substance, of principle, or of origin between the automatic forms of activity and voluntary behaviors: if these are separated, it is only by the distance between the evolutionary levels, by the less differentiated and more primitive character of the automatic reaction and the more differentiated, more complex, and also more fragile character of voluntary activity, which it owes to its more recent origin in the evolution of structures. In this way the opposition between soul and body is stamped out, finally erased, but in its place appears the false and partial unity of the "*vital*": the vital, along with all of the functional structures that it encompasses, becomes the common denominator of any human reality; lived experience only ever presents itself as its more elaborated and later form; consciousness is only the subtle structure of the final processes of adaptation. As a result, history integrates evolution in order to constitute evolution's final phase; the movement of genesis conflates itself with the processes of development, and meaning, which must not be understood as lived signification, only ever deploys itself as a vital orientation. In the anthropology diffused through the themes of evolution, the "vital" thus defines itself as the abstract form of unity. But at the same time—and completely inversely—it plays the role of a criterion which differentiates the healthy and

[7]

the pathological, the normal man and the sick man: the normal is defined by the level of adaptation, and the pathological by a backward movement, a regression in the evolutionary processes, which return to earlier stages of development. The sick man is the man who does not live at his own level: his lived experience inserts itself into previous phases of his vital evolution; his history, instead of tracing, with a bold stroke, the dotted line marked out by phylogenesis, unspools the evolutionary thread and fulfills itself in the significations that oppose it to the orientation of life. There is sickness when history becomes the archaeology of evolution.

It is therefore impossible to preserve an anthropology of life as the implicit foundation of psycho-bodily unity, and as a presupposition for a psychology of the total man. The "vital" is only ever a reductive indication in relation to lived experience, and it discriminates with regard to what is unhealthy. If it reconciles man to himself, it is by reducing him to less than what he is and by opposing him irreducibly to the pathological forms of his behavior: in this twofold manner, the theory of life alienates the reflection on man. Undoubtedly this anthropology of the "vital" is present even in the analyses which allow it to be rejected. In Freud, it denounces itself in the theory of the libido, in the conception of neurosis as fixation and regression, in the supposed analogies between the child, the primitive, and the neurotic; in Janet, it appears in the hierarchical table of tendencies, in the analysis of degrees of activation, in the notion of psychic energy; it is the clearest foundation of Jacksonism, even and especially in its more recently revamped forms.[3] Everywhere it plays the dual role of unifying man beneath himself and outside of himself, in other words of restoring the unity of man as a natural being by breaking the value of man as a historical being into two. Unification, in an anthropology of life, goes hand in hand with a fragmentation within humanism. Nietzsche's philosophy did not have, after all, any other issue . . .

*

Yet something else entirely was implied in the analyses through which, at the end of the nineteenth century, thinkers attempted to grasp human unity through the symptoms of hysteria. What we can decipher still today, in these efforts to develop a psychogenesis, is not the primacy of the vital, but the irreducible character of lived experience; it is not the incompatibility of meaning between the normal and the pathological, but on the contrary the community of their signification.

Freed from the evolutionist horizon in which theoretical reflection imprisons it, Freudian analysis offers itself as an analysis of lived experience in a style which is irreducible to that of the natural sciences.[4] Psychological genesis such as we see it developed, for example, in the *Cinq psychanalyses* does not establish a natural type of causality between processes:[d] it describes a shift of significations, a displacing of their content, a chronicle of their appearance that can have meaning only at the level of lived experience, but which remain meaningless at the level of the vital. Conduct disorders, organic deficits—coughing fits and loss of voice in Dora the hysteric—are connected to a kernel of significations that Freud describes as a style of lived experience: "symbolism" is seen as a thematic identity across the figurative contents that express it; "overdetermination" designates an infinity of reciprocal implications that have nothing to do with the

[9]

---

d [Here Foucault refers to a collection in French of Freud's case histories that includes those of Dora, Little Hans, the Rat Man, Schreber, and the Wolf Man. See Sigmund Freud, *Cinq psychanalyses*, trans. Marie Bonaparte and Rudolph M. Löwenstein (PUF, 1954 [1935])—Trans.]

spatial totality of an integrated organism, but which indicate the constancy of a horizon that one cannot manage to deploy in its totality; and the "unconscious content" of behaviors develops itself over the course of the analysis through a continuous movement from the explicit toward the implicit, from the intended effect toward the secret signification, a movement whose twists and turns eventually blur in the eyes of Freud himself, when transference and countertransference bring out significations that are common to the physician and the patient.

The decisive moment in Freud's work, undoubtedly, is when he renounces the search for a human unity in a psychology of evolution in order to uncover it instead in a psychology of genesis, when he abandons the theme of the vital in order to lay all of the weight of his analysis on the domain of lived experience. And when, for the sake of method, we obscure for a moment the evolutionist landscape that limits the horizon of Freudian thought, in order to illuminate what does not belong to the familiarity of this landscape and what has, in relation to it, a kind of exotic allure, then we see taking shape a psychology in a descriptive style, whose coherence is ensured by the notion of a genesis of significations—radically opposed to that of evolution of structures.[5]

Yet this lesson contained in psychoanalysis matches that which, in the same period, was explicit in Husserl's works. The theme of an eidetic psychology as a science of consciousness, that of a description of significations opposed to a causal explanation of conditions, that of the foundation of natural understanding on the elucidation of the absolute subject: these are all themes that have nothing in common with Freud's positivism. And yet in the *Cinq analyses* and in *Ideas* II,[e] we see Husserl and Freud working

---

e [Edmund Husserl, *Ideas Pertaining to a Pure Phenomenology and to a Phenomenological Philosophy, Second Book: Studies in the Phenomenology of Constitution*, trans. Richard Rojcewicz and André Schuwer (Kluwer Academic Publishers, 1989); hereafter *Ideas* II.]

toward the same goal: to detach the sphere of lived experience from an "immediate vital" causality without rejecting the theme of an organic articulation; to establish for the sphere of lived experience a descriptive style of analysis that borrows nothing from naturalist explanations; to recognize in this domain of lived experience a historical and intersubjective dimension that cannot be reduced to any evolutionary process. The reflection of the positivist physician, trained by his reading of Darwin, overlapped with that of a logician nourished by neo-Kantian idealism. Knowing nothing of each other, together they fixed a decisive moment in the history of the human sciences: they tore them out of their naturalist context and gave them as a primary task the return to lived experience.[6]

[11]

*

Only through a philosophical confusion can this return to lived experience be likened to a recourse to the immediate data of consciousness. Indeed, in the myth of "immediate data" we find the twofold concern for a positive understanding of consciousness in its natural dimension—an understanding as precise and rigorous as that of all of the life sciences[f]—and for an immediate, almost perceptual grasp of the qualitative contents of that consciousness.[g] Within this twofold project we find delineated something like an effort toward an Aristotelianism of psychology, in which quality would be the ultimate object of descriptive classifications, and whose counterpart, in its era, is neither the first elements

---

f *Bulletin de la Société française de philosophie* 3 (1903). [Foucault is probably referring to the session of January 29, 1903, and the discussion of André Lalande's paper "Sur l'apparence objective des perceptions visuelles" [On the Objective Appearance of Visual Perceptions], 57–93.]

g Henri Bergson, *Time and Free Will: An Essay on the Immediate Data of Consciousness*, trans. Frank Lubecki Pogson (Dover, 2001 [1913]).

of concrete psychology[7] nor the initial strides of phenomenology, but rather Duhem's attempt to restore an Aristotelianism of epistemology:[8] Bergsonism[9] is only one of the latest efforts to recover the human sciences in the style of a scholasticism.[h] Conversely, the return to lived experience in phenomenology is not an introduction to the world of qualities, but an opening to the universe of essences: an essence that dominates and manages, so to speak, all of the qualitative variations, and whose autonomy is safeguarded by the path that allows it to be accessed. This path is that of the imaginary variations which dull the immediate presence of the quality and destroy its charm by confronting it with the potentiality of all of its possible variations: sadness does not reside, isolated and massive, in this particular quality of sadness described at this particular moment, but rather it is that essential presence that appears in profiles and recognizes itself in all of the nuances of sadness, which extend from the beginning of grief to the first limits of melancholia. "Phenomenology drops only the *individuation* (*Individuation*), but it retains all of the eidetic content (*Wesensgehalt*), respecting its concrete plenitude; elevates it to the level of eidetic consciousness; and treats it as an essence endowed with an ideal identity which, like any other essence, could be singularized (*vereinzeln*) not only *hic et nunc* but also in a countless series of examples."[i] Phenomenological essence is thus

---

h Only a misinterpretation made it possible for certain psychologists and psychiatrists to believe that they could associate their analyses of schizophrenia or of lived time, for example, simultaneously with phenomenological analysis and with Bergsonian themes of the immediate qualities of duration. [Here Foucault is referring especially to Eugène Minkowski's "structural psychopathology" in *Lived Time: Phenomenological and Psychopathological Studies*, trans. Nancy Metzel (Northwestern University Press, 1970).]

i Edmund Husserl, *Ideas Pertaining to a Pure Phenomenology and to a Phenomenological Philosophy, First Book: General Introduction to a Pure Phenomenology*, trans. Frederick I. Kersten (Kluwer Academic Publishers, 1983), 168; hereafter *Ideas* I. [The translation of the quoted passage has been heavily revised to better correspond to the French translation by Paul Ricoeur, which Foucault quotes—Trans.]

grasped against the deployed horizon of the possible, rather than in the instantaneous hollowness of a real sensation.

But at the same time, this investigation of the *potential* through the pathways of imaginary variation finds its endpoint only in the unearthing of the *necessary*: the content, which lets itself be apprehended through the appearances in which it sketches itself out, is not the positive content of a fact; it is the essential structure of a right. "In its very meaning, contingency has a limit: it has a correlative to which it is linked, *necessity*; but this necessity does not designate the mere *de facto* permanence of an obtaining rule of coordination among spatiotemporal facts; it presents all of the characters[j] of eidetic necessity."[k] Across the modulations imposed by the imaginary, it is toward this foundation of eidetic necessity that phenomenology is headed, not through an inductive process of ever more abstract generalization, but through a practice of purification that strips away the extrinsic and allows the essential to emerge in the plenitude of a concrete experience. "The evidence of ideal objects is, in its effect, analogous to that of ordinary experience . . . The identity of the ideal object can be directly seen with an originality similar to that of the object of ordinary experience."[l] There, too, phenomenology turns its back on Bergsonism, since it is not an attention folded in on the positive content of the real, but rather an awakening to the necessities of essence which control

[13]

---

j [In the margin: "'Fiction' makes up the vital element of phenomenology, as of every other eidetic science; fiction is the source from which the cognition of 'eternal truths' is fed" (Husserl, *Ideas* I, § 70, 160).]

k Husserl, *Ideas* I, § 2, 7. [Foucault quotes freely from the French translation, and here I also principally reflect his wording—Trans.]

l Edmund Husserl, *Formal and Transcendental Logic*, trans. Dorion Cairns (Martinus Nijhoff, 1969), 155. [Foucault is translating, as Suzanne Bachelard's French translation of this work would only be published in 1957.]

this content and make it possible; and phenomenological intuition is not, like Bergsonian intuition, that privileged form of experience which welcomes the real in its positivity colored by a return to immediacy; it is that movement of the spirit which, in the deployment of the possible, recognizes through experience the necessity that inhabits it: direct experience and the return to the immediate cannot be confused for each other.

A Bergsonian psychology is possible only in the style of Aristotelian scholasticism: a collection of facts whose solely qualitative coordinates do not allow for the description of any real genesis, do not authorize the illumination of any effective link, and proscribe the essential forms of necessity. Coherence, in such a psychology, can come only from a classification of qualities: in other words, the concern to avoid the abstraction of essence would lead it, necessarily, to the prejudice of the species. Conversely, a phenomenological psychology can claim the rigor of a science, even if it does not seek its model in the ideal of the exact sciences. A phenomenological psychology will be an eidetic science, in accordance with the fundamental principle, "*the most universal of all methods, according to which all data has an original right*";[m] phenomenological psychology will be the elucidation of this original right as it concerns the given in the immanent flux of consciousness: it will constitute an eidetics of consciousness just as mathematics constitute an eidetics of nature.

But this eidetic psychology does not exhaust its characters in this analogy with the mathematical foundations of the exact sciences. Indeed, mathematics concerns a multiplicity that defines a system of coexistence in space: in this way, mathematics as an eidetic science rests on a definite number of principles, while

---

m Husserl, *Ideas* I, § 26, 48.

eidetic psychology, since it concerns a flux of consciousness which does not allow itself to be enclosed in any spatial coexistence, rests on an indefinite number of principles.[n] The field of eidetic psychology is not bounded, but it opens like a horizon whose elucidation cannot, by definition, have any end and which no deduction can, by essential necessity, exhaust: it will therefore present itself as a descriptive science. The essences invested in the eidetic field of mathematics have a validity defined by the exactitude of the deduction that connects them to the axiomatic principles of the system, and, in the domain of mathematics, "we can assume the equivalence of these two concepts: "*true*" and "*formal consequence of the axioms.*"[o] Conversely, the essences that psychological eidetics might bring to light cannot be subjected to the same criterion of exactitude. Sadness, for example, can never present itself as a stable process whose elements can be analyzed and tallied, nor [as] the origin which can be exhaustively deduced: what rendered sad is an event that sadness, overflowing it in its regressive movement, transformed into a "problem" that justifies the sadness. And it does not unfold in the flux of consciousness as an organic unity, but rather always presents as a contestation of itself—as an exaggerated sadness, poorly founded, accentuated by fatigue, amplified by memories that do not concern it—or on the contrary as a complicity with itself, a surrender to one's own heaviness (it is my own sadness that makes me sad, and I find in it only reasons to be sad); it announces itself even before arriving, as the intermittent and exterior sadness of unsmiling faces or as the oscillating sadness of gloomy things; it vacillates for a long time without it being

[15]

---

n Edmund Husserl, *Ideas Pertaining to a Pure Phenomenology and to a Phenomenological Philosophy, Third Book: Phenomenology and the Foundation of the Sciences*, trans. Ted E. Klein and William E. Pohl (Martinus Nijhoff, 1980), 38–39.

o Husserl, *Ideas* I, § 72, 164.

possible to determine whether it is still there, a sadness that hangs on and trails behind like rags. Even in the plenitude of experience that grasps it "in person," such an essence of sadness never presents itself as an "exact essence," in the way that a triangle or function might be, but it is always susceptible to a rigorous description that restores it in its necessity. The specificity of the essences of lived experience is to have, in this way, fluid spheres of application, but this in no way impedes an appropriate conceptual expression, so long as this expression respects the eidetic characters given in the intuition.[p]

Phenomenological psychology is therefore this rigorous understanding of the eidetics of consciousness. At first the eidetic task takes as its aim the determination of essence: fully discerning this structure that confers their unity of meaning to lived experiences whose misty unity gives itself immediately in various figures. Binswanger recalls in one of his earliest works[q] a sentence by Van Gogh: he sees in a wheat field something unspeakably pure and soft in which is expressed "a rest, like that of a young child who is sleeping."[r] Beyond this metaphor, preceding it and making it possible, a certain essence common to rest, to softness, to purity can be apprehended, for which a wheat field or the sleep of a child are only the precarious exaltations and something like the instantaneously perceptible apotheoses. This bringing to light of the essence within lived experience itself represents the static aspect of phenomenological psychology. We might find it adumbrated in some of Janet's descriptions ([the] feeling of unreality,

---

p Husserl, *Ideas* I, § 74, 166.
q [The text by Ludwig Binswanger to which Foucault refers is "Über Phänomenologie," *Zeitschrift für die gesamte Neurologie und Psychiatrie* 82, no. 1 (1923): 10–45, which Foucault will cite later as reprinted in *Ausgewählte Vorträge und Aufsätze*, vol. 1, *Zur phänomenologischen Anthropologie* (A. Francke, 1947), 13–49.]
r [Binswanger, "Über Phänomenologie," 18.]

scruples, the feeling of incompleteness) and in several pages of Sartre's *L'imaginaire*.[s]

But this static analysis necessarily gives rise to a genetic description of the way in which lived experiences are connected to each other, and in which their essential unity finally becomes what it is.[10] This genetic analysis can seek to follow and retrace the thematic evolution of lived experience, whose every phase is an eidetic moment toward the promotion of an ever-richer unity of signification. It is in this style that, before Scheler,[11] Nietzsche had already described the genesis of the values of ressentiment.[12] Ressentiment begins in hatred—in the hatred [of] the growth of values and [of] the "triumphant affirmation of the self"[t] in which aristocratic morality, in establishing itself, plays a creative role. Hatred and feeling of powerlessness, of an irreducible incapacity in the face of the affirmation of strength, exalted courage, and pride. Then the weak person denies pride as a value, he denies courage, he denies strength as a value: and in retaliations in which he lies to himself, he makes of his powerlessness a value that he calls goodness; in his fear, he discovers a value of humility, and of obedience in his cowardice. In this way, the branch of Christian love flowered on the trunk of the old Judaic hatred, and all of the new values of cowardice and slavery—which do nothing but give a derisory content to the hatred of the race of Abraham for the glorious plenitude of ancient values—flourished. Across the genetic moments of hatred, of weakness, of the negation of the reversal of values, the ethical world of ressentiment constituted itself, and its unity of

---

s [Jean-Paul Sartre, *The Imaginary: A Phenomenological Psychology of the Imagination*, trans. Jonathan Webber and Arlette Elkaïm-Sartre (Routledge, 2004).]

t [Friedrich Nietzsche, *On the Genealogy of Morals*, trans. Walter Kaufmann and R. J. Hollingdale (Vintage, 1989): "every noble morality develops from a triumphant affirmation of itself" (36).]

signification deployed itself: "Did Israel not attain the ultimate goal of its sublime vengefulness precisely through the bypath of this "Redeemer," this ostensible opponent and disintegrator of Israel?"[u]

But genesis can be understood differently. No longer as an analysis of the eidetic moments of lived experience, but as an examination of the manner in which the various eidetic domains connect to each other; as an analysis of the movement in which each regional domain of the essences discovers its own foundation: an effort, for example, to find out how the sphere of the *Geist*[v] finds its insertion in the corporeal sphere, and inversely how the domain of the body is invested by a cultural and spiritual domain in which it finds its absolute foundation. Discovering how the soul-region is articulated with the body-region was a research theme already invoked by Husserl in *Ideas* I; it is further developed in *Ideas* II.[13] There the body is described as "the copresence of what is constituted in the outer attitude and what is constituted in the inner attitude";[w] and in this way, it proves to be susceptible to two orders of reading: one which inserts it into a network of natural determinations in which it constitutes itself as an object; the other which deciphers in it the moment where spatial structures find the absolute origin, the zero point of their lived orientation, where natural causality is inverted and presents itself as a condition, this moment whose irreducible subjectivity is designated by the field of experience in its totality, in its coherence and its significations. The necessary ambiguity of any eidetics of the body and of the significations that come together in it can only be misrecognized or reduced by any composition in the style of causality, or any transcription

---

u Nietzsche, *On the Genealogy of Morals*, 35.
v ["Mind' or "Spirit."]
w Husserl, *Ideas* II [see the second section, chap. 3, § 42].

in the style of parallelism. The body must be recognized instead as a field of motivations in which the consciousness encounters its body only as that through which it steers itself toward the world which surrounds it; the meaning of the body must be read, as obstacle, or as means and instrument, or as theme of sacrifice, through the style in which consciousness relates to the world. As for this world in which the body appears to find its place, and something like its origin or its foundation, this world is not in fact a universe of causes, but a world of motifs "that I perceive, value, and treat practically as lined with pathways and barred by obstacles."ˣ And in this way the natural world of the body rests and is founded on the region of *Geist* where, as Husserl says, "nature is relative to absolute spirit."ʸ And finally such a genesis of constitutions represents, as Ricoeur states, an "effort to institute a total experience of subjectivity where the involuntary and the owned body are recovered in their subjectivity."ᶻ

[19]

We will set aside the problem of knowing to what extent an analysis of constitutions still belongs to an eidetic psychology. If it is true that the analysis of the essences of lived experience is on the same level as an eidetic psychology, since the former defines the latter's primordial theme, we can also assert that, for Husserl, the problem of constitutions pertains solely to transcendental phenomenology. At which level, in this deepening movement that goes from the eidetics of lived experience to the genesis of constitutions, does the psychological form of reflection find itself "unhooked"? This is a problem that we will not consider in this work[14] because it calls into question the whole

---

x [The quotation comes from Paul Ricoeur's essay "Husserl's *Ideas* II: Analyses and Problems," in *Husserl: An Analysis of His Phenomenology*, trans. Edward G. Ballard and Lester E. Embree (Northwestern University Press, 1967), 73.]

y Husserl, *Ideas* II, third section, chap. 3, § 64 [see Ricoeur, "Husserl's *Ideas* II," 79].

z [Foucault is referring here to Ricoeur's "Husserl's *Ideas* II," 73.]

of Husserlian phenomenology's internal economy. We would only like to highlight this fact: it was through a series of internal demands that the description of lived experience became transcendental constitution and that the problem of essence transformed itself into a question about foundation. This deepening of the level of reflection appears inevitable as soon as we undertake a "phenomenological description," in the most commonplace sense of the term, of a lived experience. Radicalized, the essence of consciousness reveals itself as its constitutive activity.

*

What is strange is that this necessity, which we grasp so easily between the lines of Husserlian analysis, does not appear in any way when the essence that we attempt to decipher in lived experience refers to a pathological experience.

[20] In phenomenological description, it was a matter of recovering the emergence of significative wholes and the manner in which the world constitutes itself from a phenomenological field defined, from the very start, by its concrete plenitude: from the static description of lived experience to transcendental constitution, each genetic movement rests on the immediate presence of a world. This presence announces itself already in the earliest phenomenological analyses, in the plenitude of the self-evident fact that accomplishes itself and comes to fill, in some way, the act in which it realizes itself; it is finally uncovered in its entirety at the end of Husserl's reflection. It is defined, in *Erfahrung und Urteil*, as a world of life, as a *Lebenswelt*, a world that is "preconstituted" ahead of any constitutive genesis, a world that is "pregiven" even before the deployment of the act in which it gives itself, a world with which consciousness is interlaced with the immediate implications, anterior to any position of

understanding, of the originary *doxa*: "The being of the world in totality is the thing that is self-evident, which can never be put in doubt, which is not first the result of an activity of judgment but which forms the presupposition of all judgment. Consciousness of the world is consciousness in the mode of certainty of belief."[aa] Therefore, if it is true that all of the significations internal to the world are dependent and pertain to a constitutive genesis, the world itself is anterior to any genesis; it is presupposed in any constitution; it is "substrate" in the strong sense.[bb]

Across Husserlian description, meaning is never born except in the homeland of meaning, and the world is never anything other than the flourishing of the world that is already there. Metamorphosis of the world's landscapes, metempsychosis of its significations; but never birth in the strict sense, absolute origin.

[21]

Yet the significations that we encounter in pathological experience do not deploy themselves starting from a world that is already there, or rather, if they take with them the presupposition of a world, it is that of another world which is a non-world. When hysterics obstruct one region or another of their motor activity or of their sensory field, the body is not then for them the originary form of presence in the world, the most immediate manner of being among things and on level footing with their objectivity; it constitutes, on the contrary, a way of absenting oneself from the world, of no longer being there; the world is no longer presupposed but rather excluded via the body. Or, to take another

---

aa Edmund Husserl, *Experience and Judgment: Investigations in a Genealogy of Logic*, trans. James S. Churchill and Karl Ameriks (Northwestern University Press, 1973), 30. [Foucault borrows this quotation from Jean Wahl, "Notes on the First Part of *Experience and Judgment* by Husserl," trans. Laurence E. Winters, in *Apriori and World: European Contributions to Husserlian Phenomenology*, ed. William R. McKenna, Robert M. Harlan, and Laurence E. Winters (Martinus Nijhoff, 1981), 173.]

bb Husserl, *Experience and Judgment*, 138.

example, in phobic fantasies the image is not a form of the quasi-presence, in the backdrop, of a reality that is always presupposed and always there in its plenitude; the image takes the appearance of an "over-presence" which repels the presence of reality and alters its meaning. It is likely not possible to grasp the meaning of a pathological experience without referring it to this implicit world for which it is only one of the possible ways of giving oneself; but the way this world has of being pregiven is radically different in normal experience and in pathological experience.[cc] In the former, any singular genesis rests against the backdrop of a same world—and in this way it avoids the problem of knowing why the world is not a non-world, and it refuses even the possibility of raising it;[dd] but the genesis of pathological experience must give an account of the appearance of a world which is a non-world, of the emergence of a meaning which is a non-meaning.

This genesis must return an absolute meaning to a certain number of notions that phenomenological constitution encompasses as a singular figure in a genetic movement. For example, phenomenology gives only a secondary and derivative meaning to negation: if forgetfulness is negation, it is only so insofar as it offers itself as a progressive neutralization into which the figures of the present sink little by little; they lose their contours, shrink, "shrivel up" and finally disappear as an implicit horizon of current presence. Hysterical forgetting has another style entirely: it is a negation at work, it constitutes itself as an operation through which the significative content of the present is crossed out, "scratched out"; it is the active moment of suppression; it is the point where "the spirit makes it so that that which was done was not done." In the same way, there is a

---

cc [*In the margin*: "the phobic world of the universe of hysteria."]
dd [This last phrase ("and it refuses . . .") was added in the margin.]

constitutive genesis of contradiction in Husserl's descriptions of the "genealogy of logic": the principle of contradiction—one of the essential dimensions of the apophantic[ee]—takes its originary meaning from the passive genesis of the associations that allow for sketches and that designate, [on the] fringes of the current horizon, the imminent presences which will immediately offer their plenitude; against the backdrop of this passive genesis, the sketches of attention bring out the expected as the theme of all of these protensions and the doxic act which is already making way for it in the world. Still, disappointments arise: the expectation is not met, so the object is scratched out—not through an act thematized in its activity, in which the object is maintained in its unity with the disappointment that crosses it out from the world; it then appears with this immediate meaning: "not this way, but otherwise."[ff]

Contradiction therefore always appears against the backdrop of a full world, spanned in its entirety by an immediate positivity. And yet in pathological experience, contradiction is not this secondary modulation of an originary plenitude: schizophrenic ambivalence is the emergence of absolutely contemporaneous contradictory terms; no arithmetic operation on the field's significations and indicators could exhaust it; the universe has singular contents only in the form of universal contradiction; the world itself is a non-world, immediate destruction of the self, and contestation of the self's existence which undoes itself at each instant, as experienced by certain schizophrenics in the delusion of cosmic catastrophe that German psychiatrists term "*Weltuntergangswahn*":[gg] [15] there life is simultaneously death, and

[23]

---

ee [The apophantic is that part of logic whose object is the form of judgment, insofar as it can be true or false.]
ff Husserl, *Experience and Judgment*, § 21.
gg ["Delusion of the end of the world."]

the being is recognized only in his non-being. Far from the contradiction defining itself at a precise genetic moment—like that of disappointment in the antepredicamental experience—it is the constitution's absolute point of reference, the form within which pathological genesis occurs. From that point on it is no longer possible to follow the significative implications of the morbid experience through a genesis whose constitution would rest on a world that is already there, on a world offering its ultimate significations, encompassed from the start. Taking negation seriously, making of contradiction the absolute reference point of genesis, means rejecting the facility of the already-there, means never letting the reflection on the "pre-constituted" stop or rest; it means posing the problem of the absolute origin, of the jump, of the appearance out of nothing, of the dimension that must crossed in a single leap. It means denying oneself any speculation on the "anterior" that already gives everything that it does not possess; it means, in taking the question of origins rigorously, tackling the problem of dialectics head-on.

*

The genesis of constitutions in the domain of psychopathology thus discovers dialectics not as "its effectively real content" but as its absolute limit. Would it be possible, by testing these limits, to measure the scope of phenomenological descriptions and to save them specifically in the name of a scope of human consciousness that would be at their scale? Can we designate, in human existence, the boundary line at which meaning loses its meaning, and the world becomes another world? This would do justice to dialectics, outside of the domain of phenomenological understanding—or rather it would eliminate dialectics as moment of genesis.

All of Jaspers's work in psychopathology can be read as this effort to free the field of phenomenological description from the problems of psychological contradiction and of absolute origin: an attempt to cut one's losses, by fixing the rightful limits between what pertains to understanding, to intuitive grasping in the manner of phenomenology, and what remains irreducible to all of these forms of recognition. The division is easily made when it comes to the static grasping of the essence of lived experience. On the one hand, we have intelligible lived experiences that we can grasp directly: "When we were children we drew things not as we saw them but as we imagined them, so, as psychologists and psychopathologists, we go through a phase in which we have our own notions about the psyche and only gradually emerge into a direct, unprejudiced apprehension of psychic phenomena as they are."hh But not all lived experiences are susceptible to this restitution that gets to the essence beyond all comparisons, symbols, indirect analogies, hypotheses, beyond all of the psychologies of the "as if."[16] Certain lived experiences remain impenetrable without a system of references that places them in a metaphorical world where they are refracted and distorted. They cannot offer themselves to comprehension as they are; they only ever present themselves through a network of superficial symbols; they only ever express themselves as allusions to themselves. The majority of delusional experiences find their expression only in the indecipherable code of symbols: one of Jaspers's patients experiences the presence of a machine "fixed in such a way that every word he spoke was put into him

[25]

---

hh [Foucault's footnote is to the French translation of the third edition of Jaspers's *General Psychopathology* (first German edition 1913), published in 1933 as *Psychopathologie générale* (Félix Alcan). Here I adapt the 1964 English translation of the seventh edition by J. Hoenig and Marian W. Hamilton (University of Chicago Press), p. 56, to reflect Foucault's phrasing—Trans.]

electrically"; the words are "formally wound round his head"; he is "interfered with daily." "Only someone who has been tortured by such a machine as I was would be able to understand . . . if only someone would tell me what it all means. I am terribly unhappy."[ii] The genetic understanding of lived experiences comes up short against such rigorous limits. While it is possible to trace certain movements of genesis (for example, certain kinds of morbid jealousy)[17] through the historical thread of biography, and while a whole existence can appear as the development and unearthing of a signification, the triggering of certain behaviors interrupts any intelligible continuity: the emergence of jealousy—whose significative content is neither prepared by any event nor anticipated by any personality trait—appears as a "morbid neo-formation, an innovation that is heterogeneous to the personality previous to the illness."[jj] This is an absolute beginning that cannot be grasped by the understanding, since what we understand must always have already begun. We find a great many of these processes in mental pathology: compulsions, unmotivated ideas, dissociation, intrapsychic ataxia; in all these terms we hear only one meaning: "unintelligibility."[kk]

Yet with these limits of phenomenological understanding we reach those of consciousness. Let us explain ourselves: when a comprehensive analysis deploys the moments of a genesis such as that of ressentiment, putting in their place the moment of hatred, the moment of negation, the movement of the reversal of values, it does not say what the consciousness of ressentiment

---

ii Jaspers, *General Psychopathology*, 579–80. [Foucault cites freely.]

jj Daniel Lagache, *La jalousie amoureuse, psychologie descriptive et psychanalyse*, vol. 1, *Les états de jalousie et le problème de la conscience morbide* (PUF, 1947), 9.

kk Jaspers, *Psychopathologie générale*, 161. [The passage appears on p. 581 of the English edition cited above, but this sentence is heavily modified from the French/third edition—Trans.]

says to itself when it formulates what it is; on the contrary, it names what this consciousness silences, it fills its silences with a hidden meaning and allows the explicit to be understood against the horizon of the implicit; we thus cannot say that the understanding does not call on the unconscious, which is like the implicit surround of the consciousness for that group of significations which are un-conscious insofar as they are intra-conscious. Yet the limits of the understanding we have just discussed touch on processes that are unconscious because they are extra-conscious: an eruption into lived experience of massive structures that the subject cannot even recognize as having been lived by himself and that he deflects onto some other existence mysteriously insinuated into himself; a triggering of psychic processes and of a whole throng of impressions that elicit another life, a new start in existence, a transposition into another world; a collapse of existence that sinks into vegetative modes of survival and that, at the end of the madness, abandons itself to the causality of organic processes.

Finally, the limits of phenomenological understanding are measured by the domain of natural causality. Between the intelligible and the unintelligible, between genesis and process, between consciousness and the extra-conscious a boundary establishes itself—a boundary that also passes between signification and causality, between phenomenological method and natural attitude. This entails forgetting that we cannot do justice to one and the other simultaneously, because they are not situated at the same level of reflection and because the methodological choice between them is decisive. The one, even if it allows itself to be completed by the other in fact, cannot avoid being its rightful foundation. And insofar as doing justice to naturalism means already admitting it in its validity, we understand how Jaspers might write that "causal understanding has no borders.

[27]

Everywhere, even in psychic events, we can seek causes and effects: on the contrary, understanding finds limits everywhere."[11] An implicit return to naturalism, but taken only according to its negative measures. A return, also, to the dualism we discussed above in relation to naturalism, but with an inversion of indicators: it is natural causality that denounces the pathological process; against the backdrop of this causality, comprehensive genesis marks the style specific to experiences lived in the normal mode. The explanation by means of nature has become the criterion of the pathological, rather than being that of the normal; but in Jaspers, as in the evolutionists, as in classic psychopathology, psychiatric humanism has split itself into a "bi-humanism."

*

Can this dualism be overcome once again? Is it not the ultimate meaning we must assign to any analysis of alienation, of morbid existence, of this pathological world that is a non-world?

The final phases of a schizophrenic evolution or the terminal stages of madness seem to no longer carry any meaning, even implicit: there is a kind of collapse of subjectivity into a mode of natural subsistence, whose only coordinates are on the order of biological automatism. Significations have been reabsorbed into causality. But does a twofold analysis—in the style of phenomenological understanding and in the style of naturalist explanation—allow us to fully understand the phenomenon? Can it restore the process in its development? Comprehensive analysis has access only to the lived experiences that serve as a prelude—and, in certain moments, almost flickering, as accompaniment—to the process by which the madness evolves:

---

11 Jaspers, *Psychopathologie générale*, 281. [This passage does not appear in the English translation of the seventh edition—Trans.]

as for the explanation in terms of natural causality, it can lay out the entire chain of objective consequences. But the transition itself remains obscure, and, with the transition, the subject accomplishing it. What is there in the shared foundation of this *lived experience* that the comprehension penetrates, and of this *life* against which it runs aground? In other words, in the movement of alienation, what is the subject that is alienating itself?

It is not the subject, as the carrier and absolute origin of significations: alienation is precisely the moment of its suppression. In alienating itself, it ceases to be an origin and becomes nothing more than the crisscrossing of significations it receives from outside; it no longer carries them, but rather supports or endures them: inanimate object of universal persecution, transitory point of a terror that shrouds it, it is given over entirely to the world and its fantastical significations. The subject in the phenomenological sense does not alienate itself; it is suppressed in the movement of alienation; and it would be a tautology to define mental illness by its erasure and the stamping out of its constitutive activity.[mm]

---

mm Yet this is what Merleau-Ponty appears to do when he defines Goldstein's patient's illness as a slackening of the intentional arc. It is true that this is not a case of alienation; but chances are that the problem of the subject of the illness is the same as that of the subject of alienation, even as it appears less clearly. [See M. Merleau-Ponty, *Phenomenology of Perception*, trans. Colin Smith (Routledge & Kegan Paul, 1962), part 1, chap. 3: "the life of consciousness—cognitive life, the life of desire or perceptual life—is subtended by an 'intentional arc' which projects round about us our past, our future, our human setting, our physical, ideological and moral situation, or rather which results in our being situated in all these respects. It is this intentional arc which brings about the unity of the senses, of intelligence, of sensibility and motility. And it is this which 'goes limp' in illness" (136). The clinical case study cited by Merleau-Ponty had been discussed by the German neuropsychiatrist Kurt Goldstein in his works of the 1920s: see "Über die Abhängigkeit der Bewegungen von optischen Vorgängen. Bewegungsstörungen bei Seelenblinden," *Monatsschrift für Psychiatrie und Neurologie* 54 (1923): 141–94; see also Adhémar Gelb and Kurt Goldstein, "Über den Einfluss des vollständigen Verlustes des optischen Vorstellungsvermögens auf das tactile Erkennen. Zugleich ein Beitrag zur Psychologie der taktilen Raumwahrnehmung und der Bewegungsvorstellungen," in *Psychologische Analysen hirnpathologischer Fälle* (Barth, 1920), 157–250.]

[29] Can the notion of personality constitute the subject of alienation? A good number of contemporary psychiatrists have sought to define it as the fundamental concept of any possible psychopathology. Manfred Bleuler[18] writes: [. . .].[nn] But this notion of personality is just as incapable as the phenomenological notion of the subject of giving an account of the processes of alienation. It is, indeed, what, in alienation, alters itself, dissociates itself and finally disappears. But it is also what subsists beyond every process; it constitutes something like the element in which they all develop; it forms its permanent decor, and they borrow their psychic reality from it:[oo] "The phenomenon always plays out against the backdrop of a me, of a person: in other words, we always see it as an expression or as a manifestation of this or that person."[pp] Any psychopathology in this style cannot avoid ambiguity: the person finding in alienation the form and its suppression; and the alienation finding in the subsistence of the person the content and the meaning of his processes.

The notions of the subject and of the person are not commensurate with that of alienation. We must find a way to access a more radical notion that can found alienation, as transition from meaning to non-meaning, as movement of psychological contradiction, as absolute origin of lived experience, in short, as primordial dialectical moment. We would need to grasp anew the point at which man abandons himself to the movement of natural causality by renouncing any form of authentic freedom, this point that indicates in his existence that he himself
[30] preempts analysis in the naturalist style by effacing himself as

---

nn [Missing quotation and reference.]
oo [The following passage has been crossed out: "We continue to find this psychopathology of the person, with its ambiguities, in texts in which Binswanger is still seeking his path."]
pp Binswanger, "Über Phänomenologie," 37. [The translation into French is Foucault's.]

the absolute subject of signification and by dispersing his personal unity. In other words, this fundamental moment must be expressed neither in terms of person nor in terms of subject, but only in terms of existence. The analysis of morbid experiences must necessarily lead to the analysis of forms of existence:[19] because only existence can alienate itself without disappearing; only existence can announce itself in a non-meaning that does not suppress it; only existence can sustain the dialectic of contradiction.

This is the decisive moment in the analysis of mental illness; this is also the decisive moment for the radical surpassing of phenomenological analysis—in its effort toward the genesis of constitutions and understanding of meaning. The dialectical content of morbid experience—and the urgency of the contradictions it encompasses—requires a different style of analysis than that of phenomenology: the deciphering of the essence of lived experience does not exhaust the reality of pathological experience, we must now have access to the truth of existence. But what content should we give to this notion of "existence"? Must we understand that it is necessary to resort to an analysis of the real conditions of concrete existence? Must we, in this spirit, try to determine what the actual contradictions are, what objectively the dialectic at the root of this existence is? Or shall we attempt an analysis of the structures of existence, as a manner of making human reality present to the world? Must we then analyze mental illnesses as modifications (*Abwandlungen*) of this "*In-der-Welt-sein*"?[qq] [20] In this way, we will need to leave the conception of mental illnesses as illnesses of the brain to the medical and clinical point of view, and decipher in morbid experience the alteration "of the fundamental or essential structure

[31]

---

qq ["Being in the world."]

and of the structural links (*Wesenstruktur*) of being-in-the-world as transcendence."[rr]

We must choose between ontological reference and dialectical reference. We will now try to show in more detail how the whole movement of *Daseinsanalyse* constitutes an option for ontological reference. But prior to that we will devote three chapters to the problems of space, time, and the experience of the other: we will try to reproduce this movement through which any phenomenological analysis is called, especially when it addresses pathological experiences, to go beyond itself and to seek its foundation in a form of reflection that defines itself as anthropological. Indeed, it is the unearthing of these anthropological implications that led the analysis of morbid existence in the direction of an existential analysis and diverted it away from the paths of dialectics.[ss]

---

rr Ludwig Binswanger, "The Existential Analysis School of Thought," trans. Ernest Angel, in *Existence: A New Dimension in Psychiatry and Psychology*, ed. Rollo May, Ernest Angel, and Henri F. Ellenberger (Basic Books, 1958), 194.
ss [Blank page.]

NOTES

1. Foucault does not provide any bibliographical indications here. He is referring to the first part of Charles Blondel's book *La psychanalyse* (Félix Alcan, 1924), which collects the articles Blondel published in 1922 in the *Revue d'histoire et de philosophie religieuses* (no. 2, 118–140; no. 3, 234–257; no. 4, 315–336), which were then collated, that same year, in the third of the special issues published by this journal.

2. The distinction between "*fonction vitale*" (vital function) and what Foucault translates alternately as "*histoire de la vie*" or as "*histoire vécue*" (lived history) is at the heart of Binswanger's thought and recurs constantly across his oeuvre. In particular, Binswanger published an article about these two concepts in 1928; see "Lebensfunktion und innere Lebensgeschichte," *Monatschrift für Psychiatrie und Neurologie* 68 (1928): 52–79; reprinted in *Ausgewählte Vorträge und Aufsätze*, vol. 1, *Zur phänomenologischen Anthropologie* (A. Francke, 1947), 50–73. Foucault dedicated a very detailed reading note to this study in the 1950s: see the file entitled "Binswanger (articles)" (BNF, Box 38, folder 1).

3. Here Foucault is referring to the "neo-Jacksonism" characteristic of "organo-dynamism," a theory developed in the 1930s by Henri Ey, who had applied the ideas of the British neurologist John Hughlings Jackson (1835–1911) to neuropsychiatry; on this topic, see Emmanuel Delille's "L'organo-dynamisme d'Henri Ey: l'oubli d'une théorie de la conscience considéré dans ses relations avec l'analyse existentielle" (*L'Homme et la société*, nos. 167–169 (2008): 203–19. According to Jackson, the functioning of the nervous system was organized hierarchically, in a series of tiered functional levels, from the most voluntary to the most automatic. The functions of the lower levels were freed when the higher levels of control failed. The term "neo-Jacksonism" first appeared in 1936 in Henri Ey and Julien Rouart's "Essai d'application des principes de Jackson à une conception dynamique de la neuropsychiatrie" (*L'Encéphale*, no. 31, 313–356; reprinted in volumes by G. Doin, 1938). The theory of organo-dynamism was developed by Henri Ey in the 1940s, starting with his article "Une conception organo-dynamiste de la psychiatrie," *Annales médico-psychologiques* 11 (1943): 259–78. In Foucault's first book, *Maladie mentale et personnalité*—a heavily revised version of which was republished in 1962 as *Maladie mentale et psychologie*,

and later in English translation as *Mental Illness and Psychology*, trans. Alan Sheridan (University of California Press, 1987)—he writes: "The error of "neo-Jacksonism" is to have turned regression into the "principle" of illness, which is to say to have wanted both to exhaust its totality and to locate its cause in regression" (*Maladie mentale et personnalité* (PUF, 1954), 33n1; this footnote was subsequently removed from *Mental Illness and Psychology*). Among the handwritten notes produced during Foucault's drafting of the book, there is a document entitled "Maladie et personnalité dans le néo-jacksonisme" [Illness and personality in Neo-Jacksonism], in which Foucault states that neo-Jacksonism highlighted "all of the personality's reactions to dissolution. The positive aspect of illness is not so much its residue as the reorganization of that residue in the form of a new personality that can mask the illness's deficits" (BNF, NAF 28803). Yet, he continues, "this idea of a reorganization of the personality following a dissolution leads to a new way of defining the notion of symptom and of illness." Finally, he concludes, "there is nothing surprising in Jackson's and Ey's work cohering so easily with that of Goldstein, Jaspers, and phenomenological psychology, since in all of these the subject is always constitutive in relation to illness." In *Maladie mentale et personnalité*, Foucault adds: "In this priority given to the notion of totality one can see a return to concrete pathology and the possibility of determining the field of mental pathology and that of organic pathology as a single domain . . . whether its first designations are organic or psychological, the illness concerns the overall situation of the individual in the world" (10–11; this sentence is unchanged in *Mental Illness and Psychology*, where it appears on pp. 8–9). Still, he concludes, "By means of the unity that it ensures and the problems that it eliminates, this notion of totality is well adapted to introduce into pathology an atmosphere of conceptual euphoria. It was from this atmosphere that those who had to any extent been inspired by Goldstein wished to benefit. But, unfortunately, the euphoria was not matched by an equal rigor" (11–12; this sentence is unchanged in *Mental Illness and Psychology*, where it appears on p. 9). It is interesting to note that, in a preparatory typescript for *Maladie mentale et personnalité*, Foucault had named some authors inspired by Kurt Goldstein; he includes Maurice Merleau-Ponty, *The Structure of Behavior*, trans. Alden L. Fisher (Beacon, 1963) and Georges Canguilhem, *Essay on Some Problems Concerning the Normal and the Pathological*, section 1 of *The Normal and the*

Pathological, trans. Carolyn R. Fawcett with Robert S. Cohen (Zone Books, 1991).

4. The arguments developed here are close to those formulated by Foucault at the beginning of chapter 3 of *Maladie mentale et Personnalité*: "the original error of psychoanalysis and, following it, of most genetic psychologies is no doubt that of failing to seize these two irreducible dimensions of evolution and history in the unity of psychological development. But Freud's stroke of genius lay in being able, so early on, to go beyond the evolutionist horizon defined by the notion of libido and reach the historical dimension of the human psyche" (37; this sentence is unchanged in *Mental Illness and Psychology*, where it appears on pp. 30–31).

5. See on this topic a fragment from Foucault's teaching notes of the early 1950s, in which he writes, "Freud, while seeking to conform to the Darwinian model, freed—probably contrary to his intention, and without always becoming aware of it—psychology from a naturalist epistemology: for explanations that sought to dispel contradiction, he substituted explanations by means of contradiction; to the central notion of the conservation of life (or of adaptation—or of utility—or of interest) which reigned over all of the life sciences, including even the science of man, he opposed a conflictual dialectic between Eros and Thanatos; for evolutionist schemas that made the present follow from the past, he substituted a mode of analysis in which present and past accumulate in an indissociable unity" (BNF, Box 46, folder 4, fragment of a handwritten manuscript entitled "General Introduction"). This is an argument that Foucault makes in almost all of his published work from this period: in *Maladie mentale et personnalité* he identifies in the Freudian concept of anxiety the point of transition from a "psychology of evolution" to a "psychology of genesis" (48–51; see the final pages of chapter 3 in *Mental Illness and Psychology*); in "La psychologie de 1850 à 1950" (1957), he situates the Freudian system as the origin of the "great toppling of psychology" through which "causal analysis transformed itself into genesis of significations"; see *Dits et écrits*, vol. 1, *1954–1969*, ed. Daniel Defert and François Ewald, with Jacques Lagrange (Paris: Gallimard, 1994), no. 2, 128. Moreover, in his introduction to Binswanger's *Le rêve et l'existence*, Foucault sees in Freud's *Interpretation of Dreams* and in Husserl's *Logical Investigations* a "twofold attempt by man to recapture his meanings and to recapture himself in his significance." See Michel

Foucault, "Dream, Imagination and Existence," trans. Forrest Williams, in *Dream and Existence*, ed. Keith Hoeller, special issue, *Review of Existential Psychology & Psychiatry* 19, no. 1 (1985); reprinted in *Dream and Existence* (Humanities Press, 1993), 34.

6. See on this topic the manuscript fragment entitled "General Introduction," in which Foucault writes: "1. Phenomenology and the naturalist psychology of evolution each led to a point of view on genesis in which they converged, yet which seemed as distant from an eidetics of consciousness that would have presented itself as the equivalent of mathematics for the natural sciences as it was from a psychological naturalism that would have borrowed its principal concepts and forms of description from the sciences. From the requirement of an ideal foundation for the facts of consciousness, Husserl arrived at the idea of an ideal genesis of significations; from the requirement of a naturalist explanation of psychological evolution, Freud arrived at the description of a genesis of behaviors, and at an elucidation of their meaning. 2. This convergence is not important only insofar as it marks a point of correspondence. What the appearance of this genesis as an essential dimension of the description of consciousness signifies is a radical change in the foundations of psychology" (BNF, Box 46, folder 4). Foucault also brings together Freud and Husserl in his introduction to *Le rêve et l'existence*, but in that context it is the *Interpretation of Dreams* and the *Logical Investigations* that Foucault cites.

7. The term "concrete psychology" refers to the project launched by Georges Politzer (1903–1942) at the end of the 1920s to reform psychology according to a "new orientation" that would reject both associationism and the "myth" of interior life, and let itself be guided instead by the principle of the "concrete," which is to say a practical understanding of human life closer to wisdom than to the scientific knowledge borrowed from physiology. Politzer's 1928 *Critique of the Foundations of Psychology*, like the *Revue de psychologie concrète* founded by Politzer in 1929, was widely read by French philosophers and psychiatrists between the 1930s and the 1950s—from Jean-Paul Sartre and Maurice Merleau-Ponty to Eugène Minkowski, Jacques Lacan, and Daniel Lagache. For the English translation, see *Critique of the Foundations of Psychology*, trans. Maurice Apprey (Duquesne University Press, 1994). During this period, the expression "psychologie concrète" was also used by philosophers outside the framework

of disciplinary psychology. In this way, Merleau-Ponty speaks of "concrete psychology" in reference to Nietzsche's description of ressentiment, which was taken up by Max Scheler. On this topic, Merleau-Ponty's 1935 review of the French translation of Scheler's 1933 book *L'homme du ressentiment* is instructive; see Merleau-Ponty, "Christianity and *Ressentiment*," in *Texts and Dialogues: On Philosophy, Politics and Culture*, ed. Hugh J. Silverman and James Barry Jr., trans. Gerald G. Wening (Humanity Books, 2000), 85–100. In 1946, Emmanuel Mounier went so far as to describe Politzer as the "Saint John the Baptist of this Good News" consisting in "denouncing the systematic objectification of psychological life by our psychologies 'in the third person'"; see *Traité du caractère* (Seuil, 1946), 44–45. In France, because of concrete psychology's anthropological vocation, it has forged a privileged link with the existential school of psychiatry since the 1930s. On this topic, see Elisabetta Basso, "Foucault entre psychanalyse et psychiatrie. 'Reprendre la folie au niveau de son langage,'" *Archives de philosophie* 79, no. 1 (2016): 27–54. On Politzer's philosophical reception more broadly, see Giuseppe Bianco, ed., *Georges Politzer, le concret et sa signification: psychologie, philosophie et politique* (Hermann, 2016).

8. Here Foucault is referring especially to Pierre Duhem's epistemological study *La Théorie physique. Son objet et sa structure*, 2nd ed. (M. Rivière, 1914 [1904–1905]), according to which a physical theory is a system of mathematical principles and of syllogisms deduced from a small number of axioms and constructed so as to order and classify a group of experimental laws in the simplest, most complete, and most precise manner possible. According to Duhem, a physical theory does not claim to grasp reality, which is inaccessible.

9. The critique of Bergsonism was at the heart of the polemical pamphlet that Georges Politzer published in 1929 under the pseudonym François Arouet: *La fin d'une parade philosophique. Le bergsonisme* (Les Revues, 1929), reprinted in *Contre Bergson et quelques autres. Écrits philosophiques, 1924–1939*, ed. Roger Bruyeron (Flammarion, 2013). In this tract, Politzer defines Bergson's thought as the very model of an idealist philosophy, unable to give an adequate account of concrete, individual human life. Politzer's text was very well received by major mid-century French philosophers, including Jean-Paul Sartre, Maurice Merleau-Ponty, Georges Canguilhem, Gilles Deleuze, and Michel Foucault.

10. Here Foucault is also referring, via Max Scheler, to Karl Jaspers's distinction between a "static" comprehension of phenomena, aimed at visualizing, defining, describing, and ordering psychic states, and their "genetic" comprehension, which includes both "affective interpenetration" (*Einfühlung*) and the "understanding of psychic relationships" or "filiation of psychic states." According to Jaspers, it is the latter that constitutes real psychology or "*einfühlende*" psychology, whose finality consists in "understanding how the psychic stems from the psychic." See "Kausale und "verständliche" Zusammenhänge zwischen Schicksal und Psychose bei der *Dementia praecox* (Schizophrenie)," *Zeitschrift für die gesamte Neurologie und Psychiatrie* 14 (1913), 158–263; reprinted in *Gesammelte Schriften zur Psychopathologie* (Springer, 1963), 330. These two forms of comprehension, which constitute "subjective psychology," are founded on a kind of understanding that pertains to evidence and are totally distinct from objective or physiological psychology (*Leistungspsychologie*), a knowledge founded on an inductive kind of understanding whose goal is to establish causal links between psychic facts, and from there, to formulate laws opening onto the construction of theories. This theme is also taken up by Jaspers in his *General Psychopathology*, which Foucault cites later on. Thanks to the archives, we know that Foucault had encountered Jaspers's 1913 article through Max Scheler, whom he mentions in a reading note devoted to his 1913–1914 work *Phänomenologie und Erkenntnistheorie*, in *Gesammelte Werke*, vol. 10, *Schriften aus dem Nachlass*, ed. Manfred S. Frings (A. Francke, 1957), 379–430. Foucault likely consulted the manuscript transcribed by Herman Leo Van Breda and Stephan Strasser which is conserved in the Husserl Archives in Paris. In his reading note, Foucault remarks: "We must therefore not confuse the phenomenology of the psyche with explanatory psychology, nor with descriptive psychology. Indeed, there is no description without observation (*Beobachtung*). Yet in the phenomenological attitude what is intended [*visé*] is "*erschaut*" [seen] and never "*be-obachtet*" [observed]. Furthermore, the description is always directed toward a fact that is transcendental from a phenomenological point of view. The phenomenology of the psyche happens to coincide with certain studies that also exclude psychologism from psychology; Bergson, W. James, Dilthey, Natorp: they understand quite clearly the task of a phenomenology of the psyche, even if they do not understand extra-psychic phenomenological *Tatsachen* [facts] (especially

Bergson). But there are connections especially between the phenomenology of the psyche and certain experimental studies: the experiments are mostly "*Veranschaulichungsexperimente*" [illustrative experiments], in which a layer found in the essence of the content of an *Erlebnis* is brought to the immediate intuition. See works of Bühler on the essence of "*Bedeutung*" [signification]; see Messer's *Empfindung und Denken* [Quelle und Meyer, 1908]; see Köhler, Katz, Jaensch (the space of visual perception), Krüger and Stumpf (acoustics): these studies pertain in part to a phenomenology of the psyche, in part to a phenomenology of the qualities, and in part to a phenomenology of the simplest physical appearances. Except for Stumpf (who clearly distinguished between phenomenology and psychology, while restricting them to the appearances that he terms sensory, "*sinnlich*")—none has been able to effectively distinguish the phenomenological attitude from the psychological attitude. Importance also of psychiatry: K. Jaspers, "Zur Analyse der Trugwahrnehmungen (Leibhaftigkeit und Realitätsurteil)" [*Zeitschrift für die gesamte Neurologie und Psychiatrie* 6, no. 1 (1911): 460–535]; "The Phenomenological Approach in Psychopathology" [*British Journal of Psychiatry* 114, no. 516 (November 1968): 1313–23]; "Kausale und 'verständliche' Zusammenhänge"; Wilhelm Specht, "Zur Morphologie der Halluzinationen und Illusionen" ["Zur Phanomenologie und Morphologie der pathologischen Wahrnehmungstauschungen,"*Zeitschrift für Pathopsychologie* 2, nos. 1, 2, and 4 (1914): 1–35, 121–143, and 481–569 respectively; reprinted in *Wahrnehmung und Halluzination* (Engelmann, 1914)]; M. Scheler, "Über Selbsttäuschungen" [*Zeitschrift für Pathopsychologie* 1 (1912): 87–163]; "Zur Psychologie der sogenannten Rentenhysterie und der rechte Kampf gegen das Übel" [*Archiv für Sozialwissenschaft und Sozialpolitik* 37, no. 2 (1913): 521–34]" (BNF, Box 37, folder 2).

11. In the 1950s, Foucault was keenly attentive to Max Scheler's work, about which he drafted numerous reading notes. At the beginning of a folder that includes about fifty pages devoted to this author, he drew up the following table of contents: "The meaning of suffering"; "Love and Knowledge"; "Repentance and Rebirth"; *Ressentiment*; "Exemplars of Person and Leaders"; *The Nature of Sympathy*; *The Human Place in the Cosmos*; "Shame and Feelings of Modesty"; *Phänomenologie und Erkenntnistheorie* (BNF, Box 37, folder 2). At the time when Foucault was writing these notes, a number of Scheler's works existed in French translation: *Nature et formes*

de la sympathie [*The Nature of Sympathy*] had been translated in 1928 by Marcel Lefebvre and published by Payot; *L'homme du ressentiment* [*Ressentiment*] had appeared in 1933 in Gallimard's NRF [Nouvelle Revue Française] collection; the first three titles in Foucault's table of contents had been translated by Pierre Klossowski in 1936 in *Le sens de la souffrance, suivi de deux autres essais*, in the "Philosophie de l'esprit" series edited by René Le Senne and Louis Lavelle (pub. Aubier-Montaigne). *Le saint, le génie, le héros* ["Exemplars of Person and Leaders"] had appeared in 1944 in a translation by Émile Marmy (pub. Egloff), while *La situation de l'homme dans le monde* and *La pudeur* [*The Human Place in the Cosmos*; "Shame and Feelings of Modesty"] had just come out in translations by Maurice Dupuy in 1951 and 1952, respectively (pub. Aubier). In this same folder on Scheler, two of Foucault's reading notes (one entitled "Acts and functions" and the other "Ambiguities in the acts-functions distinction") mention Scheler's *Der Formalismus in der Ethik und die matierale Wertethik* (Niemeyer, 1927); for an English translation, see *Formalism in Ethics and Non-Formal Ethics of Values*, trans. Manfred S. Frings and Robert L. Funk (Northwestern University Press, 1973). On this topic, Foucault analyzes the distinction between acts and functions starting with Jules Vuillemin's reading of it in his monograph *L'être et le travail. Les conditions dialectiques de la psychologie et de la sociologie* (PUF, 1949). Scheler is also mentioned in other reading notes focusing on works by Binswanger (BNF, Box 38, folder 3), Hans Kunz, and Franz Fischer (BNF, Box 42b, folder 1). Foucault especially cites Scheler's works *Die Idole der Selbsterkenntnis*, in *Abhandlungen und Aufsätze*, vol. 2 (Verlag der Weissen Bücher, 1915), 3–168; "Zur Idee des Menschen" [1914], in *Vom Umsturz der Werte. Abhandlungen und Aufsätze*, vol. 1 (Neue Geist, 1919), 271–312; and "Idealismus Realismus," *Philosophischer Anzeiger* 2 (1928): 255–324. Scheler is a constant point of reference across Binswanger's work: in his reading notes, Foucault mentions him especially on the subject of the phenomenon of shame discussed in the case study of Ellen West, as well as on the subject of the problem of space in psychopathology, more specifically the Binswangerian concept of "*gestimmte[r] Raum*" ("emotive" or "affective" space). As for Hans Kunz, Foucault devoted a reading note to the article "Idee, Wesen und Wirklichkeit des Menschen. Bemerkungen zu einem Grundproblem der philosophischen Anthropologie," *Studia Philosophica* 4, no. 147 (1944): 147–69, and cites Scheler on the problem of sexuality in relation to the determination of the essence of man. In addition, in another series of reading notes preserved in the same box, Foucault summarizes Kunz's article "Die anthropologische Betrachtungsweise in der Psychopathologie," *Zeitschrift für die gesamte Neurologie und Psychiatrie* 172 (1941): 145–80, and cites Scheler on the definition of anthropology presented in "Mensch und Geschichte," *Neue Rundschau* 37 (1926): 449–76. Finally, Foucault mentions Franz Fischer's article "Zeitstruktur und Schizophrenie," which cites Scheler's conception of time as "Tätigkeitsform des Geistes" ("form of activity of the spirit"). The Schelerian conception of anthropology is also central in Foucault's course on anthropology, given in the early 1950s at the University of Lille and École normale supérieure; see "Connaissance de l'homme et réflexion transcendantale," BNF, Box 46; and "Problèmes de l'anthropologie," notes by Jacques Lagrange, IMEC, Fonds Michel Foucault, C.2.1/FCL 2. A03–08).

12. In Foucault's archives from the early 1950s, there are two reading notes entitled, respectively, "Ressentiment" and "Ressentiment and the revolt of slaves" (BNF, Box 33a, folders 1 and 2). Let us recall that Merleau-Ponty had written a review of Scheler's book *Ressentiment* when it was published: see "Christianity and *Ressentiment*" (note 7 above).

13. Foucault dedicated a great many reading notes in the early 1950s to this work by Husserl (BNF, Box 42a, folder 3).

14. This problem is developed by Foucault especially in his manuscript entitled "Phénoménologie et psychologie (1953–1954)" (BNF, Box 46, folder 2).

15. We can deduce the missing bibliographic reference by means of a series of reading notes from the 1950s, where Foucault mentions studies precisely on the topic of the "delusion of the end of the world": Rudolf Bilz, "Die Metapher des Untergangs in der Schizophrenie," *Der Nervenarzt* 20 (1949): 258–62; and Alfred Storch and Caspar Kulenkampff, "Zum Verständnis des Weltuntergangs der Schizophrenen," *Der Nervenartz* 21, no. 3 (1950): 102–108 (BNF, Box 42b, folder 1). These articles are also cited by Foucault in another reading note about Binswanger's essay "Daseinsanalytik und Psychiatrie," *Der Nervenarzt* 22 (1951): 1–10, reprinted in *Ausgewählte Vorträge und Aufsätze*, vol. 2, *Zur Problematik der psychiatrischen Forschung und zum Problem der Psychiatrie* (A. Francke, 1955), 279–302, which tackles the relationship between *Daseinsanalyse* and psychopathology, and especially the "metaphors of schizophrenics" (BNF, Box 38, folder

1). Foucault also mentions the "*Erlebnis des Weltuntergang*" in a reading note examining Alfred Storch's study "Die Daseinsfrage der schizophrenen," *Archiv für Neurologie, Neurochirurgie und Psychiatrie* 59 (1947): 330–85 (BNF, Box 42b, folder 1). It is interesting to recall that in Paris in 1948 François Tosquelles defended his thesis in medicine on the topic of "the lived experience of the end of the world in madness"; see *Le vécu de la fin du monde dans la folie. Le témoignage de Gérard de Nerval*, preface by Jean Oury (Jérôme Millon, 2012).

16. Here Foucault is referring to Jaspers's critique of psychoanalysis in chapter 3 of *General Psychopathology* (in the French translation based on the third edition) as well as in his 1913 article "Kausale und "verständliche" Zusammenhänge." According to Jaspers, the "meaningful connections" in psychic life always emerge from an individual life, whose interpretation can only be conjectural. However, in numerous cases, Freud imagines "extraconscious" connections as the basis of meaningful connections, which are always at the level of the "unremarked," which is to say at the level of consciousness. Yet, since these connections are by definition unknowable, Freudian understanding then presents itself as an "as if" understanding (*"als ob" Verstehen*), which is to say a conjectural, "imprudent" and "unconvincing" interpretation ("Kausale und "verständliche" Zusammenhänge, 338). Foucault was likely recalling this argument in his introduction to *Dream and Existence* when he wrote, about the interpretation of dreams, that "psychoanalysis gets only to the hypothetical . . . the link uniting image to meaning is always defined as a possible, eventual, contingent one" (36).

17. Foucault is referring to Jaspers's study on delusional jealousy, "Eifersuchtswahn. Einer Beitrag zur Frage: 'Entwicklung einer Persönlichkeit' oder 'Prozess'?" *Zeitschrift für die gesamte Neurologie und Psychiatrie* 1 (1910): 567–637; reprinted in *Gesammelte Schriften zur Psychopathologie*, 85–141. Foucault knew it through Lagache's work on romantic jealousy, which is cited later in the manuscript. In Foucault's archives, a folder from the 1950s on Jaspers contains a reading note devoted precisely to this study (BNF, Box 42b, folder 1).

18. Manfred Bleuler (1903–1994): son of the famous psychiatrist Eugen Bleuler, he was professor of psychiatry from 1942 to 1969 at the University of Zurich, where he also directed the Burghölzli psychiatric clinic. In 1937, he took over editorship of the psychology digest *Lehrbuch der Psychiatrie*

from his father; this journal had appeared for the first time in 1916. In a reading note from the 1950s, Foucault summarizes Manfred Bleuler's book *Krankheitsverlauf, Persönlichkeit und Verwandtschaft Schizophrener und ihre gegenseitigen Beziehungen* [Progress of the illness, personality, and affinity of schizophrenics and their mutual relationships] (Thieme, 1941) and notes, "According to Ellenberger, Swiss psychiatry. Ev. Psy. 1951" (BNF, Box 44b, folder 1). Indeed, Henri F. Ellenberger published a series of articles in *L'Évolution psychiatrique* between 1951 and 1953; these were reprinted in *La psychiatrie suisse* (Poirier-Bottreau, 1954). Ellenberger also devoted some pages to Manfred Bleuler in "La psychiatrie suisse (II)," *L'Évolution psychiatrique* 16, no. 4 (1951): 627–29. In them, he focuses on Bleuler's studies concerning the analysis of heredity in schizophrenia and the influence of endocrine factors in psychosis.

19. See on this topic the introduction to *Le rêve et l'existence*: "It has seemed to us worthwhile to follow *for a moment* this path of [Binswanger's] reflection, and to see [alongside it] whether the reality of man may not prove to be accessible only outside any distinction between the psychological and the philosophical; whether man, in his forms of existence, may not be the only means of getting to man" ("Dream, Imagination and Existence," 32).

20. In a reading note entitled "Totality and existence," Foucault quotes Binswanger: "No element of the structure of the *In-der-Welt-sein* as a whole can be modified without the whole being modified, and inversely" (BNF, Box 38, folder 1). This quotation is from Binswanger, "Anthropologie, Psychologie, Psychopathologie," *Schweizerische medizinische Wochenschrift* 66 (1936): 680, and is cited by Hans Kunz in "Die anthropologische Betrachtungsweise in der Psychopathologie," 176.

CHAPTER ONE

The Ellen West Case

Theoretical construction and clinical observation in phenomenological psychopathology. I. The Ellen West case (Ludwig Binswanger): 1. The patient's history; 2. Comparison between the Ellen West case and the Nadia case (Pierre Janet); 3. The psychoanalytic interpretation of Ellen West; 4. The world of Ellen West; 5. The style of existence of Ellen West. II. Ontic and ontological.

Kurt Schneider[1] once reproached[a] psychopathologists inspired by phenomenology—he was thinking of Erwin Straus[2] and of Viktor Emil von Gebsattel[3]—for not sufficiently attending to clinical practice and for offering, where one might expect a psychological method, a *"philosophische Deutung."*[b][4] Binswanger would probably have agreed with Gebsattel's response:[c] that one must not speak of theoretical construction in situations where clinical observation does not confirm what it is not in its nature to confirm; and that in any case *theôria*, the intuitive exam, which the

[33]

---

a Kurt Schneider, "Allgemeine Psychopathologie im Jahre 1928," *Fortschritte der Neurologie, Psychiatrie und ihrer Grenzgebiete* 1 (1929): 145. [This article is also mentioned by Foucault in "Dream, Imagination, and Existence," (trans. Forrest Williams, in *Dream and Existence*, ed. Keith Hoeller (Humanities Press, 1993), 32n3.]
b ["Philosophical interpretation."]
c Viktor Emil von Gebsattel, "Die Störungen des Werdens und des Zeiterlebens im Rahmen psychiatrischer Erkrankungen," in *Gegenwartsprobleme der psychiatrisch-neurologischen Forschung: Vorträge auf dem Internationalen Fortbildungskurs*, ed. Christel Heinrich Roggenbau (Enke, 1939), 54–71.

blossoming of meaning presupposes, is in no way a hypothetical construction of the understanding. Nothing could confirm these ideas better than the clinical studies published by Binswanger: at the same time as the pursuit of clinical detail is pushed as far as possible, the arbitrary frameworks of symptomatology are set aside; classifications and relations that pertain only to the understanding are dispensed with; and what one seeks throughout these pathological existences, in the jumble of details that they accumulate, is to allow their most originary meaning to speak. *Theôria* does not exclude experience and is not its inverse: it is, on the contrary, the content of experience that must be opened to the "theoretical" gaze of the intuition, without going through the detour of the categories of discursive understanding.

Among the examples of analyses Binswanger's writings offer us, we will choose the Ellen West case to examine at greater length.[d5] This is because, in this first example of a study of schizophrenia, the author still attaches a particular importance to problems of method, and invites a comparison with these methods, which we could describe as pertaining to understanding, which are psychoanalytic interpretation and clinical commentary.

HISTORY OF THE PATIENT

Ellen West belongs to a Jewish family; the domineering father plays the role of the man of action; yet he has depressive episodes and at night, occasionally, anxiety attacks. In the father's family,

---

d [Ludwig Binswanger, "Der Fall Ellen West: Eine anthropologisch-klinische Studie," *Schweizer Archiv für Neurologie und Psychiatrie* 53 (1944): 255–727; 54 (1944): 69–117 and 330–360; 55 (1945): 16–40; reprinted in *Schizophrenie* (Günther Neske, 1957), 57–188; for an English translation, see "The Case of Ellen West: An Anthopological-Clinical Study," trans. Werner M. Mendel and Joseph Lyons, in *Existence: A New Dimension in Psychiatry and Psychology*, ed. Rollo May, Ernest Angel, and Henri F. Ellenberger (Basic Books, 1958), 237–364.]

we can note several psychoses (manic depression in Ellen West's great-grandmother). The mother of the patient, a gentle woman, good, pliable, a dreamer, had a long depressive episode during her engagement. Ellen West has two brothers: the eldest resembles his father, while the other, younger than her, is an effeminate aesthete; when he was approximately seventeen, he exhibited suicidal thoughts and was placed in a clinic for a few weeks.

When she is nine months old, she refuses milk and will not be able to tolerate it in the years that follow. Despite two courses of psychoanalytic treatment, she has almost no memory of her childhood; according to her relatives she was lively, capricious, stubborn. When she is ten, she comes to Europe, where her parents settle; she attends school and shows herself to be diligent, proud, and distant. Her childhood and teenage amusements are boys' games and in one of the poems of her seventeenth year she writes of her wish to be a boy in order to become "a warrior" and "to die, sword in hand."[e] Until then, she had been very religious, which opposed her to her father. But at seventeen she reads *Niels Lyhne*,[6] becomes enamored of his religious nihilism, and fascinated, repeats after him, "*Kein Heim auf Erden, kein Gott in Himmel, kein Ziel in Zukunft.*"[f] She also follows him in his exaltation of individuality—this pathetic essence of man: "the strength and independence of the human race in its belief in itself."[g] She takes up all of the themes of Nietzsche's imitators, and, going through the same gestures as so many young bourgeois of the early

[36]

---

e [Binswanger, "The Case of Ellen West," 239. Despite the use of quotation marks, in most cases Foucault's translations of the passages he cites from Binswanger in this manuscript are quite loose. (Here I use the English translation of Binswanger's text by Mendel and Lyons as a bibliographic reference; while I draw on the vocabulary of this translation more generally, I have reproduced Foucault's wording wherever possible—Trans.)]

f ["No home on earth, no God in heaven, no goal in the future." Binswanger, "Ellen West," 272.]

g [Binswanger, "Ellen West," 273.]

twentieth century who want to emancipate themselves, distances herself from her family whose material comfort and bourgeois status she disdains, dreams of social action, and becomes enamored of liberatory myths. Within these daydreams, a very labile affectivity sets in: her poems sometimes swell with a senseless joy; sometimes also they become very dark, in the old-fashioned and touching style of the most desperate romanticism: at twilight . . . "old pictures rise up before us. The old plans and hopes, none of which have been realized, the boundless emptiness of the world and our infinite minuteness stand before our tired soul. Then the old question crowds to our lips, 'What for—why all this? Why do we strive and live, only to molder in the frozen earth?'"[h] But the work is there, like "an opiate for this suffering."[i] She travels, she probably experiences the bitterness of interrupted romance, since her parents force her to break off an engagement, but all in all it is the happiest period of her life. Her daydreams are always trapped in the contradiction between her "longing for darkness" and "the brightness of the sun and the smiling spring."[j] But the love of life wins out: she wants to love a man who "must be tall, and strong, and have a soul as pure and unblemished as the morning light. He must not dream life, but only live it, in all its seriousness and all its joy."[k]

When she is approximately twenty she travels to Sicily: these are the first shadows. She is not understood; she is abandoned; she wants to act but knows only how to lose herself in useless words; she is mocked because she is fat; she refuses sweets, no longer eats in the evening, goes on very long walks. Once she returns home, her depression escalates: she experiences anxiety

---

h Binswanger, "Ellen West," 240.]
i [Binswanger, "Ellen West," 240.]
j [Binswanger, "Ellen West," 240–41.]
k [Binswanger, "Ellen West," 241.]

around everything, sunshine and darkness, day and night. She complains that her inner self *(inneres Selbst)* is too narrowly linked to her body: "I despise myself"; "every day I get fatter, older, more loathsome."[1] She no longer fears death: "If the great friend, death, makes me wait too long I shall go seek her."[m] The luxury that surrounds her, bourgeois life oppress her: she pounds the walls with her fists so long that she ends up collapsing, spent. Alongside the fear of growing fatter then appears the violent desire to eat, and to eat mostly sweets, especially when the presence of others has made her nervous.

At the university she attends, she has met a student to whom she becomes engaged; her depression dissipates, but gives way to a kind of exalted love of death: she wants to die as "the birdling does, in highest jubilation, and not to live like a worm, loathsome and dull."[n] Her parents, who disapprove of the marriage, send her away; her refusal of food intensifies; in order to lose weight she takes 36 to 48 tablets of thyroidine a day;[o] in the United States, where she is traveling, she is diagnosed with Basedow's disease[7] and stays in bed for six weeks. Upon her return to Europe, she weighs seventy-five kilograms. One of her cousins courts her; for two years [she] hesitates between him and the student; finally it is the cousin she marries. She is twenty-six years old.

[38]

---

l [Binswanger, "Ellen West," 242.]

m [Binswanger, "Ellen West," 242. In his French translation of the text (28n1) Philippe Veysset observes that the German term "death" (*Tod*) is gendered masculine, which is why he chooses to refer to death as the "grand ami" rather than the "grande amie." Veysset's remark is important because, according to Binswanger, there is a connection between Ellen West's love of men and her love of death, in which death takes a masculine—even paternal—face. (Different from German usage, "death" is a feminine noun in French. Foucault uses the feminine in his quotation, and I have followed his choice here—Trans.)]

n [Binswanger, "Ellen West," 246.]

o [Sentence added in the margin: Thyroidine is a treatment for obesity.]

The entirety of the period that will follow, until her thirty-third year, is characterized by progressive decline, barely slowed by a few transitory improvements. During the year that follows her marriage, Ellen West is torn between the desire to have a child and the anxious fear of gaining weight. At meals she does not consume any food, but occasionally she throws herself avidly on any foodstuff that she believes is not fattening; sometimes she eats everything she has bought for the household: each of these "binges" throws her into deep remorse. At thirty-two, she weighs forty-two kilos. She attempts psychoanalytic treatment with a young doctor who does not follow Freudian orthodoxy; she regains hope, aspires to health, goes to the theatre and to concerts. But all of this is on the order of effort rather than of actual improvement for her: "The only real improvement," she writes to her husband, "which must come from within, is not yet here; Nirvana has not yet been reached."[p] She notes, "Now I have the will (*Will*) to become fatter, but not the wish (*Wunsch*). It is a conflict between duty (*Pflicht*) and desire (*Neigung*) in the Kantian sense."[q] She is willing to heal, but does not want to "pay the price."[r] In short, the psychoanalysis does not take, and for external reasons it is interrupted. She then experiences the desire to spend time with her parents, not because of her father who is hard and severe, but because of her mother in whom she would like to confide and with whom she would like to cry. The beginning of her visit goes well, but after two weeks, she begins to wander the city, whose streets she roams while crying; she hardly stops crying all day. A doctor wants to admit her to a

---

p [Binswanger, "Ellen West," 251. Foucault cites only part of Binswanger's quotation of Ellen West: "Nirvana in a figurative sense, 'the extinction of greed, hate, and delusion' has not yet been reached."]

q [Binswanger, "Ellen West," 251.]

r [Binswanger, "Ellen West," 250.]

clinic. She refuses, and consults a psychoanalyst who follows Freudian orthodoxy.

Soon after the beginning of the treatment, she attempts suicide by taking a large dose of Somnacetin. The psychoanalyst does not attach much importance to this gesture and continues the treatment. Her state worsens, she continues to wander the streets, always in tears; it is at this time that she writes, "The sun shines, but there is emptiness within me. . . . Two things torture me: hunger, and the dread of getting fatter."[s] This is how she describes one of her mornings: "I sit at my desk and am pleased about all I have to do. But a tormenting restlessness keeps me from finding quiet. I jump up, walk to and fro, stop in front of the cupboard where the bread is. I eat a little piece; ten minutes later I jump up again and eat some more. I naturally have enough willpower to stop eating, but I cannot suppress my desire; all day long, I cannot get the thought of hunger out of my mind. It fills up my brain, and there is no more room for other thoughts. I can no longer work, nor concentrate on my reading. Most of the time this is how it ends: I run into the street. *I run away from the bread that is in my cupboard*"[t] (her emphasis). "My life is full of dread: dread of food; dread of hunger; dread of the dread."[u]

Less than two months after the start of her second psychoanalysis—we are in the month of November—and because of the risk of suicide, she checks into an open clinic, where she continues her treatment. She eats much better and, for the first time in a long time, she consumes meat, potatoes, chocolate. On arrival, she weighed forty-seven kilograms; two months later, fifty-two. While living at the clinic, she attends university courses and

[40]

---

s [Binswanger, "Ellen West," 253.]
t [Binswanger, "Ellen West," 253–54.]
u [Binswanger, "Ellen West," 254–55.]

goes out to the theatre at night. Hope is reborn in her, and in her poems she expresses the desire to "become once again a human among humans."[v] The night of November 18–19 is the peak of this upward trajectory: "I see the golden stars dance; it is still night, a chaos as there has never been before. With the morning and its sparkling clarity, will rest come, as well as harmony?"[w] She asks herself, "Is love coming back into my life?"[x] She is reassured, and her ailments themselves take on a more serene aspect: "I am no longer afraid of what is coming. It is sweet to fear and to suffer, to become and to grow."[y] On the morning of the 19th, everything has vanished; she has never felt so alone: "My illness isolates me more and more from people. . . . I see them through a glass wall; I have an unutterable longing to get to them; I scream, but they do not hear me; I stretch out my arms toward them, but my hands merely beat against the walls of my glass cage."[z] From that day on, she is one with her illness, and the only hope lies in death: the thought of eating "pursues her, just as the thought of a murder pursues the murderer until he denounces himself to the police. In the punishment, he seeks redemption. I can free myself only in death."[aa] She begins to write the history of this illness which has now closed in on her like a fate, to trace it like a finished thing, like the very truth of her life: around (my) thirty-second year "I felt that all inner development was interrupted, because a single idea was filling my entire soul: I could no longer free myself from it. . . . Thus I came to psychoanalysis. I wanted to know the unknown urges which were stronger than my reason

---

v [Binswanger, "Ellen West," 255.]
w [Binswanger, "Ellen West," 255.]
x [Binswanger, "Ellen West," 256.]
y [Binswanger, "Ellen West," 256.]
z [Binswanger, "Ellen West," 256.]
aa [Binswanger, "Ellen West," 256.]

and which forced me to shape my entire life in accordance with a guiding point of view: to be thin. The analysis was a disappointment. I analyzed with my mind, and everything remained theory. . . . To this something far worse was added: the need to always have to think about eating. This pressure has become the curse of my life. It pursues me, as the Furies pursue a murderer, and makes my life a hell."[bb] From now on she experiences her unhappiness as the necessity of a tragedy: she is like one of those theatrical heroes who seek to leave the scene, but encounter warriors drawing their swords against them at every turn: "Life has become a prison for me and I aspire to death."[cc] The psychoanalyst wants her to leave the clinic and "return to life";[dd] the clinic's physician opposes this plan. On January 14th, he forbids the continuation of the psychoanalytic treatment and sends her to Bellevue Hospital with a report that speaks of depression coupled with obsessions. At the moment of departure, she writes to her younger brother: "Life burdens me like a cloud."[ee]

[42]

She stays at the hospital for two months (January 14–March 13). The first day, she provides some details about her illness: she differentiates between her "obsessions" (necessity of thinking about food) and her "fixed idea" (becoming thin); it is the conflict between them that turns each of her meals into an inner drama. She has the feeling that everything is unreal, without signification. She continues to feel the impulse to eat: one night, she consumes seven oranges in succession. She attaches herself, in a manifestly homosexual mode, to another young, elegant, thin female patient. She alternates between periods of rest and periods of agitation, but the desire to die stays constant: the doctors

---

bb [Binswanger, "Ellen West," 257.]
cc [Binswanger, "Ellen West," 258.]
dd [Binswanger, "Ellen West," 257.]
ee [Binswanger, "Ellen West," 259.]

are sadists because they do not want to allow her to end her suffering. She offers fifty thousand francs for someone to kill her.

The patient is in an open ward; the risk of suicide is so great that the husband is asked to choose between having his wife transferred to a locked ward or having her discharged from the hospital. The husband will consent to internment only if there is hope for a cure, or at least for improvement. Binswanger calls Bleuler in to consult, as well as a foreign psychiatrist far removed from Bleulerian conceptions.[8] Binswanger has already made the diagnosis of schizophrenic psychosis; Bleuler identifies schizophrenia, and the foreign doctor speaks of a psychopathic constitution. All three agree to reject the diagnosis of obsessional neurosis or of a manic-depressive cycle. The prognosis therefore does not portend any amelioration.

The patient's departure is set; she is externally calm, but inwardly she is very agitated. Outside the hospital, the symptoms deepen. Seeing what she left behind underscores her illness in her own eyes: she feels even more unable to live. She arrives home: on the third day of her return, she eats appropriately; she accepts sweets, chocolate; for the first time in thirteen years, she feels full. That afternoon, she reads poems by Rilke, Goethe, Tennyson; she goes for a long walk with her husband; she takes pleasure in reading George Bernard Shaw's critique of *Christian Science*; that evening, she writes letters; the last is addressed to the young woman she met at the hospital and grew so attached to there. In the morning, she is found dead; she had poisoned herself; she looked "as she had never looked in life, full of calm, happiness, and joy."[ff]

*

---

ff [Binswanger, "Ellen West," 267.]

Binswanger compares the case of Ellen West to a quite similar [44] case narrated by Janet in *Les obsessions et la psychasthénie* [Obsessions and Psychasthenia].[gg] [9]

Nadia had been referred to Janet with a diagnosis of hysterical anorexia: each day, the only food she was consuming was two portions of bouillon, one egg yolk, one spoonful of vinegar and one cup of extremely strong tea, with lemon juice. Yet Nadia's is not one of these hysterical anaesthesias that suppress the very sensation of hunger; on the contrary, she is so hungry that she spends entire hours thinking about food: "I was swallowing my saliva, I was biting into my handkerchief, I was rolling on the floor, so much did I want to eat."[hh] If she forbids herself food, it is for fear of gaining weight and of becoming as heavy as her mother: "I do not want to be pretty, but I would be too ashamed if I were to swell up; I could not bear it."[ii] This shame does not concern only her size, but the very act of eating (mastication "makes a specific, ridiculous, ignoble noise"),[jj] sex (she dresses like a boy, not because she would like to be sexed male, but because she "would like to have no sex"),[kk] and finally the body as a whole: she would like to be without a body.

Let us leave the differences between the Nadia and Ellen West cases in the background for now; we will return to them later.[10] What matters to us here are the methods through which Janet and Binswanger approach them. Janet first notes about Nadia that the obsession does not focus so much on food as an

---

gg   Pierre Janet, *Les obsessions et la psychasthénie*, vol. 1, *Études cliniques et expérimentales sur les idées obsédantes, les impulsions, les manies mentales, la folie du doute, les tics, les agitations, les phobies, les délires du contact, les angoisses, les sentiments d'incomplétude, la neurasthénie, les modifications du réel, leur pathologie et leur traitement* (Félix Alcan, 1903), 33.

hh   [Janet, *Les obsessions et la psychasthénie*, 35.]

ii   [Janet, *Les obsessions*, 37. Foucault's quotation differs slightly from Janet's text.]

jj   [Janet, *Les obsessions*, 38.]

kk   [Janet, *Les obsessions*, 39. Foucault cites Janet's text freely.]

object, that it does not crystallize around any particular foodstuff, but rather that it concerns a behavior:[ll] the act of eating, and, through it, all of the acts that make up bodily behaviors. In the obsessive idea, what is primary is not the object, despite all the worries it elicits in the patient, but the behaviors associated with it. Yet these behaviors—and it is in this way that they are obsessive—are not accompanied by the feelings that normally regulate action, that give rise to it at its start (desire) and stop it at its completion (satisfaction); on the contrary they [have] for affective context a feeling that perturbs them, stopping them in their course and making them start again indefinitely: in this way, the body shame that constrains all bodily conduct interrupts dietary behavior by leaving it, so to speak, unsatisfied.[mm] There is therefore obsession only insofar as a disturbance of feeling halts the sequence of behaviors in their earliest stages. But what accounts for this disturbance of feeling? It is because the psychic energy is no longer strong enough to get to the end of the most complex forms of behavior; then the feeling—as a good regulator of behaviors, as a good distributor, we might say, of psychic energy—interrupts them and reiterates only their simplest phases. In this way, Nadia is no longer capable of complicated behavior such as the ingestion of food in situations of social control: she is [no longer] able to eat while knowing that she is being seen to eat; then the shame of being surprised in her dietary functions forbids her from eating in any way other than hastily, swallowing some liquid surreptitiously, or throwing herself on food as soon as others' backs are turned. We see how easy it would be to analyze the Ellen West case along these lines: the

---

ll [Both "conduite" and "comportement" are translated by "behavior" in this section; see the translator's note.]

mm [Foucault uses the French expression "laisser sur sa faim"—Trans.]

reduction of psychic tension is manifest in her incapacity to act [46] and in the feeling of unreality that she often expresses. Eating as a behavior of assimilating the real is impossible for her: she can eat only hurriedly, gluttonously, and always anticipating the torment of a remorse that will immediately interrupt her.

Let us not dwell on the easier critiques of Janet (mysterious nature of psychic tension and energy, obscure finalism of regulatory feelings); not because they are not valid, but because they are not radical. Janet's analysis, insofar as it voluntarily occurs at this psychological level, is like a project of backing the pathological away from its own limits. Transposing the problem of obsessive representation into behavioral terms, then into terms of feeling, and finally into terms of energy: this frees the psychological sphere from fundamental interrogation by redirecting this interrogation to a bio-physiological sphere that we know in advance cannot be explored. When it does not content itself with offering a diagnosis—which is to say, referring a patient immediately back to illness—the clinic has as its only role, even when practiced by Janet, to evade the essential question by redirecting it from like to like until the point where everyone acknowledges that it can no longer be resolved. The clinic, fundamentally, aims to avoid forcing the patient to answer for his own illness. What is at the root of the illness is not the patient, but the disturbance of an obscure sphere: the patient, in his pathological behaviors, [47] is nothing but the consequence of his own illness. The entire value of the clinic lies in its ability to draw its conclusions with all of the rigor that psychology is capable of. And reciprocally, all of its weakness lies it its conception of pathological conduct, of the pathological universe, of the pathological man, only in the register of consequences.

*

Despite appearances, psychoanalysis perhaps does not go much farther. Ellen West had the privilege of undergoing two courses of psychoanalytic treatment that seem, perhaps because of the illness's psychotic structure, to have had little influence on her. But what is important here is the manner in which the psychoanalytic interpretation was carried out. The second treatment, which seems to have been more far-reaching than the first, begins by establishing a system of symbolic equivalencies: thinness, with all of its affective content, conceals a certain kind of libidinal object whose incarnations in the patient's life were the student to whom she became engaged, the friend she met in the hospital, and maybe her younger brother; fatness, on the contrary, designates a type within the Jewish bourgeoisie in which it is probably easy to see the paternal image taking shape, and maybe that of her older brother. In all likelihood, none of this can be denied, and there is indeed in all of Ellen West's lived experiences this cleavage between two opposed types, one that attracts and the other [that repels].[nn] All of this is exact, except precisely the notion of "symbol." To say that thinness is a symbol of "spirituality" is to presuppose a theory of the image; it implies a philosophical conception of the primacy of sensations. The only thing that we can say with certainty is that thinness, spirituality, and a certain type of ethereal figure hold a common signification for the patient, and that in this way they constitute a universe opposed on every count to the universe where the significations common to fatness, materiality, and a type of figure solidly attached to the values of life meet.

There is therefore no way, except through a detour, to speak of symbolism where there is only convergence of meaning, and this even if one supposes a process of repression at play between

---

nn [This is a conjecture; the word is illegible.]

the symbol and the symbolized. Ellen West's psychoanalysis oriented itself toward the theme of food as a symbolic expression of the repressed theme of conception, the first serving only as a substitute for the second, and the fear of becoming fatter being nothing but a derivation of the fear of becoming pregnant;[oo] infantile mythology invites such a hypothesis. But in the case of Ellen West, the hypothesis lies not in the identification of these two themes, but rather in the existence of a process of repression between them. The theme of fatness and that of pregnancy are on the contrary always intertwined within her; and the separation does not occur between a vast unconscious on one hand and a consciousness haunted by symbols on the other, but rather between two worlds: one of youth, thinness, vitality; and the other of heavier age, of ugliness, of the weight of the body that pulls toward the earth and gives life only at the expense of life.

In any case, the psychoanalytic interpretation of a permanent reference between the symbolic and the symbolized can never lead to the necessary understanding. All we need to do is take the example of the dream. Here is one of Ellen West's dreams during her hospital stay: during "a sea voyage, she jumps into the water through a porthole. Her first lover (the student) and her husband both attempt resuscitation. Afterward she eats many chocolate candies and packs her trunk."[pp] In the dream's symbolic system, the leap into the water is a birth fantasy, or that of a second birth, where the ship symbolizes the body of the mother: this birth can be either the birth of the dreaming subject or the birth of the

---

oo These are repressive and substitutive mechanisms that likely led the second analyst to offer the diagnosis of *Zwangsneurose* ["obsessional neurosis"]. [In French, "devenir grosse" primarily means to become fat, but it is also used in reference to pregnancy; as a result, the French text uses almost identical wording (*peur de grossir, peur de devenir grosse*) to describe the two conditions—Trans.]

pp [Binswanger, "Ellen West," 263, 321.]

subject's child;qq the reanimation is a symbol of fertilization and conceals her desire to have the children of her first lover and of her current husband; the trunk is the symbol of the female body and the food consumed recalls the old infantile myth that it is by eating that one can have children. As in many cases, we have to read this dream backward, and we can see an entire portion of the patient's affective history traced out, starting with her first childhood desires: "I ate in order to calm my sexual desire and to have children; but now I know that a man is necessary, and I wish for this to occur: if I have a child, I will be resuscitated."rr

But a second interpretation is possible, this time starting not from the theme of birth, but from the theme of death: "I have the wish to die; the student and my husband must help me (in the dream, the proposition's meaning has been reversed and, following a frequent mechanism, turned into its opposite); it is only then that I will be able to eat without suffering."ss This double possibility in interpretation is not a problem for psychoanalysis, and through the notion of overdetermination, it makes room for this plurality of meanings. And there are many chances for a course of psychoanalysis to see in the ambiguity of this dream the convergence, toward a same symbolic expression, of the two opposed instincts of life and death, like the imaginary counterpoint of Eros and Thanatos. But the fact remains that overdetermination will always be a lesser determination if it juxtaposes the potential meanings of a single psychic symbol in the form of a double instinctual drive. What gives a dream such as Ellen West's the plenitude of its signification is specifically the necessary

---

qq Binswanger has analyzed a fantasy of this kind, in conformity with the Freudian perspective, in "Analysis of a Hysterical Phobia." "Analyse einer hysterischen Phobie," *Jahrbuch für psychoanalytische und psychopathologische Forschungen* 3, no. 1 (1911): 228–308.

rr [Binswanger, "Ellen West," 324.]

ss [Binswanger, "Ellen West," 324–25.]

unity between the various interpretations that analysis proposes: a unity that we do not need to look for in some obscure contradiction of the unconscious, because it is immediately expressed by the patient herself as nostalgia for a death which would simultaneously be a second birth: "Create me once more," she cries out to the Almighty, "but create me new."[tt] The meaning of the dream [51] must not be sought in interpretations that mediate it, but rather grasped immediately in the expression in which it takes shape.

The major error of psychoanalysis is to break up the unity with which the patient expresses himself, and distribute it on one side or another of a line that separates the symbol from the symbolized, the conscious from the unconscious, the manifest expression from the instinctive drives that subtend it.[11] For psychoanalysis the truth is always by definition hidden, and the effort to understand is always a matter of not being fooled. But in a psychosis such as that of Ellen West, at least, the truth is not on the order of an enigma: it is there in its entirety, present in the patient's sphere of expression.[12] To seek it in the hypothetical domain of the unexpressed is to be fooled by one's very concern not to be fooled: the truth of psychosis is precisely where it expresses itself and nowhere else. The illness must not be situated in the back-world of the sick person; it is entirely in his world.[uu]

*

---

tt [Binswanger, "Ellen West," 247, 325.]

uu There is something like a common prejudice in a clinical analysis in the manner of Janet and in psychoanalytic interpretation: the refusal to take seriously the dimension of behavior and expression where the illness manifests itself, and the preoccupation with locating the truth of the illness in a psychic energy ostensibly feeding the behaviors, or in an unconscious that would be concealing the undisguised truth of the expression. In phenomenological psychiatry, the manifest, insofar as it is manifested, takes up its rightful place: the physician's chief concern is not to avoid being the dupe of the patient; rather, the physician first seeks not to be duped by himself. Phenomenological psychiatry is a return to seriousness.

[52] Let us return to Binswanger and to the manner in which he analyzes Ellen West's world. It is a world in which a compartmentalization, which will later become more and more rigid, appears very early: the precocious refusal of certain foods, the capricious stubbornness that her relatives remember already demonstrate a rupture between the material milieu (*Umwelt*), the social milieu (*Mitwelt*) on one hand, and on the other this world proper to the individual, which encompasses his organic life as well as his psychological life, and which the Germans call the *Eigenwelt*. Between this world and the two others, the opposition is asserted from the start, but this condition of independence is only seeming; this retreat of the *Eigenwelt* actually prevents the subject from controlling the situation, from considering all of its relations of signification, and from freely opening himself to the possibilities they invite: he can confer upon the situation only the definitively foreclosed meaning of his own opposition, and this is what the vocabulary of mainstream psychology denounces as stubbornness or obstinacy in children. But there is yet more: the subject's interior world collides not only with the world that surrounds it, but it is opposed to this world which he himself is as an objective individual, which he is for others, and which is like the external inverse of his own history; what he thus pushes away is his fate, and in a more precise manner, to the extent that "anatomy is destiny,"[vv] he rejects

---

vv [This is a famous formula of Sigmund Freud's in "The Dissolution of the Oedipus Complex" (1924). The French edition includes the following note: "*Die Anatomie ist das Schicksal.* Cf. *Die Politik ist das Schicksal:* Destiny is politics. Napoleon's phrase reported by Goethe (Meeting with Napoleon on 2 October 1808 in Erfurt, in Goethe, *Paralipomena zu den Annalen, Jubiläums-Ausgabe*, vol. 30, 414)." See Sigmund Freud, *Oeuvres complètes*, vol. 17, *1923–1925: Psychanalyse*, ed. André Bourguignon, Pierre Cotet and Jean Laplanche (PUF, 1992), 31. The first French translation of this essay by Freud was "Le déclin du complexe d'Oedipe," trans. Anne Berman, *Revue française de psychanalyse* 7, no. 3 (1934): 394–99.

his sexuality.[ww] Until her seventeenth year, Ellen West will play boys' games, she will dream of being a man and will transpose her own existence into the labile, transparent, airy world of fantasy; as Binswanger remarks, "*Schein* substitutes itself for *Sein*."[xx]

[53]

Her life now fixes itself in this existence of opposition and fantasy: the abandonment of her religious beliefs and her enthusiasm for Niels Lyhne's romantic nihilism merely specify and enrich the style of this existence: she now knows that it is necessary that "a soul be always alone,"[yy] that heaven is not inhabited, and that man has no other recourse than to the belief he has in himself. For real relationships with real people, she substitutes, under the same influence, vague humanitarian dreams where her hostility toward her family melds with a diffuse pity for the "sufferings of the masses":[zz] she is not able to find an authentic homeland in her social consciousness; she encounters only the perpetual exile and worry that tear her from her home.

True action is no longer possible for her, but rather only this action that she dreams in her words and that she reproaches herself for not accomplishing, as if its essence did not lie specifically in its inability to be accomplished. At the same time, it is a whole dimension of the world that collapses: this solid world where the steady relationships between things, the confident relations between men give action its security, this world of familiar landscapes where habit has traced its pathways, and where the road that goes from the possible without excess to the satisfied

---

ww See Hegel: "Destiny is myself become my own enemy" [sometimes translated into English as "Destiny is consciousness of oneself, but consciousness of oneself as an enemy." Foucault borrows the quotation from Jean Hyppolite, *Introduction à la philosophie de l'histoire de Hegel* (M. Rivière, 1948), 52, who in turn refers to Herman Nohl, *Hegels theologische Jugendschriften* (Mohr, 1907), 283 note a.]

xx ["Being is replaced by illusion." Binswanger, "Ellen West," 271.]

yy [Binswanger, "Ellen West," 272.]

zz [Binswanger, "Ellen West," 274.]

plenitude of the real is known, this terra firma, this world of the imagination at ground level, of full-color dreams of the present has now disappeared for Ellen West. From now on only marginal worlds will have value for her: the ethereal world where the fantasies of the imagination soar, carrying impossible dreams that the imagination exhausts in the infertile instant; and the dark, crushing, frozen world of things that crawl under the earth, a world that opens like a tomb only to close over the past. The ethereal world will carry every hope, the underground world every threat, but we must note right now that one is not the world of happiness while the other is the world of anxiety; rather, for Ellen West there is a fundamental anxiety[13] in the face of both worlds: in neither does she recognize her homeland, and each is foreign to her existence. One of her writings that we have cited opposes and connects in the same anxiety the "boundless emptiness of the world" and the "cold earth" in which we must "molder";[aaa] in another poem, she evokes the fiery sinking of the sun into the sea, and then the sky slowly obscured by a thick cloud: "Is there no rescue anymore?" *(Gibt's keine Rettung mehr?)*.[bbb]

Yet this anxiety can still be controlled: the reassuring struggle, the living and human struggle *against* both of these worlds, is lived more deeply than the anguishing struggle *between* these two worlds. This is the period during which she travels with her parents, when she is thrilled by long horseback rides, when she dreams of a friend who would really love life, "in all its seriousness and all its joy."[ccc] The subject here is not entirely given over to anxiety; the contradiction does not saturate the subject, but the subject struggles against it and exalts in its desire to control it.

---

aaa [Binswanger, "Ellen West," 240.]
bbb [Binswanger, "Ellen West," 239.]
ccc [Binswanger, "Ellen West," 241.]

Some time later, during the voyage to Sicily, the fear of gaining weight appears. For the psychiatrist, this is the beginning of the symptoms of obsession, of the idée fixe and of pathological withdrawal; but looking at things from farther away, it is more like the end of a whole existential cycle. The cosmological contradiction reaches the *Eigenwelt*; the ethereal world becomes the world of thinness, spirituality, youth; the underground world becomes the world of heaviness, age, the body's degrading instincts. As a result, the possibilities of existence close up—and this very effort by which Ellen West, in the final moments of her happy life, tore herself away from contradiction and anxiety, through an exaltation of life, this effort is now exhausted; the fallout will be only nostalgia. Anxiety and contradiction are now inscribed at the heart of her existence. There is nothing left that does not cause her anxiety: darkness and sunshine, silence and noise, tranquility—vertiginous void—and agitation—pointless din. Death would be the only issue, and death itself is experienced in the mode of contradiction: to die to avoid becoming ugly and old, laden with the weight of the years; but, if one dies, to rot under the heavy, cold earth. Existence is overrun and from now on torn apart by the contradiction of the worlds she had projected.

At this point of her existential development, time seems to have closed on its own impossibility; the future has no meaning because it opens onto the contradiction of death: "every day I feel myself getting older and more loathsome"; and the past can no longer be assumed in its plenitude: in a poem from this period, she describes a long horseback ride in which she is pursued by the shadows of the past, pale ghosts, regrets of time lost, and impossible dreams, like so many spirits of the wicked night. As for the present, cut off from the future and threatened by the ghosts of the past, it is empty, colorless, and joyless. Starting with her trip to Sicily, an anecdote illustrates this time which henceforth "goes around in circles": Ellen has gone on a long walk with her friends; having reached a scenic point, her friends stop and admire the view; but Ellen does not stop—rather she keeps walking in circles, because she is not walking toward a goal, but only to lose weight. The present cannot flourish in a sensory plenitude, and its emptiness can be filled only via incessant agitation.

That lived time has lost its meaning[ddd]—in both senses of the term, as "orientation" and as "signification"—does not stop the existential structures from continuing to evolve. It is around the twenty-fifth year that a new psychiatric symptom appears, which the patient, on her end, takes great care to distinguish from her fear of gaining weight: it is the impulsive desire to eat. This is a distinctly obsessional trait: repetition or even constant presence of a single idea; a tendency to act that takes on, for the patient, the aspect of a constraint; dissatisfaction; and remorse when the action has been accomplished. But the problem is not resolved when this new obsessional symptom has been appended to the older clinical chart; rather, the problem has only been posed. The definition of the symptom is not a solution; it is a starting point.

In one way, the conflict between the desire to eat and the fear of gaining weight is like an extension of the conflict between the ethereal world and the subterranean world: it is its echo in the sphere of the *Eigenwelt*. But in another, this conflict in its newness reveals a recent stage in the existential development; it is the discovery of a death that would consist not in the expiration of a graceless old age, and moldering in the tomb, but rather in taking flight toward the ethereal world and the dawn of its triumph.

---

ddd [Here Foucault uses the French "sens," which means both "meaning" and "direction"—Trans.]

The contradictory and simultaneous anxiety before the light and the dark, before the empty dreamworld and the massive universe of earthly forces—this anxiety escapes its contradiction by finding in the ethereal world the hope for a death that will allow her to escape the prison of the body and of the tomb. Anxiety will no longer be a fascination in the face of the contradictory equivalency of the two worlds: it will now be the acute feeling that the translucent world of death and hope is threatened by the thick world of life, of the instincts, and of the earth. It is indeed at this time that death stops being loathsome to Ellen West and that she invokes it as "the great friend," "the only chance of life," whom she would like to join if it does not come to her quickly enough.[eee] In the face of this world—where she now fixes the happiness of her existence and where she believes she has discovered her authentic destiny—the earthly world appears as a fundamental, ever-growing threat: the internal threat of hunger which, cropping up at any time, prevents her from working, thinking, accessing a disembodied spirituality; the external threat of her luxurious bourgeois existence, against which she rebels by pounding the walls with her fists until she collapses, depleted. The anxiety is now crystallized around this existence that threatens to be crushed, that threatens to be swallowed up by the earthly forces of life. It is not by chance that the period in which this obsessional symptom appears [is] also the period in which death appears to her as the only escape; in which she attends university again, in a great fit of intellectual asceticism; in which she befriends a student who to her eyes represents the very model of disembodied spirituality. And it would be a mistake to believe that the obsessional symptom is deeper, more real, more originary than these behaviors: in the psychiatric

[58]

---

eee [Binswanger, "Ellen West," 242–43.]

perspective, it is the symptom, because it is abnormal, that has the task of giving meaning to the individual's normal behaviors once he is recognized, named, labeled as "sick," but that entails rupturing the unity of existence in the name of a criterion which is more moral than it is psychological, and more pejorative than it is discriminating. It is not for the abnormal in its strangeness to give an account of the normal: it is not *because* she has the obsessive idea of food that Ellen West wants to escape it via a more or less neurotic escalation of her intellectual life. Rather, all of these behaviors—the liaison with a student, the intellectual asceticism, the obsession with food—"symbolize" with each other, as Leibniz would say;[14] and all of them assume their meaning in the existential development that makes of death the point of fulfillment of existence.

This existential development is crucial, because it allows us to penetrate the cycle of the tragedy: indeed, there where existence can realize itself only under the condition of sacrificing one's life, it becomes a tragic existence.[fff] But this existence, now destined for death, is not yet submitted or offered to it. Death is now the issue, but its doors are still closed. The world of the earth still has its weight, and this is what, in the face of empty death, still gives her vertigo: for two years she hesitates to marry the student she loves, and finally she decides to marry her cousin, a man who belongs to her family, to her earthly home. The universe of shadow and of instincts still threatens her from every direction, anxiety turns into panic, and she already flees hunger, as one day she will flee life. On this subject Binswanger quotes Valéry: "The man who eats ... nourishes both good and bad in his body. Every bite which he feels melting and spreading in himself will bring new force to his own virtue, just as it does to his own vices.

---

fff Binswanger, "Ellen West," 298.

It sustains his turmoils as it fattens his hopes, and it divides somewhere between passion and reason. Love needs it as well as hatred; and my joy and my bitterness, my memory and my plans, share as brothers the same substance of the bite."[ggg] For Ellen West, on the contrary, food nourishes only her vices and her ailments, her torments and her hatred, her passions and her bitterness. And in a strange paradox, the more food she consumes, the more avidly she devours, the more also she experiences a feeling of emptiness and insatiety. Janet would call this a feeling of incompleteness specific to psychasthenia. But it is this feeling itself that is the problem and that we must understand. How can this fullness, this "*Vollsein*" of the body, have as its necessary correlative the *Leersein*[hhh] of the spirit and the heart? Except, of course, that the contradiction that tore apart Ellen West's existence has now taken the rigorous, almost mathematical form of complementarity, and that everything that is given to one of the terms is refused to the other: what is fulfillment and sensory satisfaction on one side is desiccation and torture on the other. It is this complementarity that explains why Ellen West *does not commit suicide*, and that while she calls out to death, she does not manage to give it to herself, and begs others to end her suffering: she has not yet found the serenity that will deliver her from the earthly world; in the mode of refusal, she is still tied to it. This is perhaps the meaning that we must give to this strange image in which she depicts herself like a character in a tragedy who, at the moment of escape, encounters at each

[60]

---

ggg Paul Valéry, *Dance and the Soul*, trans. Dorothy Bussy (London: John Lehmann, 1951), 8. [Foucault reproduces Binswanger's quotation and reference from "The Case of Ellen West," 293; for this reason, I am using the version of the text found in the English translation of Binswanger, rather than Bussy's translation—Trans. Paul Valéry's poem was first published in 1921 in a special issue of *La revue musicale*.]

hhh ["Being-empty."]

exit the threat of death: but what threatens and imprisons her is, for her, life.

She escapes it, however, more each day: attesting to it is the dream of death and of rebirth that she has at the hospital, and her homosexual fixation on the young woman, the last fugitive apparition of the model of disembodied spirituality. But it is in all likelihood at her hospital discharge that she feels absolutely incapable of living: reencountering her past as a stranger reveals that she no longer belongs to it. Then she is free to die: she can accept all of the desires that have tortured her without contradiction; they can no longer threaten the world that is now open to her. In a few years, she has undergone a whole development that has led her to a sort of existential old age, which curiously anticipates biological old age: in the same way that an old age that feels the ripening of death frees itself little by little of all of life's necessities, she who already feels "dead among the living," has her desires desert her, and she can reencounter the real taste of food—not of insatiable desires, but of a hunger that, for the first time in thirteen years, is satisfied.

But as ripe as this death may be, however called forth by a life that leaves itself behind more each day, in order for it to occur, both as an event and as a denouement, a new spurt of existential maturation is necessary. The meaning of all of this existence, in the end, was not the project of being herself (*sie selbst zu sein*), but always that of not being herself:[15] neither herself in her body, nor herself in her sexuality, nor herself in her social situation, to not be *there*, in a word, in the world where she is. It is this project that psychoanalysis conceptualizes in what it calls "the fantasy of new birth" (*Wiedergeburtsphantasie*), but through which it would be wrong to try to explain suicide, because it is only its instantaneous expression. And now Ellen West's existence is free for death and opens onto it as onto its fate: then, in the single decision to die, she is able simultaneously to fulfill her aim to not be herself, and to be fully herself, because it is in complete freedom that she now goes to meet her true fate: her existence—her *Dasein*—becomes authentically itself in the act through which she eliminates herself; for the first time, in choosing herself, she has found herself. And this is why the day of her death is like a day of celebration: celebration of farewell as well as of birth, of departure and of beginning; celebration where the bread that is shared satisfies the appetite—where one starts to reread beloved things, where an impossible love can come together and then come apart in a final letter. The present regains its flavor because it is full of the reconciled past, and entirely open onto a new future. In suicide, existence has found its dawn once again. [62]

What is there, after all, that is so new in the analysis of a case [63] such as that of Ellen West? For a long time the psychiatric tradition had tended to describe these disturbances in the patient's universe through which the illness announces, expresses, and, as it were, realizes itself.[iii] We need only cite Bleuler and his description of schizophrenia: a world that is cold, colorless, chaotic, a world that the presence of others and the shifting significations of immediate comprehension have left behind. And why not recall the text, little known by psychiatrists, in which Halbwachs[jjj] analyzes the phenomena of aphasia: he demonstrates an essential link between the use of language—as a structured assemblage, as a kernel of significations and as a mobile communications network—and the insertion into a social time whose slow maturation frames and supports the historical language of a society: the aphasiac lives in a world where time, which is determined by its social coordinates, has disappeared, rendering unusable a

---

iii Bleuler [in all likelihood Foucault is referring to Eugen Bleuler, *Dementia Praecox; or, the Group of Schizophrenias*, trans. Joseph Zinkin (International Universities, 1950)].

jjj [Foucault is referring to Maurice Halbwachs, *Les cadres sociaux de la mémoire*; for the English translation, see On *Collective Memory*, ed. and trans. Lewis A. Coser (University of Chicago Press, 1992)].

language that has meaning only when plunged into this time, linked to its past in the mode of narration and to its future in the mode of an anticipation that predicts, orders, or promises.

[64] These analyses verge on existential description and, at first glance, they diverge from it only in terms of terminology. However, the difference is vast, at least at the level of the problem: what psychiatrists such as Bleuler want to determine is how the illness has modified the subject's world. What they describe are processes such as the "discoloration" of the world, the "derealization" of the other, the "fragmentation" of the perceived universe and of the meaning that can be read into it: a normal world is presupposed, and the morbid world is analyzed according to a subtractive logic, as the result of processes that have altered, perverted, or obliterated one region or another of this normal world. This is not how *Daseinsanalyse* considers the schizophrenic person's universe: it is not a question of knowing which alterations of his universe now denounce him as schizophrenic, but only in which universe this man, whom the psychiatrist designates as schizophrenic, lives.[kkk] This is not only to say that the analyst must bracket any distinction between normal and pathological, and that such an opposition can be of no help in existential analysis; this is not only to say that the space or the time of the patient, rather than being a narrowed space or an altered time, is *another* time and *another* space; it is simply to say—but this is the crucial point—that the world of this schizophrenic to whom

[65] we give the name of Ellen West is nothing other than *her* world, with *her* time, *her* space, and *her* human entourage. It is to refuse to ask the illness to give an account of this universe, and instead to look for its foundation in the patient himself: and not insofar

---

kkk See a remark along these lines by . . . [Here Foucault has begun a footnote but left it incomplete.]

as he is sick, but only insofar as he is a man, as he is existence, as he is free. The world of a sick man is not the process of the illness; it is the project of the man.

This is where we encounter one of the major difficulties of *Daseinsanalyse*: the difficulty of the task to be accomplished, which will perhaps reveal itself, one day, as a difficulty in the method to follow; the extreme ambition that can appear, at its core, as an ambiguity. The structure of the manic world, or the tempo of schizophrenic time, or even still the hierarchical segmentation of obsessional space are among those clinical facts that pertain to experience (*Erfahren*) and that are at the level that Heidegger calls the "ontic": there man is considered only as a "being" [*étant*] among other "beings" [*étants*]. There his world is not only confronted by the world of other men, but also by the world of life and of animality. In this way, the time of the schizophrenic unfolds the duration of vital processes in slow motion, whereas that of the manic person accelerates them to a fever pitch; the living space of the obsessive is strewn with barriers and prohibitions, which shatter the coherent unity of this milieu, defined by von Uexküll[16] as the *Umwelt*[lll] of any animal existence. But this [66] reflection begun at the level of the ontic must extend to the ontological and reach the understanding (*Verstehen*) of the project to which the originary freedom which is existence commits itself.

The analysis of existentials such as the temporality or the spatiality of the human world must therefore call into question both the experience of "beings" and the understanding of existence. As Kunz[17] observes, the anthropological interpretation of psychoses implies a reflection on both the ontic and the ontological: because human existence is both ontic and ontological.[mmm]

---

lll ["Ambient world."]

mmm Hans Kunz, "Die anthropologische Betrachtungsweise in der Psychopathologie," *Zeitschrift für die gesamte Neurologie und Psychiatrie* 172 (1941): 176–77.

NOTES

1. Kurt Schneider (1887–1967): In 1931, after medical studies in Berlin and Tübingen, he became director of the Institute for Psychiatric Research (Institut Kaiser-Wilhelm) in Munich, an institution founded by his teacher Emil Kraepelin. He left the Institute because of the Third Reich's eugenicist policies. After the war, he was named professor and director of Heidelberg University's psychiatric clinic, where he practiced until his retirement in 1955. In his reading notes from the 1950s, Foucault cites two of Kurt Schneider's works: *Psychiatrie heute* (Thieme, 1952) and *Über den Wahn* (Thieme, 1952) (BNF, Box 42b, folder 1).

2. Erwin Straus (1891–1975): A neurologist and psychiatrist, he cofounded the journal *Der Nervenarzt* in 1928. He held a position as professor of psychiatry at the University of Berlin before being forced, as a Jew, to emigrate to the United States in 1938. He taught philosophy and psychology at Black Mountain College in North Carolina until 1946 when he obtained authorization from Johns Hopkins University to practice medicine in the United States. He subsequently became a professor at the University of Kentucky in Lexington. After the war, he reconnected with his German and Swiss colleagues—notably Viktor Emil von Gebsattel, Eugène Minkowski, and Ludwig Binswanger—with whom he regularly met in Europe. In the early 1950s he was a visiting professor in Frankfurt, and then in Würzburg in 1961–62. Straus's thought is a constant reference point in the work of Binswanger and, in general, in that of all the authors associated with the phenomenological approach to psychopathology. Foucault devoted numerous reading notes to him in the 1950s. A folder entitled "Erwin Straus," in particular, contains twenty-eight pages dedicated to the book *The Primary World of Senses: A Vindication of Sensory Experience*, trans. Jacob Needleman (New York: Free Press, 1963) (BNF, Box 42b, folder 1). Foucault dedicated other reading notes specifically to the problem of the pathology of time and space according to Straus's perspective; on this topic, the works he mentions are "Das Zeiterlebnis in der endogenen Depression und in der psychopathischen Verstimmung," *Monatsschrift für Psychiatrie und Neurologie* 68 (1928): 126–40; "Die Formen des Räumlichen: Ihre Bedeutung für die Motorik und die Wahrnehmung," *Der Nervenarzt* 3, no. 11 (1930): 633–56; *Geschehnis und Erlebnis. Zugleich eine historiologische*

Deuteung des Psychischen Traumas und der Renten-Neurose (Springer, 1930); "Die aufrechte Haltung: Eine anthropologische Studie," *Monatsschrift für Psychiatrie und Neurologie* 117, nos. 4–6 (1949): 367–79; and "Ein Beitrag zur Pathologie der Zwangserscheinungen," *Monatsschrift für Psychiatrie und Neurologie* 98, no. 2 (1938): 61–81 (BNF, Box 38, folder 1; Box 42b, folder 1).

3. Viktor Emil von Gebsattel (1883–1976): From 1915 to 1920 he worked as an assistant physician in Munich in the psychiatric clinic directed by Emil Kraepelin. He then trained as a psychoanalyst and opened a private practice in Berlin. After the fall of the Nazi regime, he worked as chief of medicine at the Badenweiler sanatorium, in Baden-Württemberg, before obtaining a position teaching medical psychology and psychotherapy at the University of Freiburg im Breisgau. In 1950, he was named interim professor, holding the chair in psychiatry and neurology at the University of Würzburg, where he also taught courses in medical psychiatry. In Würzburg he also founded the Institut für Psychotherapie und Medizinische Psychologie, the first in Germany. Gebsattel is an important reference in Binswanger's work, and Foucault dedicated a great many reading notes to him (see especially the folder that bears his name in BNF, Box 42b, folder 1).

4. Foucault borrows this observation from Hans Kunz's article "Die anthropologische Betrachtungsweise in der Psychopathologie." In the reading note he dedicates to it, he records specifically: "K. Schneider reproaches Straus and Gebsattel for not paying sufficient attention to the clinic and for offering a method that is barely psychological: it is a *"philosophische Deutung.*" Hans Kunz, "Die anthropologische Betrachtungsweise in der Psychopathologie," *Fortschritte der Neurologie, Psychiatrie und ihrer Grenzgebiete* 1 (1929): 145 (BNF, Box 42b, folder 1).

5. Foucault wrote many reading notes on the clinical case study of Ellen West, as well as on particular concepts developed by Binswanger in his existential analysis of this case, specifically those of "eternity and love," "anxiety," "temporality," and "temporalization" (BNF, Box 38, folder 1). The file dedicated to the summary of the case study and to its analysis is located in Box 42b (folder 1, 23 pages).

6. *Niels Lyhne*, a novel published in 1880 by the Danish writer Jens Peter Jacobsen (1847–1885), narrates the life of a young poet, an idealist and a dreamer torn between his quest for the absolute and his total faith in Darwin. A prisoner of his nostalgia for an idealized life, incapable of acting,

Niels Lyhne is destined for a mediocre existence, marked by a feeling of defeat (*Niels Lyhne*, trans. Tiina Nunnally, Penguin Classics, 2006).

7. Basedow's disease [better known in the United States as Graves' disease—Trans.] is an autoimmune disorder of the thyroid characterized by hyperthyroidism. It is accompanied by specific clinical symptoms, including weakness, weight loss, and excessive sweating, as well as neuropsychological symptoms (fatigue, irritability, tachycardia).

8. The reference here is to Eugen Bleuler (1857–1939), who succeeded Auguste Forel as chair in psychiatry at the University of Zurich and director of Burghölzli, the psychiatric clinic affiliated with the university, from 1898 until 1927. Among his many students were Hermann Rorschach, Carl Jung, Ludwig Binswanger, Karl Abraham, and Eugène Minkowski. Bleuler met Sigmund Freud in 1904 and participated in the first International Psychoanalytical Congress in Salzburg in 1908. In 1909, he and Freud cofounded the *Jahrbuch für psychoanalytische und psychopathologische Forschungen*; in 1910 he contributed to the creation of the International Psychoanalytical Association. Prior to the falling-out between Freud and Bleuler around 1913, Burghölzli was the first university psychiatric clinic to use Freudian theory. In Foucault's reading notes from the 1950s, he often mentions the Swiss psychiatrist, especially his two major works: *Dementia praecox oder Gruppe der Schizophrenia* (Deuticke, 1911) and *Lehrbuch der Psychiatrie* (Springer, 1916) (BNF, Box 38, folder 1). It was in the first of these that Bleuler introduced the terms "schizophrenia" and "autism" to the vocabulary of psychiatry.

9. In Foucault's archives from the 1950s, there are numerous reading notes dedicated to Janet and especially to *Les obsessions et la psychasthénie* (BNF, Box 38, folder 3).

10. Foucault composed a reading note on this subject entitled "Comparison of the Ellen West, Nadia, and Jürg Zünd cases," in which he remarks, "1. All three established the ideal for their existence. This ideal carries more weight for them than their *Dasein*. Renouncing it arouses dread in them. But in this struggle they exhaust their *seelischen und körperlichen* [psychic and physical] strength. They shrink from a *geistig* [spiritual] point of view. 2. Now this ideal does not concern impersonal values (nation, science, philosophy, art), but values that are purely personal, purely "*selbstlich*": for Ellen W. the ideal of being thin; for Nadia of being *körperlos* [without a body]; for

Jürg Zünd that of social elevation. The ideal is not in the service of love, but in that of this *Selbst-Liebe* [self-love] to which it is diametrically opposed, which is the contrary of the *"Du-Offenheit"* [openness to the you] and which is the product of anxiety. Consequently, this ideal—and its modes of realization—are incompatible with the *"Grundverhältnisse der menschlichen Existenz"* [fundamental relations of human existence] in general, and the individual existences that contain them. 3. All three desperately want to remain themselves, but *"als ein anderer Selbst als sie sind"* [as a different self from what they are]. They cut off their own access to the foundation of their being, to this "force which established them," in order to sink further into the violence (*Gewalt*) of their egotistic ideal. In this way they separate themselves both from the grace of love and from independent action and lock themselves into defensiveness. 4. They are thus condemned (*verfallen*) to the world (*Eigen-, Um-* and *Mitwelt* [personal world, surrounding world, and world of coexistence]); this is the world that absorbs their force. It is why they join society (*verweltlichen*): i.e., from independent, loving, and free people, they become creatures that are *weltgebundene, vom Vergleichen-müssen lebende* [bound to the world, living from the duty to compare], unfree, anxiety-ridden (*angstgeplagte*). 5. In all three cases, this is what explains the transformation of the *Scham-und-Schuld-Gefühl* [feeling of shame and guilt] into *Gefühl der Schande* [feeling of shame], i.e., the transformation of existential dread into fear of something. Nadia is afraid of being seen, Ellen West of becoming fat, Jürg Zünd of being observed and disdained (*beachtet-verachtet*). The range of action decreases; despair increases. 6. They close themselves off not only from their *Daseinsgrund* [raison d'être], but also to communication. They are closed off to themselves and to others. Free *Offenbarung* [revelation] is succeeded by unfree *Offenbarung*: for Nadia and Ellen West, in the fact of wanting to eat good food; for Nadia and Jürg Zünd, in the production of always-new *Angriffsfläche* [surfaces of attack]" (BNF, Box 42b, folder 1).

11. The critique of the psychoanalytic conception of the "symbol" is also central to "Dream, Imagination and Existence," where Foucault states precisely that at the origins of the flaws of Freudian theory, there is an "inadequate elaboration of the notion of the symbol": "Freud takes the symbol as merely the tangential point where, for an instant, the limpid meaning joins with the material of the image taken as a transformed and transformable

residue of perception. The symbol is that surface of contact, that film, which separates, as it joins, an inner world and an external world; the instantiation of an unconscious impulse and of a perceptual consciousness; the factor of implicit language and the factor of sensible image" ("Dream, Imagination and Existence," trans. Forrest Williams, in *Dream and Existence*, ed. Keith Hoeller [Humanities Press, 1993], 36–37).

12. The "analysis of the expressive act in its necessity" is at the heart of "Dream, Imagination and Existence" (36). Here, Foucault expands on his critique of the Freudian hermeneutics of the dream precisely by insisting on the necessity and immediacy of meaning. He stresses that in the *Daseinsanalytic* approach, "the essential point of the dream lies not so much in what it revives of the past as in what it declares about the future": "more than an obligatory repetition of the traumatic past," the dream "anticipates"; it is "a prefiguring of history"; it "is already this future making itself" (58). On this topic, Foucault mentions a dream analyzed by Binswanger in a collection of lectures published in 1928 about the "changes in the conception and interpretation of dreams from the Greeks to the present"; see *Wandlungen in der Auffassung und Deutung des Traumes: Von den Griechen bis zur Gegengenwart* (Springer, 1928). Foucault dedicated a reading note to this dream study (a dream about a customs agent), which was found inside an annotated copy of Binswanger's book in Foucault's personal library. (As we can see from the call number on its cover, he borrowed this volume from the École normale supérieure's library.) He writes: "the situation with regard to the customs agent is the same as that with regard to the physician: it is his own conscience with regard to the physician. The dream is an anticipation of a situation that has not yet occurred: the patient has not yet found the primary trauma. Therefore, the dream is not always a repetition of the past, as Freud claims, but also an anticipation of an expected discourse." It is interesting to note, moreover, that Foucault has underlined the passages in *Wandlungen* in which Binswanger refers to Hegel. In particular, in Chapter 3, where two series of dreams are analyzed ("Aus der Analyse zweier Traumserien"), Foucault has underlined a passage in which Binswanger presents a dream that he considers to be "a particularly beautiful and significant example of the analytical treatment itself": "This 'die and become,' which represents any serious psychoanalysis and makes of it an instrument that demands so much responsibility and

[that is] sometimes dangerous, expresses itself in the dream with marvelous clarity. Or, to use another image, Hegel's 'triadic approach' of thesis, antithesis, and synthesis is shown in all its clarity: the 'tormented' life before the analysis is the thesis; the being who has been exhausted and emptied by the analysis is the spiritual void; the spiritual death, which is always an equally important and dangerous phase of the treatment, signifies the antithesis. In the final synthesis at the end of the treatment or after the treatment, death in life is once again 'surmounted' (*aufgehoben*); spiritual rebirth has been accomplished. The goal of the analysis is not the so-called 'freedom from complexes,' which would in reality signify spiritual death, but rather a full life that pulses, which this dream represents in such a plastic manner, a life that is no longer tormented, but free and freely *chosen*" (82, our translation). The BNF holds another, quite schematic reading note that Foucault wrote about the *Wandlungen* (Box 38, folder 1).

13. On this subject, see a reading note dedicated by Foucault to anxiety in the case of Ellen West, where he remarks, ""Man can no more escape his fate than he can escape his foundation. But where, as in the case of Ellen West, we noticed a circular movement (*Kreisbewegung*) of the *Dasein* in order to escape one's foundation, and then to fall back into it as one would an abyss (*Ab-grund*), it is then that *Dasein* exists in the mode of anxiety. Rather than an authentic temporalization in the mode of a *Selbstwerden* [becoming oneself], . . . there occurs an '*Entwerden*' [un-becoming]" (Gebsattel) (Binswanger, "The Case of Ellen West," 299)" (BNF, Box 38, folder 1). On the meaning of the "fundamental" character of anxiety in the existential perspective, Foucault expresses himself very clearly in *Maladie mentale et personnalité*: "If anxiety fills an individual's history, it is because it is its principle and foundation; it defines, from the outset, a certain style of experience that marks the traumas, the psychological mechanisms that they trigger, the forms of repetition that they affect during pathological episodes: it is a sort of *a priori* of existence"; see *Maladie mentale et personnalité* (PUF, 1954), 54. A slightly different version of this sentence appears in *Mental Illness and Psychology*, trans. Alan Sheridan (University of California Press, 1987), 42.

14. Here Foucault is alluding to §61 of the *Monadology*, in which Leibniz states that "composites are analogous to [in French, "symbolize with"] simples "; see Gottfried Wilhelm Leibniz, *Die philosophischen Schriften*, ed.

Carl I. Gerhardt, vol. 6 (Olms, 1965), 617; see also *Philosophical Essays*, ed. and trans. Roger Ariew and Daniel Garber (Hackett, 1989), 221.

15. The phenomenon of "not wanting to be yourself" is central to the *Daseinsanalysis* perspective. Binswanger borrows this concept from Søren Kierkegaard, an author whose works the Swiss psychiatrist always considered to be fundamental landmarks for existential analysis. The works by Kierkegaard that Binswanger cites most often in his writings are *The Concept of Anxiety* (1844) and *The Sickness Unto Death* (1948). In his reading notes on the cases of Ellen West, Lola Voss, and Jürg Zünd, Foucault mentions the Danish philosopher quite often (BNF, Box 42b, folder 1). He also mentions him in connection with Hans Kunz's essay "Idee, Wesen und Wirklichkeit des Menschen," *Studia Philosophica* 4, no. 147 (1944): 147–69 (BNF, Box 42b, folder 1). For a deeper understanding of Kierkegaard's presence in Binswanger's thought, see Elisabetta Basso, "Kierkegaard's Influence on Ludwig Binswanger's Work," in *Kierkegaard Research: Sources, Reception, and Resources*, ed. Jon Stewart (Ashgate, 2012), 29–53.

16. Jakob von Uexküll (1864–1944): In 1925, after studying zoology and physiology at the University of Tartu (Estonia) and in Heidelberg, he founded the Institute for Environmental Research in Hamburg, which he directed until 1940. From 1940 until his death, he worked at the Naples Zoological Center. His thought, across works such as *Umwelt und Innenwelt der Tiere* (Julius Springer, 1909) and *Theoretische Biologie* (Paetel, 1920), was widely taken up by philosophers, especially in the field of phenomenology. The concept of *Umwelt* in particular was used by Max Scheler, Martin Heidegger, and Helmuth Plessner. Binswanger cites von Uexküll especially in his study "The Existential Analysis School of Thought," in *Existence: A New Dimension in Psychiatry and Psychology*, ed. Rollo May, Ernest Angel, and Henri F. Ellenberger, trans. Ernest Angel (Basic Books, 1958), 191–213. In Foucault's archives from the 1950s, there is a reading note called "The *Umwelt* according to von Uexküll" (BNF, Box 44b, folder 3), in which the following works are mentioned: *Theoretische Biologie*, 2nd ed. (Springer, 1928 [1920]); *Niegeschaute Welten: Die Umwelten meiner Freunde* (Fischer, 1939); *Umwelt und Innenwelt der Tiere*. Foucault groups these under the heading "D'après [After] Binswanger, *Vorträge*, p. 198." This citation points precisely to the article by Binswanger that we have just mentioned.

17. Hans Kunz (1904–1982): After having undertaken legal studies at the University of Basel and in Heidelberg, he was impressed by Jaspers's courses in Heidelberg and abandoned law in favor of psychology and philosophy. In 1934, he defended a thesis dedicated to "phenomenology and the analysis of expression" (*Zur Phänomenologie und Analyse des Ausdrucks*) under the direction of Paul Häberlin at the University of Basel. For many years he worked at the Institute of Anthropology of the Lucerna Foundation, which had also hosted, in March 1927, Binswanger's course on the history of dreams that led to his 1928 study *Wandlungen in der Auffassung und Deutung des Traumes*. After completing his professorial thesis on the anthropological meaning of fantasy (*Die anthropologische Bedeutung der Phantasie*) in 1946, Kunz continued to teach at the University of Basel, despite having received an offer in 1957 from Hans-Georg Gadamer and Karl Löwith to join them at the University of Heidelberg. Foucault was well acquainted with Kunz's work, to which he dedicated a folder in the 1950s containing many reading notes (BNF, Box 42b, folder 1; see also Box 38, folder 1). In the final pages of his 1957 article "La psychologie de 1850 à 1950," Foucault writes, "To grasp man as an existence in the world and to characterize each man by the style proper to this existence is, for L. Binswanger, for H. Kunz, to reach, beyond psychology, the foundation that gives him his possibility and offers an account of his ambiguities"; see *Dits et écrits*, vol. 1, *1954–1969*, ed. Daniel Defert and François Ewald, with Jacques Lagrange (Gallimard, 1994), no. 2, 136.

CHAPTER TWO

Space

I. Spatiality: 1. The originary lived experience of space: Husserl; 2. Spatiality founds itself on "being-in-the-world"; 3. Affective spatiality. II. The space of patients: 1. The Franz Weber case (Roland Kuhn): the "delusion of limits"; 2. The subject's mode of spatialization. III. The link between space and time: analyzing spatiality leads one to ask how existence is temporalized.

In originary lived experience, space does not offer itself as a geometric structure of simultaneity: a space of this kind—that in which the natural sciences unfold the coherence of objective phenomena—is constituted only through a genesis. We can retrace the moments of this genesis, starting from sensory experience in its dense colorations and contents: we might, in this way, first describe the originary "pre-spatial" fields of organic sensibility; then the absolute orientation that structures them in a simple and rigid matter, around the body which is undeniably "here"; then the layering of perspectives onto which visual exploration opens, especially as it begins to relate to kinesthetic and tactile experience, and as the moments of each of these two domains articulate themselves on each other; finally, the constitution of a system of physico-mathematic invariants that strip the body of its referential primacy.[a] The genesis could also be

[67]

---

a Oskar Becker, "Beiträge zur phänomenologischen Begründung der Geometrie und ihrer physikalischen Anwendung," *Jahrbuch für Philosophie und phänomenologische Forschung* 6 (1923): 385–560.

sketched out through historical profiles of its various moments: this is [what] Husserl attempted in "Ursprung der Geometrie,"[b] by showing how, through practices of measuring, a Euclidian universe of geometry was constituted, which Galileo's genius reinvested into nature, by revealing the mathematical eidetics of the laws of the falling of bodies and of movement in general.

[68] The possibility of these two genetic analyses—and the equivalence of both of their necessities—sufficiently highlights the insufficiency of phenomenological description: the current content of an experience always refers to a becoming that constituted it; but the temporal horizon of that becoming remains implicit in phenomenology. Is it a becoming that develops one's powers and unfolds in the mode of maturation? Is it a becoming that promotes realities and is accomplished as a dialectic of history? The letter of Husserlian phenomenology does not allow us to decide one way or another; we must go beyond it to access a kind of necessity that will give spatial experience its decisive meaning. It is not to the origin that we must return, because with the very word "origin" we take away the ambiguity of the meaning given to the word "genesis"; instead, we must return to this native soil of all significations and all shifts in signification, to the world itself, or rather to being-in-the-world.[c] If the tridimensional and geometric spatiality of the world is the fulfillment of a genesis,

---

b [Edmund Husserl, "The Origin of Geometry," in *The Crisis of European Sciences and Transcendental Phenomenology*, trans. David Carr (Northwestern University Press, 1970), 353–78.]

c "L'espace n'est pas dans le sujet, ni le monde dans l'espace. L'espace est bien plutôt dans le monde, dans la mesure où l'être-dans-le monde constitutif du *Dasein* a fait épanouir l'espace." [This is Foucault's translation of a passage from Martin Heidegger, *Being and Time*, trans. John Macquarrie and Edward Robinson (Blackwell, 1962). The English translation is "*Space is not in the subject, nor is the world in space.* Space is rather 'in' the world insofar as space has been disclosed by that Being-in-the-world which is constitutive for Dasein" (146)].

it is insofar as spatiality has original meaning only against the backdrop of a world. This is the point that phenomenology had left in the shadows; it is what existential analysis gives itself the task to elucidate.

Saying that spatiality is founded on being-in-the world, or that the world is the native soil of spatiality, means acknowledging from the start that it has a content, a plenitude, a dense coloration, a thickness, and finally a familiar consistency that [69] phenomenological genesis carefully stripped away from it; it is to let space be a full space; it is to let it be near or distant, strangely far away, foggy, lost in the horizon, or immediately there, solid, docile or resistant to the touch; it is to let it be, from its origin, to my right or to my left, at my back or before my gaze. It is to let it be, already changed, this implicit invitation to action, this openness to my gesture, which makes it offer itself, on its own, to my hand—and which allowed Heidegger to characterize it first and foremost as the spatiality of the "*Zuhandenen.*"[1]

At this level, spatiality defines itself by the distinction between the space of the body and the space of the *milieu* or environment (the *Leibraum* and the *Umraum*). But this distinction only exists and has meaning if it is constantly being taken up in the form of unity: and this unity is that of the gesture, executed toward a goal, which knows how to circumvent an obstacle or model the thing that [bends]; it is that of the action that structures a series of movements in the direction of a task; this unity is that of "realization," of "*Leistung,*" as von Weizsäcker[d][2] says. But this unity that occurs in the act implies a space that is focused on a goal, a space whose lines of force converge toward

---

d Viktor von Weizsäcker, *Der Gestaltkreis. Theorie der Einheit von Wahrnehmen und Bewegen*, 4th ed. (Thieme, 1950 [1940]). [Foucault will later translate this book with Daniel Rocher: *Le cycle de la structure*, preface by Henri Ey (Desclée de Brouwer, 1958).]

a point, in short a "finalized space," and, to quote E. Straus's expression, a *"Zweckraum."*[e] The debate with the world that establishes itself in such a space is a vital debate, in which the only question is organic functioning, or at least the deployment of bodily activities. This is why it is hardly at issue outside of neurological disorders, those that range from segmentary disturbances such as hemianopsia or partial asomatognosia,[f] to intoxications that transform it completely, such as intoxications due to mescaline or hashish. These disorders have been studied by Schilder,[3] Gelb,[4] Goldstein,[5] Van Woerkom;[6] and we will not return to them except to show that, at the heart of all these disorders, there is mostly a dissociation between a near space—the space of the body, of the immediate gesture, of adjacent objects that we literally have at hand—and a faraway space from which the body is absent, that we can designate by allusion only as an over there, foreign and objective. These two categories of objective space have been defined by Grünbaum.[7]

Grünbaum describes it as follows in his article "Aphasie et motricité" [Aphasia and Motricity]:[g] "The individual space (*Eigenraum*) is the dynamic link between the body proper and its closest surroundings. This individual space is given as a unit of functioning that is simultaneously kinesthetic, optic, and motor, and it constitutes the background of the body's motricity. The movements of the limbs differentiate themselves from this space, at the moment of action, as relatively independent instruments,

---

e Erwin Straus, "Die Formen des Räumlichen. Ihre Bedeutung für die Motorik und die Wahrnehmung," *Der Nervenarzt* 3, no. 11 (1930): 633–56.

f [Hemianopsia is the diminution or loss of vision of half of the field of vision; partial asomatognosia is the loss of awareness of part of one's own bodily schema.]

g Abraham A. Grünbaum, "Aphasie und Motorik," *Zeitschrift für die gesamte Neurologie und Psychiatrie* 130, no. 1 (1930): 385–412. [Foucault borrows the quotation that follows from Binswanger, "Das Raumproblem in der Psychopathologie," *Zeitschrift für die gesamte Neurologie und Psychiatrie* 145 (1933): 609; reprinted in *Ausgewählte Vorträge und Aufsätze*, vol. 2 (Francke, 1955), 185–86.]

and in this way they allow for the constitution of foreign space (*Fremdraum*). By foreign space we must understand the milieu of objective representation.... The individual space and the foreign space are not absolutely separate from each other, but they perpetually flow into one another through the mediation of motricity."

In neurological illnesses, their relationship is disturbed. At [71] times there sets in such a distance between them that the unity can never be reestablished: the aphasiac can "grasp," but cannot "show";[8] he spontaneously regains the use of an object placed close at hand, but he is not able to recognize it when it is presented to him at a distance. Must we—following Cassirer—move from this fact to a theory of "functions" and analyze it as a loss of symbolic function; or, following Goldstein and his theory of "attitudes," see in it the disappearance of the categorical attitude?[9] Might it not more simply be, in line with the closest phenomenological meaning, a disassociation between the near space and the faraway space, the *Eigenraum* and the *Fremdraum*—the inability of motor activity to reopen the pathways to unity between them? At other times, on the contrary, there arises an immediate confusion between these two spaces, and something like an invasion of the near space by the faraway space. One of Binswanger's patients,[h] lying down in his bed, has the impression that an element of the railway track that is there, below his windows, enters his room, reaches him, and pierces his head: he feels his brain being run through, he has atrocious migraines and anxiety attacks. Carl Schneider[i][10] quotes an observation of Mannheim's in this

---

h Ludwig Binswanger, "Das Raumproblem in der Psychopathologie," 634 [in *Ausgewählte Vorträge und Aufsätze*, 2:210].

i Carl Schneider, "Über Sinnentrug. I. Beitrag," *Zeitschrift für die gesamte Neurologie und Psychiatrie* 131 (1931): 773; see also "Über Sinnentrug. II. Abschnitt: Die Frage der Klassifikation des Sinnentrugs und die Voraussetzungen zur Erforschung seiner Entstehungsbedingungen und Erscheinungsgesetze," *Zeitschrift für die gesamte Neurologie und Psychiatrie* 137 (1931): 458–521.

same direction: a subject is intoxicated with mescaline: "Abruptly, he sees his dip pen—which seems to be surrounded by a nebulous halo—crawling toward him with undulating movements, like a caterpillar. It appears to be getting closer."[j]

[72] But this extreme lability or rigidity in the relationship between faraway space and near space are not the furthest-reaching phenomena. Binswanger's example is enough to demonstrate it. The invasion of near space is not experienced as a disruption of oriented space in itself and for itself. It is experienced instead as the manifestation of a "superior power" that magically makes and unmakes the solid links between near and far, that shortens and elongates in an instant, that upsets distances and penetrates the impenetrable. The space of this disruption is a magical space.

But this space refers to a spatiality that is more originary and more fundamental than oriented spatiality: it is affective spatiality, which is to say a spatiality that is no longer centered on the body, nor distributed on the basis of organic coordinates, but that is structured according to the affective qualities of lived experience. It is a spatiality that does not coordinate itself in relation to the themes of action, but that finds its plenitude as a direction of expression—a space that does not open onto pathways toward a goal, but that accomplishes itself in its entirety in the moment in which it is experienced. This affective space is [to] the space of orientation a bit what the space of dancing is to the space of walking: this is a space which, at each instant, is absolutely full and current, and whose diversity is not on the order of geometric plurality, but on the order of qualitative and symbolic variety;[k]

---

j [In the manuscript, an arrow points from Schneider to Binswanger, who is quoted earlier. Foucault probably intended to cite Schneider's example before Binswanger's.]

k See Straus, "Die Formen des Räumlichen." [In a bibliographical note entitled "Pathology of space," Foucault also cites Straus's article "Die aufrechte Haltung, Eine anthropologische Studie," *Monatsschrift für Psychiatrie und Neurologie* 117, nos. 4–6 (1949): 367–79 (BNF, Box 42b, folder 1).]

high and low, right and left [do not] depend on a relative distribution around a central point, but have in themselves an absolute signification, one we would like to call "autochthonous." [73]

It would suffice to take up once again the spatial thematics of dreams, of myths, or of fantasies or delusions: there we would find these absolute significations. In this way, Binswanger analyzes two of Gottfried Keller's dreams.[1] He sees an eagle soaring above a valley; he experiences great, calm joy to see, for the first time, an eagle soaring completely freely. The eagle approaches the window Keller is leaning against; the dreamer observes that it has a crown on its head. Gottfried Keller then hides in order to let it come in through the window: the eagle, which has finally entered the room, fills it for a moment with a dazzling brightness and the whirling of its feathers; Keller closes his eyes; when he opens them again and comes closer, there is nothing on the ground other than a piece of black paper; he is filled with melancholy.

A dream of this kind—much like the patient's illusion described earlier—deploys itself in the affective space: the moment of ethereal space, of the great bird's free flight, and that of whirling and falling express something like the pulse of existence, its expansion and depression, "its systole and its diastole," as Binswanger puts it: and we can, in this alternation, decipher the project of an existence that is realized in the fullness of an instantaneous liberty, and continually threatened by a fall that would obliterate it in a derisory objectivity. We can easily find a pulse of this kind in the case of Ellen West: the same unreal flight of jubilation, and the analogous fall without it ever being possible, in this affective space, to establish the solid, consistent dimensions of a space where one walks, a [74] firm ground that ensures continuous progress.

---

1 [See Ludwig Binswanger, "Dream and Existence," trans. Jacob Needleman, in *Dream and Existence*, ed. Keith Hoeller (Humanities Press, 1993), 81–105. For the French translation, see *Le rêve et l'existence*, trans. Jacqueline Verdeaux, introd. and notes by Michel Foucault (Desclée de Brouwer, 1954).]

Not that this space of solid ground belongs by right to the healthy man: illness also knows how to raise fences there, how to parcel out areas that are something like the concrete image of a fate in which existence shuts itself away. Individual space and social space are always marked by systems of limits, thresholds, borders, which are superimposed over their geographic distribution. We know the role that the transition from one region of the world to another (the Argonauts), from one level of the universe to another (Orpheus; Theseus's descent to the underworld), plays in religious myths; we know the importance of rites of passage (ritualism of the crossing of the threshold in Greek and Roman religions) or of rites that delimit, enclose, protect a defined space (division of the sacred space in the form of a *temenos*, or of a *templum*: rogation processions that circumscribe the city to ensure its protection). This mythical division implies an opposition between the sacred and the profane, between a space charged with religious power and a space deprived of it; or even between a space of familiarity, of the homeland, of hospitality, and that hostile space of the foreign.[m] It also implies the specific and highly valued cohesion of the space that has thus been delimited: the space of the *templum* encloses within its limits a sacred charge that enters into relation with the profane and spills out only at the moments of transition ritualized by religion; the city is bounded by the cycle of the processions that protect it and it is thereby reinforced, in its internal cohesion, in the inseverable unity that it opposes to adversity.

We find these two themes reflected in the space of patients, not in the form of implicit myths, but rather deployed as the

---

m See Ernst Cassirer, *The Philosophy of Symbolic Forms*, vol. 2, *Mythical Thought*, trans. Ralph Manheim (Yale University Press, 1965).

structures of a space in which their effective existence projects itself. R. Kuhn[11] studied in this sense the "delusion of limits";[n] [12] he became especially interested in a schizophrenic patient, Franz Weber, who after having presented ideas of persecution starting when he was twenty-eight, was finally institutionalized at the age of forty-four with a diagnosis of schizophrenia (he presents with a certain dissociation of language marked by neologisms and a disturbed syntax; he is very autistic; he also presents with a delusion of influence, coupled with a delusion of grandeur which is quite discreet, but explicit). He draws often and, across his drawings, a single theme is manifest: he had begun by drawing a boat—a boat, he emphasized, that he could walk all the way around, and in which he himself could complete a whole expedition, returning after a long journey to his home port. Then the theme of the boat transformed itself; that which could still [be] [76] unstable and perilous in navigation disappeared: the patient's secure space anchored itself in solid ground and now he begins to draw a castle, a "*Burg*" which, from the shore, dominates the sea; it is a "treasure," "more beautiful than anyone has ever seen," a place in which "men could live a hundred years."[o]

At first, this castle whose design Franz Weber draws tirelessly orders itself in accordance with the proportions of the human body. The patient establishes a precise relationship between the broad architectural lines and the elements of the human skeleton: this space, which he privileges and protects, is still only the space of the body proper. But as the illness develops, and with it the delusion of grandeur, the design becomes more grandiose: it is now an entire city, which must house millions

---

n [Roland Kuhn, "Über die Bedeutung vom Grenzen im Wahn," *Monatsschrift für Psychiatrie und Neurologie* 124, nos. 4–6 (1952): 354–83.]

o [Kuhn, "Über die Bedeutung," 363.]

of people, and eventually encompass the entire world; it would be a place of refuge during war, it would store all cultural goods, it would shelter "an ordered society against modern chaos,"ᵖ it would be "security before the void."ᵠ At the same time that the design takes on gigantic proportions and the delusion that subtends it increases, the structure becomes impoverished—the design becomes more schematic and soon orders itself solely in accordance with the principle of an indefinitely repeated symmetry; between the different neighborhoods and the various edifices there is no longer any organic link; they are juxtaposed to form geometric structures from which any concern for living utility has been banished: next to drawings that are meant to represent a pharmacy, or a hair salon, there are designs bearing captions such as "chemistry, mathematics, person, city, nation, continent."ʳ

[77]

This is where we undoubtedly grasp what is most originary and most fundamental in the subject's mode of spatialization: space is no longer for him this extension across which objects establish links through which they are mediated into instruments and then organized in relationships of means to ends; the object is now thrown there, for itself, without relation to its context, in an amorphous relationship; individuality ends in indifference. The object no longer indicates lines of use for itself: it no longer extends itself, in space, toward external relationships nor, in time, toward potential transformations; it is before the gaze, but the hand no longer knows how to reach for it. There are no longer things to do, only things to see. Or, to use Heidegger's

---

p All of these resources it can now draw from itself; previously it was by the seaside, and a railway track supplied it; now it no longer has any link with the outside; it lives entirely on itself; it has its gold mines inside its walls.

q [Kuhn, "Über die Bedeutung," 367.]

r [Kuhn, "Über die Bedeutung," 370.]

terms, the "*Zuhandenen*" have transformed themselves into "*Vorhandenen*."[13]

There is no organization that is internal, and whose meaning is carried by the objects themselves: to prevent a dispersal into the arbitrary and the absurd, to guarantee a cohesion for this plurality, without principle and without form, of isolated things, the patient has at his disposition little more than the structures of an elementary geometry and the magical protection that he ensures via the multiplication of walls, ramparts, and fortifications all around his mythical city. But all of these precautions are in vain, and their reduplication only manifests their uselessness: outside the city, chaos threatens it still and always; inside, the heaping-up continues, and with it appears the necessity of perpetually enlarging the protective limits, ultimately extending them to the very edges of the world.

And in this contradiction, in this kind of sandy flow of space that requires it to be entirely enclosed if one is to retain a part of it, we find the existential root of this delusion of limits. If indeed space disperses itself and escapes, it is because time, by contrast, is no longer able to flow. Temporal orientation no longer has any meaning for the patient; he takes care, when going on walks, to trace rigorously circular routes; and when he writes, he does not trace words one after another but rather distributes them in columns, so as to establish a table in which formal symmetry has been substituted for meaningful connections. Instead of existence opening onto a future toward which it transcends itself, it allows itself to submerged by a past that alienates it from itself; existence temporalizes itself in the form of an existential "hoard"[s] that accumulates in a single treasury all of constituted knowledge, every living man, all accumulated riches—not in

[78]

---

s *Existenzhortung* [Kuhn, "Über die Bedeutung," 367].

order to throw them into a promising future, but to keep them, conserve them, allow them only to subsist. From then on, the future appears only as an undifferentiated danger that must be prevented from getting its teeth into the present: it is potential war, it is destruction that threatens, it is chaos. Cut off from the future, time turns back ceaselessly on itself, in this circular process whose image is the "expedition," a constant theme in the patient's delusion; [it is] a kind of departure that from the start has meaning only in the return that it makes possible, a repetition that lets time march only insofar as the illusion of its immobility arises beneath each of its steps, a nostalgia that accompanies the traveler from the beginning. Time has no more meaning[t]—no orientation, no signification. And it is in order to find its meaning once again, to define its undifferentiated course, that the patient imposes limits on space that he wishes to be impassable, that he breaks space down into artificial and rigid structures, that he seeks, in his delusion of limits, to give an absolute meaning to "the beginning" and "the end," below and above, to the "already done" and the potential. Spatial delusion is only an attempt, oblique and always unsuccessful, to recover the lost meaning of an authentic temporality.

But here we find ourselves already led to another domain of the analytic of existence. We have been led quite naturally from spatiality to the manner in which existence is temporalized. Is it, as Binswanger states,[u] because no element of the existential analytic can be separated from the others, and that they form a totality where a partial change has meaning only within a global change? Is it because temporality is situated at a more fundamental level of the ontological structures of existence?

---

t [Here, too, Foucault uses "sens" in its double meaning of "signification" and "orientation"—Trans.]

u Binswanger. [Foucault does not indicate which of Binswanger's texts he is referring to.]

SPACE 95

These two questions likely amount to one, since the affirmative answer that we cannot avoid giving to the first rests on that which we are led to give to the second. [80]

NOTES

1. The French translation of this term has given rise to lively debates among philosophers. We limit ourselves here to noting Emmanuel Martineau's solution; in his translation of *Sein und Zeit*, he renders the substantive form of the verb "*zuhanden*" as "ce qui est à-portée-de-la-main," "what-is-at-hand's-reach" (Martin Heidegger, *Être et Temps*, trans. Emmanuel Martineau (Authentica, 1985). [In their English translation of *Being and Time*, John Macquarrie and Edward Robinson translate this same term as "readiness-to-hand"—Trans.]

2. The German physician and anthropologist Viktor von Weizsäcker (1886–1957) is often mentioned in Foucault's reading notes of the 1950s. Indeed, this author is very present in the German-language psychiatric literature on which Foucault was working at the time. Foucault refers to von Weizsäcker especially in his notes concerning two of Binswanger's studies: "Über Psychotherapie," *Der Nervenarzt* 8 (1935): 113–21 and 180–89; reprinted in *Ausgewählte Vorträge und Aufsätze*, vol. 1, 132–58; and "Über die daseinsanalytische Forschungsrichtung in der Psychiatrie" ["The Existential Analysis School of Thought," trans. Ernest Angel, in *Existence: A New Dimension in Psychiatry and Psychology*, ed. Rollo May, Ernest Angel, and Henri F. Ellenberger (Basic Books, 1958), 191–213] (BNF, Box 38, folder 1). In a reading note entitled "Le *Gestaltkreis*," Foucault refers specifically to this article by Binswanger (BNF, Box 44b, folder 3). The concept of *Leistung*, especially—which Foucault translates as "realization" in this manuscript—is central to the book von Weizsäcker published in 1940, *Der Gestaltkreis. Theorie der Einheit von Wahrnehmen und Bewegen*, 4th ed. (Thieme, 1950 [1940]). In another reading note entitled "*Der Gestaltkreis*. Introduction," Foucault translates the term *Leistung* as "activity": "For activities (*Leistungen*) we must use the principle of the accomplishment of a single act by different means: *Leistungprinzip*" (BNF, Box 43, folder 1). Foucault translated this book for the Bibliothèque neuro-psychiatrique de

langue française, a French-language neuropsychiatric book series edited by Henri Ey. Ey's interest in this work is evident in the preface he wrote for it, in which he returns to an article he had published the previous year on the occasion of von Weizsäcker's death ("À propos de "Cycle de la structure" de V. von Weizsäcker," *L'Évolution psychiatrique*, no. 2 (1957), 379–89). Here, he observes that "contemporary bio-anthropological conceptions such as those of V. von Weizsäcker are able to give us a conceptual model much [better] adapted to human pathology *par excellence*: that of man altered in his humanity" (387–88). Ey also stresses the proximity between these ideas and those developed by Merleau-Ponty, which he considers to be the "prolegomena" to a French audience's reading of the *Gestaltkreis* (383). Indeed, von Weizsäcker's ideas appear in Merleau-Ponty's works of the 1940s, especially in *The Structure of Behavior* (Beacon, 1963), to which Foucault dedicated a large number of reading notes in the 1950s (BNF, Box 33a, folder 0). In any case, if we trust the archives, Foucault must also have become familiar with von Weizsäcker's thought through the German-language psychiatrists. For example, in a reading note about Medard Boss's *Sinn und Gehalt der sexuellen Perversionen. Ein daseinsanalytischer Beitrag zur psychopathologie des Phänomens der Liebe* (Huber, 1947), he writes, "To avoid any abstraction, any construction, any objectivizing hypostasis of concepts, we must interrogate the manner in which, in the *Dasein*, *Selbstheit* [selfhood] and *Weltlichkeit* [worldhood or worldliness] are originarily founded; the different modes according to which man in general is and can be in the world; which representations and which images he projects onto what he encounters in the world and which *Weltentwürfe* [world projects] he thereby attains. We find this form of interrogation in von Uexküll, in von Weizsäcker, in Heidegger" (BNF, Box 42b, folder 1). In 1951, the psychiatrists Charles Durand and Pedro Folch dedicated an article in *L'Évolution psychiatrique* to von Weizsäcker; they highlighted the "revolutionary" tenor of his conception of medicine, which "in such a perspective ends up becoming an anthropology to which nothing that touches man can remain foreign, the objective of the medical diagnosis being in the final instance the understanding of man. . . . Its goal will no longer be the suppression of illness, but on the contrary it will be given a positive signification"; see "À propos de "Cas et problèmes" de Viktor von Weizsäcker. Théorie et pratique de la médecine anthropologique," *L'Évolution psychiatrique* 3 (1951): 519. Von

Weizsäcker's work, especially *Der Gestaltkreis*, also plays an important role in Frederik J. J. Buytendijk's *Attitudes et mouvements. Étude fonctionnelle du mouvement humain*, trans. L. Van Haecht, pref. Eugène Minkowski (Desclée de Brouwer, 1957). Buytendijk was very close to Binswanger, to whom he dedicated a course at Utrecht University in the 1950s; see Julia Gruevska, "Von der Tierphysiologie zur Psychologie des Menschen. Ein Einblick in Werk und Wirken Frederik Buytendijks," *Internationales Jahrbuch für Philosophische Anthropologie* 8, no. 1 (2018): 87–106.

3. Paul Schilder (1886–1940): An Austrian psychiatrist, he joined the Vienna Psychoanalytic Society in 1919. Having been appointed the chair of psychiatry at the University of Vienna in 1925, he emigrated to the United States in 1929, where he became the clinical director of the psychiatric section of Bellevue Hospital in New York and professor of psychiatry at New York University's College of Medicine. His work on the body schema is an important reference for Binswanger, but also for Merleau-Ponty's studies of the 1940s. In Foucault's archives of the 1950s, Schilder appears in reading notes dedicated to phenomenological psychopathology. In a note entitled "Genesis and essence," Foucault mentions the book *Seele und Leben. Grundsätzliches zur Psychologie der Schizophrenie und Paraphrenie, zur Psychoanalyse und zur Psychologie überhaupt* (Springer, 1923) (BNF, Box 42b, folder 1). Schilder's name also comes up in notes concerning neuropathology, where Foucault lists works on the topic of "The image of the body in neurology," especially the notion of "body schema" (BNF, Box 44b, folder 1).

4. Adhémar Gelb (1887–1936): After studying philosophy in Munich and Berlin with Carl Stumpf, he became an assistant at the Institute of Psychology housed within the University of Frankfurt-am-Main's Academy of Social Science. Starting in 1915, he worked alongside Kurt Goldstein with soldiers with brain injuries. In 1929, he became a professor at the University of Frankfurt, where he directed the Institute of Psychology with Max Wertheimer. He was recruited to the University of Halle in 1931, but was forced to abandon his post in 1933 for racial reasons. Having emigrated to the Netherlands, where he joined Kurt Goldstein, he waited for a visa to enter the United States. Sick with tuberculosis, he was forced to return to Germany, where he died in 1936.

5. Kurt Goldstein (1878–1965): After studies in philosophy and literature at the Universities of Wrocław and Heidelberg, he studied medicine

(neurology and psychiatry) in Frankfurt-am-Main, first under the direction of Carl Wernicke, and then under Ludwig Edinger. In 1916 he founded a research institute dedicated to the study of the consequences of brain injuries. Here began his collaboration with Adhémar Gelb. In 1930, after having succeeded Edinger to the chair in neurology at the University of Frankfurt, he decided to leave for Berlin to direct the new Department of Neurology at Moabit General Hospital. After the National Socialists' seizure of power in 1933, Goldstein was forced to leave Germany. Thanks to a grant from the Rockefeller Foundation, he lived in Amsterdam for one year, during which he wrote his most important work: *The Organism: A Holistic Approach to Biology Derived from Pathological Data in Man* (American Book Company, 1939). In 1934 he left Europe for the United States, where he taught clinical psychiatry at Columbia University in New York and directed the neurophysiology laboratory at Montefiore Hospital. He was an invited professor at Harvard and, from 1940 to 1945, professor of neurology at Tufts University School of Medicine, near Boston. The anthropological approach to medical thinking developed by Goldstein had an important impact on numerous French philosophers and psychiatrists starting in the 1930s, especially because of its reception by Aron Gurwitsch, Georges Canguilhem, and Maurice Merleau-Ponty. The French translation of Goldstein's major work, *La structure de l'organisme. Introduction à la biologie à partir de la pathologie humaine* (Gallimard), was published in 1951 by E. Burckhardt and Jean Kuntz. In his review published in 1952 in *Les Études philosophiques* 7, no. 3, the psychiatrist Georges Lantéri-Laura underscores the way in which Goldstein's perspective encourages the clinician to "understand . . . the illness which alters in its totality a concrete man's manner of being in the world" (291). Lantéri-Laura concludes, "This is why his book is not a collection of philosophical reflections related to neurology, but rather an effort to take up from the get-go the aim of a rigorous understanding of concrete man" (291). In the 1950s, Foucault dedicated about a dozen reading notes to Goldstein (BNF, Box 44b, folder 3). In particular, he cites the work *Human Nature in the Light of Psychopathology* (Harvard University Press, 1940), as well as other studies by Goldstein (based on Henry Hécaen and Julian de Ajuriaguerra's *Le cortex cérébral. Étude neuro-psycho-pathologique*, pref. Jean Lhermitte (Masson, 1949). He also cites Ernst Cassirer's *Philosophie der symbolischen Formen*;

for the English translation, see *The Philosophy of Symbolic Forms*, vol. 3, *The Phenomenology of Knowledge*, trans. Ralph Manheim (Yale University Press, 1965).

6. Willem Van Woerkom (1881–1931): A Dutch neurologist and psychiatrist active in Rotterdam, he studied intelligence deficits in aphasia, with particular emphasis on disorders of spatial and abstract thinking. His work has a central place in Kurt Goldstein's writings on aphasia, especially his study *Über Aphasie* (Orel Füssli, 1927). Van Woerkom published many essays in French during the 1920s: "Sur la notion de l'espace (le sens géométrique), sur la notion du temps et du nombre," *Revue neurologique* 35 (1919): 113–19; "La signification de certains éléments de l'intelligence dans la genèse des troubles aphasiques," *Journal de psychologie normale et pathologique* 18 (1921): 730–51; "Sur l'état psychique des aphasiques," *L'Encéphale* 18, no. 5 (1923), 286–304. These works were often cited by French psychologists, including Ignace Meyerson in *Les fonctions psychologiques et les oeuvres* (Vrin, 1948), Pierre Pichot, and Merleau-Ponty. His work was also taken up by André Ombredane, with whom Foucault collaborated in the early 1950s at the Hôpital Saint-Anne. In his reading notes, Foucault mentions the thesis Ombredane defended at the Sorbonne in 1947, *L'aphasie et l'élaboration de la pensée explicite* (PUF, 1951) (BNF, Box 38, folder 2). In this work, Ombredane emphasizes Henri Bergson's influence on Van Woerkom's ideas in *L'aphasie et l'élaboration de la pensée explicite* (243–48). Ombredane's work on language disorders also appears in a series of Foucault's notes grouped in a folder entitled "Intelligence and neurology," and has special prominence in a reading note on the subject of the "Pathology of perception," in which Foucault mentions the first volume of the *Études de psychologie médicale* published by Ombredane in 1944, *Perception et Langage* (Atlantica Editora) (BNF, Box 44b, folder 1). Van Woerkom's work on disorders related to spatiality is also mentioned by Ernst Cassirer in *The Philosophy of Symbolic Forms* (vol. 3, chap. 6), which Foucault references in this manuscript as well as in his reading notes. Foucault also cites Van Woerkom on the subject of tests on aphasics, in reading notes dedicated to Pierre Pichot's studies of mental tests (BNF, Box 44b, folder 1).

7. Abraham Anton Grünbaum (1885–1932): A professor of developmental psychology at Utrecht University, where he also directed the psychiatric and neurological clinic. His work on aphasia, spatiality, and gesture are an

important reference in the writings of Binswanger, Merleau-Ponty (in the 1940s), and Ombredane (see previous note).

8. Here Foucault is referring to Kurt Goldstein's study "Über Zeigen und Greifen," *Der Nervenarzt*, no. 4 (1931): 453–66, which he mentions in a folder dedicated to Merleau-Ponty (BNF, Box 33a, folder 0).

9. In a reading note, Foucault mentions, citing Merleau-Ponty, that "the subject can use words in an automatic language; what he has lost is the power of naming; in the act of naming, the object and the word are taken as representatives of a category, considered from a certain point of view. It is this categorical attitude that is no longer possible. 'What is inaccessible is not then a certain stock of movements but a certain type of acts, a certain level of action'" (BNF, Box 33a, folder 0; English trans. of Merleau-Ponty from *The Structure of Behavior*, 64). Foucault will return to this phenomenon in the preface to *The Order of Things*, where he uses the example of the aphasiac and his inability to classify multicolored skeins of wool in a coherent manner to illustrate Jorge Luis Borges's heterotopia. The clinical experiment mentioned by Foucault was described by Gelb and Goldstein in a study about amnesia relative to the names of colors: "Über Farbennamenamnesie," *Psychologische Forschungen* 11 (1924): 1127–86, which Goldstein discusses further in a chapter of his 1940 volume *Human Nature in the Light of Psychopathology* (69–84). Foucault cites both of these studies in a file dedicated to Goldstein (BNF, Box 44b, folder 3).

10. Foucault draws the example, as well as the bibliographical reference, from Binswanger's "Das Raumproblem in der Psychopathologie," *Zeitschrift für die gesamte Neurologie und Psychiatrie* 145 (1933): 598–647, reprinted in *Ausgewählte Vorträge und Aufsätze*, vol. 2, 174–225. The German psychiatrist Carl Schneider (1891–1946) is cited by Foucault in a bibliographical note drawn up at the time he was drafting this manuscript, entitled "On normal and pathological perception." He also devotes a reading note entitled "On spatiality" to this article by Schneider (BNF, Box 42b, folder 1). Carl Schneider was professor and chair of the Department of Psychiatry at the University of Heidelberg and actively participated in "Aktion T4," the Nazi program euthanizing the mentally ill. After the war, while awaiting judgment by the German authorities, he died by suicide in his prison cell in Frankfurt.

11. The Swiss psychiatrist Roland Kuhn (1912–2005) was active at the Münsterlingen psychiatric clinic in the canton of Thurgau starting in 1939, first serving as chief of medicine and later as director (1970–1979). A great expert on the work of Hermann Rorschach and of the "psychodiagnostic" technique, he discovered Imipramine, the first antidepressant medication (which came to market in 1957 under the name Tofranil). In the 1940s, Kuhn became very close to Binswanger, whose anthropologico-phenomenological approach to mental illness he welcomed and developed. Foucault met Kuhn personally for the first time in March 1954, when he visited Münsterlingen with Georges and Jacqueline Verdeaux. The Verdeaux had met Kuhn there for the first time in 1947 (through Henri F. Ellenberger), and had been especially eager to do so because of his work on the Rorschach test. Indeed, André Ombredane's French translation of the *Psychodiagnostik* (Presses Universitaires de France) had appeared in 1947, when Ombredane was working with Georges Verdeaux in Jean Delay's department at the Hôpital Sainte-Anne. Conversely, Kuhn took advantage of this exchange with the French couple to learn more about the EEG technique, of which he had been a pioneer in Switzerland in the late 1930s. It was thanks to Kuhn that the Verdeaux also made contact with Binswanger. For more information on the first meeting between Foucault and the Swiss psychiatrists, which occurred during Carnival at the Münsterlingen clinic, see Jean-François Bert and Elisabetta Basso, eds., *Foucault à Münsterlingen. À l'origine de l'Histoire de la folie*, with photographs by Jacqueline Verdeaux (EHESS, 2015). Kuhn reported that, after the visit to Münsterlingen, there were other meetings between the philosopher and the psychiatrist in Paris during this period (this information was passed on by Liselotte Rutishauser, Roland Kuhn's former secretary in Münsterlingen).

12. See the very detailed reading note that Foucault devotes to "R. Kuhn. Daseinsanalytic study on the meaning of limits in delusion," in a folder entitled "Roland Kuhn" (BNF, Box 42b, folder 1). The clinical case study of Franz Weber, like that of Rudolf R. which is analyzed later in this manuscript, are also mentioned by Foucault at the end of chapter 4 of *Maladie mentale et personnalité* (PUF, 1954), 63–68.

13. Emmanuel Martineau translates the substantive corresponding to the verb *vorhanden* as "ce qui est sous-la-main," "what is at hand" in Heidegger's *Être et Temps*. The same passage—still about the Franz Weber

case—appears in *Maladie mentale et personnalité*: "The meaning of "utensility" has disappeared from space; for the patient, the world of *Zuhandenen*, to use Heidegger's term, is merely a world of *Vorhandenen*" (64; this sentence is unchanged in *Mental Illness and Psychology*, trans. Alan Sheridan (University of California Press, 1987), 52. [In their English translation of *Being and Time*, Macquarrie and Robinson translate this same term as "presence-at-hand"—Trans.]

CHAPTER THREE

Time

I. *The problem of time: 1. Time in mental pathology; 2. The common root of history and of temporality at the existential level. II. Analysis of two cases of schizophrenia: 1. The Georg case (Roland Kuhn); 2. One of Alfred Storch's analyses. III. Phenomenological description and existential analysis: 1. The morbid experience of time in the context of a purely phenomenological description; 2. The Rudolf R. case (Roland Kuhn); 3. Psychotherapy as a verification of the world-project.*

In mental pathology, the problem of time presents itself in a twofold manner: the problem of time insofar as it constitutes the thread of the subject's biographical history, and the problem of time as the lived signification of the past and the future, as the subject's mode of insertion into the present. A symptom like phobia ably illustrates the duality of the problem.

At the origin of a phobia, psychoanalysis always locates a traumatic event, inscribed in the history of childhood, and a real anxiety that prolongs its echo. It is this anxiety which is repressed along with its original object, and which reappears behind the symbolic substitutes that the unconscious has given to this primitive object. In the phobia of empty space, or in that, also so widespread, of impurity and dirtiness, there is the permanence of an anxiety that has extended a continuous thread all

[81]

through the individual history and which, from the first trauma to the ultimate symbolic metamorphosis, gives its stamp to the real becoming of the patient and of his illness. But phobic anxiety manifests another aspect of temporality: the agoraphobe who cannot cross an empty space, who attaches himself to each of the solid holds he encounters and has an anxiety attack that throws him to the ground when he sees himself alone, without support in the middle of an empty space, such an agoraphobe does not experience his anxiety as the repetition of an infantile anxiety. The space in front of which he shrinks does not have the signification of a symbol; that in front of which he currently worries is not an imaginary substitute: it is in front of this future deployed before him as a spatial structure, it is in front of this space that must be crossed and that one can cross only while anticipating what is at the end, when one has reached the other side. If a bordered space, punctuated by solid markers, does not produce the same anxious vertigo, it is because there the future does not make itself as pressing, and does not manifest itself as so open: the future of a full space is a future within reach, a future in which one can advance step by step, in a succession of presents that touch each other; the future that deploys empty space is a future that must be assumed as an open possibility, in a solitary resolution that heads directly toward it; in empty space, the future can neither be masked nor escaped.[a][1] We might see a same refusal of the future in other phobic syndromes:[2] the patient with zoophobia does not fear the animal itself as much as the type of undifferentiated, potential danger sketched out behind it; the patient who fears dirt does not fear dirt itself, but rather

---

a See Viktor Emil von Gebsattel, "Zur Psychopathologie der Phobien. I. Teil: Die psychasthenische Phobie," *Der Nervenarzt* 8, no. 7–8 (1935): 337–46, 398–408 [reprinted in *Prolegomena einer medizinischen Anthropologie. Ausgewählte Aufsätze* (Springer, 1954), 47–74].

is never sure that it will be possible to erase it. The future is neither certain nor open enough for him to be able to expect the suppression of the past, or the repair of the present: the smallest polluting contact risks being a definitive impurity, a stain that cannot be washed away, that therefore cannot be absolved (one can perceive, in this dread of the irreparable, the connection—ubiquitous among phobics—between physical impurity and the moral impurity of sin); it perpetually remains this stain that no Arabian perfume can erase . . .

Through its symbolic content, phobia manifests the thread of individual history; but through its current signification, it also reveals the singular structures of temporality. A common style can easily be discovered between this history and this temporality: in one as in the other, the future has lost its sense of openness and its content of free possibility. History develops itself in the form of stereotypical repetition: even if the symptoms transform themselves, even if the symbolic objects undergo metamorphosis, the anxiety reiterates itself identically from the origin; and temporality, on its side, closes on a future foreign to the subject, constitutes itself as an accumulation of the past. History and temporality have no dimension beyond that of the anterior, and in this way they both tend toward immobility, as if to their destiny and their truth: this is probably what Straus meant when he described neurosis as a "*Stillstand.*"[b]

The problem is to reach the fundamental point where historicity and temporality meet, the source from which both draw their shared signification. Freud, no doubt, and others after him oriented their investigations toward this pure origin of time—of the time of history, as of lived time. But neither Freud nor

[84]

---

b ["Stop."] Erwin Straus, *Geschehnis und Erlebnis. Zugleich eine historiologische Deutung des psychischen Traumas und der Renten-Neurose* (Springer, 1930), 78.

psychiatrists like Minkowski were able to avoid the oversimple solutions of a readymade metaphysics.³

Freud shows in neurosis a kind of intoxication of the present by the past, and seeks to find in the notion of repetition the point where history and temporality meet: if the neurotic man has become a stranger to his own future, and even to his immediate present, if his time is no longer an open time, it is insofar as the blockage of the past, its crystallization around a trauma and its fixing at an archaic stage of development, have stopped the time of history and forever immobilized its living dynamism. The disturbance of temporality is only an effect of the interruption of history. And this interruption itself is the effect of an even deeper disorder: a rupture in the equilibrium between the life instinct—principle of vital development, factor of evolution, spatial and temporal, individual and specific, in any case "transmortal"—and the death instinct—principle like the inertia of living matter, its tendency to repetition, its temptation to rest. The illness, its historical iterations, and its impossibility of opening onto the future, are like the eddies, on the surface of existence, of the triumphant struggle of the death instinct, in the depths of life.

[85]

Minkowski's analyses are opposed to Freud's. It is not the repetition of history that anchors them, but the disturbances of temporality. Minkowski thus observed a sixty-six-year-old man who presented ideas of persecution, in whose rhythm one could distinguish a very characteristic alternation:ᶜ at times, bouts of melancholia, in which he was stricken by the threat of imminent ruin, were dominant; his universe was at each moment vulnerable to a catastrophe that would obliterate him. At other

---

c To his doctor who shows him that his fears are unfounded because they have not yet realized [themselves], he responds, "You have always been right, but it does not follow that you should be right tomorrow."

moments, the anxiety of imminence gave way to a delusional interpretation: the entire world was conspiring against him. Every newspaper article was directed against him and designated him for public retribution; people wanted to mutilate him, to hammer nails into his head, open his body and ram into it all of the rubbish that can be set aside in the world: all that is ash, crumbs, detritus, rot, all that no longer had any use and must disappear—all of that was carefully preserved by his persecutors in order to be introduced into his body. Between these two pathological themes, the unity of meaning is obvious: if the patient feels perpetually threatened by a catastrophe and if this imminence is renewed at every instant, it is insofar as the past contains no assurance about the future;[d] the solid security of a past which has not yet involved any catastrophe, and which has rendered vain all previous anxiety, does not allow anticipation in relation to a future that appears entirely open to catastrophe. Between the past and the future, there is no more living and dynamic link, and this is why the past no longer seems to pass: it weighs on existence with all of its threatening accumulation; and the remains, in slivers of the past, no longer able to disappear, pile up to crush the present. In the common origin of anxiety and delusion, there is therefore a weakening of personal momentum: time is no longer able to progress, it disaggregates itself and accumulates in fragmentary and disorganized materials. The continuity of its flux has stopped, dissociating an empty future from a crushing past. Duration has ceased to endure.[e] [4]

[86]

---

d [There is no note for this reference.]

e See Eugène Minkowski, "Findings in a Case of Schizophrenic Depression," trans. Barbara Bliss, in *Existence: A New Dimension in Psychiatry and Psychology*, ed. Rollo May, Ernest Angel, and Henri F. Ellenberger (Basic Books, 1958), 127–38. [Minkowski returns to this case study in *Lived Time: Phenomenological and Psychopathological Studies*, trans. Nancy Metzel (Northwestern University Press, 1970), 180.]

Despite their differences, Freud's and Minkowski's interpretations converge, at least at the level of their implicit postulates: both of them—and this is how they are radically opposed to phenomenological elucidation, despite Minkowski's original project—propose metaphysical solutions; symmetrically, on either side of concrete existence, one brings in the *élan vital* and the other, the death instinct. Both suppose that temporality and history are connected at a deeper level than that of authentic individual existence, that they are born from a vital sphere still unaware of the time of history and that of consciousness, because this vital sphere develops according to the creaturely laws of evolution. Despite appearances, there is hardly any difference between Freud's interpretation and Minkowski's save one: Freud perceives, in the form of a specific instinct, this death of time, which Minkowski views only as a failure of instinct: where the latter sees a stoppage of the life force, the former discovers a force that stops. Minkowski describes a dialectic of exhaustion, where Freud's genius is able to decipher, even through the worst of metaphysics, a dialectic of contradiction. Bergsonism did not give Minkowski the keys to phenomenology; it brought him back to the level of Freud's most contestable speculations—and even, to be frank, slightly lower. On the contrary, what must be shown, through existential analysis, is how at the level of man himself, rather than in the depths of some metaphysics of life, history and temporality (the time of life and the time that one lives) find a common root, how in a single movement of existence the individual's real history is carried out and becoming takes on, for him, a lived signification.

The always-achieved direction of phenomenological description is to liberate this signification from the metaphysical myths in which psychology alienates [it]:[f] the rigorous work of

---

[f] [Here Foucault writes "les aliène" [alienates them], but the context suggests that the referent for the pronoun is "cette signification," "this signification," i.e. "it"; I have corrected the text accordingly—Trans.]

description must discharge time, release it from the weight of repetition in which death announces itself, free it from the flux in which life gushes up in momentum and flows out in duration. Taken precisely, the lived signification of time designates, from its very manner of offering itself, the unity of the existential structure. From the start, history and temporality define themselves there in a style of unity.

Georg, one of Roland Kuhn's patients,[g] is hospitalized with a diagnosis of common hebephrenia.[h][5] He is now twenty-two years old and is the son of an unmarried mother, a schizophrenic now long hospitalized. He was raised in an orphanage. At seventeen, he steals a large sum of money from his guardian; he leaves the technical institute where he is completing his training after fighting with his professor; then he abruptly leaves the tailor to whom he was apprenticed. Affective disturbances had appeared a little while earlier, accompanied by feelings of depersonalization and anxiety; he had manifested various phobias, illusions, false memories, ideas of persecution, feelings of influence.[i] At the hospital, Georg draws: one of these drawings shows a coffin resting on the earth, next to a weeping willow that has lost its leaves; in the air, above the coffin and already contracted as if to grasp it, is a hand: it is the scraggy hand of a skeleton. In another drawing, a similar coffin: but it is almost suspended in the air, encircled by a halo of light, and on each side [there is]

[88]

---

g [Although he does not cite it, the study by Roland Kuhn to which Foucault refers is "Daseinsanalyse eines Falles von Schizephrenie," *Monatsschrift für Psychiatrie und Neurologie* 112, nos. 5–6 (1946): 233–57.]

h [Hebephrenia is a severe form of schizophrenia that generally begins during adolescence and entails intellectual and relational deterioration.]

i [The following passage was crossed out by Foucault: "The analysis reveals an incapacity to assume his own past, or rather the dominant feeling of not having a past that belongs to him properly: his illegitimate birth deprives him of the insertion into a social past that is belonging to a family; he feels like 'no one's son,' deprived of this continuity."]

a line of mountains that form a narrow canyon.[6] At the hospital, he develops previously established delusional themes; he had, at eighteen, distinguished one young woman from the others because she had refused to go to the ball, because she did not much like the company of others. One day as she accompanies him to the train station, he suddenly sees in her place a young woman with brown hair, dressed in black; the fantasy does not leave him throughout the journey: he sees in her Goethe's Iphigenia. Soon, Elfriede and Iphigenia begin to overlap and, little by little, to blur: first, Georg sees above Elfriede's left eye a small image of Iphigenia, like the figurine of his divided love, a tiny kore that already designates, sketched on the fleshy figure, the sacred world of delusion. Then the image grows and spreads: the face and finally the body of Elfriede are entirely covered; in rare instances, Elfriede's real body reappears under that of her tragic double; the myth has eluded reality, but it is always encircled, threatened, compromised by it. Illusion and reality are in constant tension, and in a kind of relationship of contestation expressed by the language of delusion: the world, with all the reality with which it is charged, threatens the patient; work becomes prejudice, and dialogue, persecution. Georg would like to force Elfriede to become one with her own myth: she must enter the convent. But she sees other young men and becomes engaged to a student. These new relationships strip her of the charm that bound her to the figure of Iphigenia; when he sees her, he seeks in vain to find the double: the fiancé, the physician, the hospital director, the old employer, all of these men have conspired to erase from Elfriede's face the distinguishing mark in which the past of her destiny could be read, the calm face that no longer belongs to men.

[90]   The abstraction of traditional psychiatry could easily distinguish biographical time, developed in the objective frameworks

of anamnesis, from lived time, detected between the lines of delusional expressions. In fact, this biographical time and this mythic time have a shared signification. His illegitimate birth deprived the patient of the social insertion in which solidified time acquires, from family tradition and the security of renewed rituals, the reassuring thickness of the past; he would not be able to support the time of his memories on the "social frameworks of memory" that the family maintains with its links of loyalty and blood: the loyalty of Iphigenia, in tragedy, which goes all the way to self-sacrifice and which lasts, fraternal, welcoming, until the dark shores of Tauris. He has no father and no name; even his first name was changed by his guardian. He is a street kid, taken up at each moment by the rush of the present; he is like a pile of sand that changes with each strike of the shovel leveled at it; and at the least puff of wind, he flies away and becomes dust in the street. "*Ich bin ein Chaosmensch.*"[j] The present grabs him incessantly, pulls him in every direction, outside of himself, in automatic gestures: he does not recognize his hand; it does not belong to him, but hangs from his arm like a dead branch. He does not find himself in his work, tools do not obey him, the needle pricks on its own, the scissors cut too quickly and too wide: they snip, slice, slash; they do not know how to resist the desire to reduce the pieces into fragments, and the fragments into tiny bits. Their spontaneous liveliness is much like the present, maker of dust. This cut-up present makes authentic dialogue or true love impossible: conversation is nothing but a "fleeting connection between two telephone posts,"[k] and love is played like a game with a ball that must be kicked away in order to keep it at a distance and send the threat back to the opponent. Georg has never

---

j ["I am a man of chaos"; Kuhn, "Daseinsanalyse eines Falles von Schizophrenie," 243.]
k [Kuhn, "Daseinsanalyse eines Falles von Schizophrenie," 245.]

had the present in himself, but always beside himself, like those things that caution sets apart: delusion, along with persecution, has slipped into this distance between himself and his present reality. But this delusion—whose scope measures the distance to the time of *reality*—strives toward a recovered time, that of *truth*: the true past, that of human community, of trusting familiarity, is that of bounded, enclosed spaces, it is the warmth of the family space; and Georg cites Kleist's drama *Die Hermannsschlacht*[l] to recall the opposition between the Teutonic world, enclosed by the shadows of the primitive forest and folded in on the group formed by the natural community (*Gemeinschaft*), and the Roman world, universe of society (*Gesellschaft*), crisscrossed by roads that spread the present in a geography of dispersion and anticipate the future which, by rendering men uniform, alienates their individuality. This world of the primitive forest and that of the military road are like the spatial landscape of a same temporal signification. Common signification in Georg's biographical history and in its delusional myth: time tears the past from the present and vice versa; the first withdraws into a henceforth impossible community, into the familiar life of the Teutons, into Iphigenia's renunciation, into this immediate presence of man to himself and to his destiny, into this beautiful unity of the Aryan tribe or the Greek polis; the other, the present, opens onto the uniform chaos of great societies, on the rivalry between men who fight over women, on tools that function spontaneously, and on the freedom that one must defend like one's life: "When a man has lost his right, it is not only his right but his singular "me" that has fallen into the hands of another."[m] For Georg, the time of his

---

l [Heinrich von Kleist, *The Battle of Herrmann*, trans. Rachel MagShamhráin (Königshausen & Neumann, 2008 [1808]).]

m [Kuhn, "Daseinsanalyse eines Falles von Schizophrenie," 240.]

life and the time that he lives in his illness are not articulated on each other as an effect is to a cause, or a consequence to an antecedent: a unity of meaning designates them both and invites any reflection to find their foundation in a more radical and originary form of temporality. In its rigor, phenomenological description promotes an analysis of the structures of existence; without this in-depth approach it would remain abstract. Only the artifice of an objectivizing thought can dissociate temporality and history. The first step of understanding must respect their identity of meaning and grasp them in a unity of style whose semantic themes and syntactic rhythms they both share.

This unity of history and temporality is not the euphoric, reconciled unity of a ready-made constitution; what this meaning signifies, in its unity, is an opposition, or at least a tension between two terms: a transitive, solid, regular time that opens to reflection all of the possibilities of return and anticipation, because it leaves on things the wrinkles of aging and the dust where the past fades away, because it announces in them its future as an imperceptible youth—this is the time that accomplishes the apotheosis of the modifications of the world. And a time[n] with an intransitive style, because it is that through which my consciousness goes beyond itself as flux: it is the temporal unity of the immanent content of consciousness which sinks into the past and, there, is retained as such, and which sketches itself out in successive profiles on the open horizon of the future; it is only through this flux and starting with this flux which

[93]

---

n [Here, all of the following passage is crossed out: "And a time without measure because it is grace and movement, intransitive because it is that in which my consciousness surpasses itself as originary flux: this flux from which time engenders itself is not itself in time, but it is the temporal unity of the immanent content of consciousness that sinks into the past, to be retained as such. Husserl defines it in the following way: "the living present is the present of the movement of flowing, of having flowed."]

anticipates the self in the "protentions" of the consciousness, and recollects itself in its "retentions," that the unfolding of time can be apprehended.[o] [7]

The pathological experience alters this directionality [*visée*] of [temporal] unfolding through the flux: it blurs its constitutive moments.

One of Storch's[8] analyses provides a very clear example of these pathological disturbances.[p]

The patient was the child of a fairly disunified couple: the mother directs the family authoritatively; the patient would like to have maintained a trusting relationship with his mother, but has only a distant admiration for her; he has the feeling of being both dependent on her and rejected by her. He is fifteen when she dies, leaving his family in inextricable difficulty. He sees her again in dreams that constantly recur. He is more and more conscious that he is homosexual. His life is a series of failures: he cannot find a stable situation, he wishes for a household but lives alone. One day, he makes a declaration to a former student who is domineering and decisive like his mother: he would like to marry her. Stunned, she refuses. Soon afterward, he exhibits the first signs of illness; then there is a crisis: depression, desire to die, then sensory illusions, feelings of a change in personality. He is hospitalized; the crisis subsides. Soon, a second crisis arises: he has the impression that the world has died and that he himself has become God. During his second hospital stay, he narrates these two crises to the physician. It is from this narrative that

---

o See Husserl. It is perhaps in an analogous way that Straus distinguishes "*Erlebnis immanente Zeit*" from "*Erlebnis transeunte Zeit.*" See Erwin Straus, "Das Zeiterlebnis in der endogenen Depression und in der psychopathischen Verstimmung," *Monatsschrift für Psychiatrie und Neurologie* 68 (1928): 640–56.

p Alfred Storch, "Die Daseinsfrage der Schizophrenen," *Schweizer Archiv für Neurologie und Psychiatrie* 59, no. 1 (1947): 330–85.

we will draw the elements allowing us to characterize the alterations in his experience of time.

In his first crisis, he experienced two kinds of state: he had the impression that another spirit had introduced itself into his head, which had become like a sphere of fire and radiated an absolute knowledge of all things. But at the same time, he experienced remorse for a sin as grave as that of Prometheus: he had stolen the divine spark. [95]

The second state constitutes the punishment for this crime: it is as if the patient were dead, although he persists in living; he has fallen into an abyss where man is no longer there, the Earth is a planet from which every human face had been erased, where God himself no longer exists. He feels outside of time: nights and days are equivalent, the sand no longer flows.q In the second crisis, he has taken God's place: he is no longer on equal footing with men, he possesses a fully-deployed divine knowledge—he knows the secret relationships between numbers and names, between names and persons; the most hidden things have become transparent. Men have died, without exception: he is alone; the planet next to him has become tiny; he can sit on it, but the weight of his body threatens at each instant to throw it out of balance; the entire universe risks collapsing. He has the violent experience of the *Weltuntergang*.r

In these two pathological crises, the experiences of time are polymorphous, and each of them designates an alteration in the constitutive moments of the temporal flow, and in the manner in which the temporal flow is aimed [*visé*], starting with the temporal mobility of the horizons of consciousness.

---

q [in the hourglass—Trans.].
r ["End of the world."]

1. By the entry into the "kingdom of light," the time of the world stops: its aging takes on the rigidity of death and the history of men is swallowed up in the end of time. But it would be insufficient and incorrect to see in this death of history, as Minkowski would, the effect of a stoppage in vital duration. Rather, it is correlated to a kind of discrepancy in the flux of consciousness: the present instant no longer extends itself toward the twofold horizon of a past that is still retained in the intention [*visée*], and of a future it can anticipate through outlines and profiles. This plenitude of the present, which defines simultaneously its positive content and the moment of its suppression, guarantees the instant's reality as the present: it is that which makes it possible to distinguish in the constitution of the present these two moments that Husserl designated as the "*Jetzt*,"[s] enclosed, submerged by the "*Präsezfeld*."[t] [9] Yet, in the case of our patient, these two constitutive structures are altered in their correlation: the field of presence that articulates itself in multiple temporal horizons is detached from its instantaneous point and from the mobility of the instant which little by little moves, modifies, shifts the general lines of its orientation. In this way, the horizon loses its structure, which is full of implicit content whose eventuality the temporal flux uncovers little by little: it is there, now entirely given, deployed in the mode of a totality deprived of implicit moments; by uncovering itself the horizon empties itself; detached from its present, history completes itself in death. But the present instant, the *Jetzt*, is then lived in the mode of empty repetition, of a kind of life that survives its own

---

s ["Present, now."]

t *Zeitbewusstsein*. [Foucault refers to Edmund Husserl, "Vorlesungen zur Phänomenologie des inneren Zeitbewusstseins," ed. M. Heidegger, *Jahrbuch für philosophische und phänomenologische Forschung* 9 (1928), which he cites in his reading notes. In German, "Präsenzfeld" literally means the "field of presence."]

death and prolongs itself like the existence of the last man after the end of the world, in a night in which life no longer has any meaning. The patient's existence will therefore divide itself into two ways of existing: that defined by a knowledge deployed in the transparency of absolute light, and that defined by a life of obscurity, in the abyss.

2. This temporal experience resembles Ellen West's in many ways: there is the same opposition between the world of light and the world of darkness, the same alternation between the myths of ethereal existence and the plunge into the abyss. For Binswanger's schizophrenic, as for Storch's patient, the world of light is a deployment of every existential eventuality, where the shadows are contained and open up a transparency within the future that eliminates that future by allowing it be totalized: the future is no longer a landscape limited by the thickness of temporal horizons; it takes on the aspect of a mythic geography whose continents have all already been explored, a sort of Icaria eternally soared over. [97]

The universe of the tomb, of the pit into which life falls, has the same signification for both patients: it is the world of a past that is no longer able to flow through, that accumulates in the form of guilty desire or of the wrongdoing that must indefinitely be put right.

One difference, however, and it is essential: Ellen West's guilt is not focused on her mythical existence in the world of light, but on her real existence, on her being-there, on the presence of her flesh, and she expresses it quite naturally through her anxiety about gaining weight and her refusal to eat: everything that separates her from ethereal existence is guilt-inducing; this culpability will lead her to suicide. Storch's patient, on the contrary, is guilty only of this mythical existence: it is not his salvation, but actually his wrongdoing; he falls in having wanted to realize it, and he naturally claims the promethean attitude for himself. But [98] healing, or at least remission, remains possible insofar as guilt is internal to the delusional system, insofar as the world of light is not the only means of escaping the fall, but rather the real origin of the fall itself.

3. This dissociation of the "instant" and the "field of presence" is connected to another temporal experience often encountered in psychosis: the experience of the "*Weltuntergang.*" The world as a place of insertion for the subject and as a domain of possible experiences implies, beyond a spatial structure with privileged lines of orientation and horizons, a temporal structure linked to it that expresses the moments of exploration, of process, of discovery, of journey. For Storch's patient, all journeying has already been accomplished and all discoveries are complete: the world in its entirety exhausts itself in its immediate presence, it is finished (*vollendet*) in the ambiguity of a perfection that eliminates it. It disappears in the moment where it is fully itself. There we have an experience that is somewhat reminiscent of R. Kuhn's patient Franz Weber and his "delusion of limits":[u] we find in both cases the same delusional effort to totalize the world and access a "*Weltregierung*"[v] that stops and freezes the universe. But for Franz Weber, this end of the world is only an end of history, which promises the indefinite extension of existential security; for Storch's patient, the end of history is only one aspect of the cosmic catastrophe that obliterates the order of the world and makes any life in the universe impossible. In the first, stopping history is a way of controlling the anxiety of an existence too open onto space; in the second, the end of the world is the expression of anxiety before the presence of a world that the living instant no longer animates.

---

u See above.

v ["Government of the world."]

In one case, it means perpetual security; in the other, it means permanent death.

4. In this finished time, the field of presence has become the empire of all-presence, and the living instant has taken on the aspect of an empty eternity. Temporality has retransformed itself into simple movements and the present is now only their incoherent explosion: the subject and the world are caught up in the same whirlpool, time is now only lived as the jolts of a universal chaos. Storch's patient recalls that during his nighttime walks on the hill overlooking the city, he sometimes heard thunder and the banging of an earthquake, then the crash of water roaring out of the mountains: above this din, he perceived God's voice, about which it is said in the Bible that it floats on the waters. It is an experience of this kind that Franz Fischer cites.[w]

We will encounter a similar experience of chaos in relation to one of Binswanger's clinical observations, the Jürg Zünd case.

[100]

*

In [the] context of a purely phenomenological description, the morbid experience of time is diversified in the form of a deployment of the field of presence outside of the instant, of a passage to the limit of culpability, of a delusional experience of the end of the world, and of a collapse into chaos.

These constitutive moments of the experience of time are not foundational. If they elucidate the general meaning of a

---

w Franz Fischer, *Zeiterlebnis* . . . [Foucault confuses this title with the title of Erwin Straus's article that he quoted earlier: "Das Zeiterlebnis in der endogenen Depression." In his reading notes, he mentions the following two studies by Franz Fischer: "Zeitstruktur und Schizophrenie," *Zeitschrift für die gesamte Neurologie und Psychiatrie* 121, no. 1 (1929): 544–74; "Raum-Zeit-Struktur und Denkstörung in der Schizophrenie," *Zeitschrift für die gesamte Neurologie und Psychiatrie* 124 (1930): 241–256 (BNF, Box 42b, folder 1).]

pathological experience, like that of Storch's patient, they do not give it a foundation. The error of the psychiatrists inspired only by phenomenology was to confuse the eidetic structure of an experience with its foundation, and to assimilate the constitutive moments of genesis with the radical origin of experience. There, phenomenological description and existential analysis diverge: the first examines how genesis can give an account of itself in a constitutive description (this is [in the] end the meaning of Husserl's last attempts, such as *Erfahrung und Urteil*, in which the "genealogy of logic" is described as its foundation; it is also the meaning of the "descriptions" of the pathological experience of time wherein the disturbances in the ideal genesis of experience must found its pathological character, which implies a reference to a normativity of temporal experience and a definition of the pathological as disorder, disturbance, variation on this ideal theme). The second seeks to ground these constitutive moments in a problem that goes beyond descriptive genesis and requires a more radical reflection, by defining the pathological as a form of existence.

[101] Indeed, each of the moments that we have just described indicates in itself a certain manner of directing oneself toward the world, of opening oneself to it, of projecting oneself onto it. The collapse into chaos is a manner of alienating oneself in a world in which time is no longer time, where movement disappears in its own wake, and where the explosion of each instant no longer has to account for its past and its future: it constitutes something like a renunciation of temporal destiny. The end of history is a way of escaping anxiety in the face of the future by totalizing it, and by making existence coextensive with it, in the myth of eternity: there is there something like [an] eternalization of the world correlating to the divinization of the self. Guilt is a way of totalizing the past, when it is no longer possible to

move beyond it toward the future: it is the weight of a world that no longer has a future. Beyond the phenomenological content of all of these pathological experiences, we sense the outline of projects that are entangled in their contradictions: the contradictory project of abandoning oneself to the time of the world, to its chaotic fractioning—and also of taking it back in the form of an immediately given totality; the project of dominating and governing the world in a quasi-divine omnipotence—and also of assuming all of its imperfections, sins, wrongdoing: a kind of simultaneous apotheosis of Demiurge and holocaust.

The description of temporal structures therefore takes us back to the analysis of the fundamental project of existence from which we can grasp their signification and their necessity. We will use a clinical observation by R. Kuhn[x] [10] that shows through mourning behaviors and criminal behaviors [how] existence can temporalize itself, can constitute itself both as temporality and as history, and decipher its own project in its various temporal experiences. [102]

On March 23, 1939, Rudolf R. attempts to kill a prostitute: they had just had sexual intercourse and, after they had dressed, he had shot her with a revolver. He is sent to a psychiatric hospital. We learn through his relatives that his mother had never recovered after his birth and that she had died when Rudolf was two and a half years old. For the previous six months Rudolf had slept in the same bed as his mother and spent the days next to her. One night, the mother died after lengthy death throes; the father moved the body into another room, but traces of blood remained on the bed. In the morning, Rudolf, as was his habit, goes into his mother's bed, looks for her and unmakes the whole

---

x Roland Kuhn, "The Attempted Murder of a Prostitute," trans. Ernest Angel, in *Existence: A New Dimension in Psychiatry and Psychology*, ed. Rollo May, Ernest Angel, and Henri F. Ellenberger (Basic Books, 1958), 365–425.

bed to find her. An older sister tells him that she is dead. He continues to look for her and finally discovers the body in [the other] room: he climbs onto the bed, kneels on the corpse and touches the dead woman's face with his hands, speaking to her: "You are not dead, as Marie says; you are sleeping."[y] An older sister catches him; he is taken away. He shows no anxiety. But according to his sisters, starting from the day of the burial he becomes entirely different.

Rudolf's childhood memories go back to his fourth year, a time when his mother is dead and his father is not yet remarried; he sleeps in the same bed as his father. He has very vivid memories of certain details, such as deep scars on [his father's] leg. His father marries, in [a second marriage], an alcoholic who would send Rudolf to buy her wine in the village: when drunk, she became mean. She was eventually hospitalized in Münsterlingen. He was not yet attending school when he saw the corpse of an old man with a long beard, their neighbor. From that moment on he had night terrors: he imagined he was encountering the devil, and when the wind howled in the cellar, he thought he recognized the sighs of men who are doomed to die.

During his schooling, he gets into the habit of stealing money from the church: he buys cigarettes, which he gives to his classmates so that they will like him. He also acquires a firework. But he is caught, punished by the teacher and by his father, reprimanded by the priest. Soon afterward he becomes attracted to the wife of a neighbor who is the same age as his mother, but after she denounces him in a new church scandal, his love is transformed into hatred. At the end of his time at school, he is sent to work for a maternal uncle who is a butcher: with friends his own age, he practices mutual masturbation and

---

y [Kuhn, "Attempted Murder," 376.]

homosexuality. He then apprentices with another butcher. He brings meat into [customers'] houses, gets to know the housewives; he likes to draw them out on the topic of their private life. He has an affair with his boss's wife: when his boss finds out, Rudolf is fired. He works in other places, and when his apprenticeship is over, he finds a job: he spends most of his money on prostitutes, or at the cinema. His occupation as a butcher allows him to practice bestiality: he accepts to be paid as a "*Strichjunge*"[z] by a homosexual doctor.

His father dies; he had just had violent discussions about money with him. He feels no grief. However, he returns to the paternal home; he is anxious approaching his father's body: he opens and closes his father's eyes, wants to shave him and to bring the corpse to one of his brothers who does not dare enter. The morning of the burial, at the moment when the coffin leaves the home, Rudolf has a crying fit; it intensifies when [the coffin] is placed in the tomb. Passing by the school, he remembers that, as a child, he envied the members of funeral processions who were on vacation and could go for a walk. The next day, he returns to Zurich and solicits [a prostitute], intending to strangle her. She tells him that she does not want to undress: immediately the murderous impulse disappears. Some weeks later, he abruptly leaves work, looks for prostitutes in bars. He finds a blond woman who brings him to her room. At the end, he gives her twenty Swiss francs and takes out a revolver; the woman believes he is joking and tells him to try. He fires and wounds her slightly. He leaves, goes to a restaurant, orders meat and red wine; then he phones the police and shares his location. Before he can begin his meal the police have arrived; he is taken away, he complains about being hungry. He is calm and cold.

[104]

---

z ["Young prostitute."]

On Easter, he hears the bells ringing and sees a blue sky; he begins to cry. The guard tells him that the moment of madness is short, and that remorse is long.

[105] In a case like Rudolf's, the major form of temporality appears, at first sight, to be repetition: all through his life—from the glimpse of the old man's corpse to the attempted murder, no doubt by way of his professional activity—we encounter the reediting of the initial scene next to his mother's corpse. We might see something like a life of mourning there, or rather something like an existence that refuses the "work of mourning" in the Freudian sense. "*Trauerarbeit*,"[aa] for psychoanalysts, consists of a series of behaviors that aim to avoid melancholic reactions to the loss of the libidinal object: progressive detachment of the libido, protection against reactions of hate, idealization of the object. Yet this "work" does not seem to have been done by Rudolf: the libido remains attached to the material reality of a corpse, that of the mother, against whom all the attempted murders of other women are symbolically directed. Rudolf's life is like a psychoanalytic illustration of the theme that there are corpses one must kill. None of this, undoubtedly, is wrong, but the problem remains if we ask why this *Trauerarbeit* could not be accomplished, why Rudolf never stopped seeking anew the anxious turmoil he had experienced for the first time when faced with his mother's body. Fixation, repetition, the iterative tendency of the death-instinct are terms that signal the problem but cannot resolve it.

---

aa Sigmund Freud, "Mourning and Melancholia" [1915] [in *The Standard Edition of the Complete Psychological Works of Sigmund Freud*, vol. 14, ed. and trans. James Strachey (Hogarth, 1957), 237–58]. Lagache [no specific reference is given. In his reading notes on psychoanalysis from the 1950s, Foucault refers to Daniel Lagache's article "Le travail du deuil. Ethnologie et psychanalyse," *Revue française de psychanalyse* 16, no. 4 (1938): 693–708 (BNF, Box 38, folder 4)].

From the existential[bb] point of view, the work of mourning dissociates, in the concrete reality of the departed person and in the whole of that person's living significations, the corporeal presence—that presence of flesh and sound that acknowledges its own disappearance in funeral rites—and the essence that fixes its destiny in collecting its truth. Mourning is the labor that undoes the thread of perceptive familiarity and leaves, on either side of its path, the "*Gestalt*"[cc] in which the present is abolished and the "*Wesen*"[dd] where the past is conserved, maintained, and reconciled: this promotion of the past to essence, in mourning behaviors, constitutes both something like the way back and something like the concrete genesis of that dialectic of abstract essence that made Hegel say, "*Wesen ist was gewesen ist.*"[ee]

[106]

Mourning, for Rudolf, does not have this signification: his maturation never distinguished between essence and presence; memory remains a quasi-existence (his fear of ghosts, of the devil, when he was a child; his recurring dreams of corpses). Behind any living presence the corpse is there, like his potential past, like the peril that time might incur. This latent presence of the corpse is sufficiently attested by an episode dating back to his apprenticeship: he took a sleeping servant to be dead and attempted to reanimate her. As a result, the past will take on a new aspect: it is no longer the site of the assumption of essence, but rather the obscure world where corporeal presence is maintained in a secret existence that is both promised and threatening; it

---

bb Ludwig Binswanger, *Grundformen und Erkenntnis menschlichen Daseins* (Niehans, 1942); R. Kuhn [no specific reference].
cc ["Form."]
dd ["Essence."]
ee [Literally, "being what has been." Here Foucault is referring to Hegel's *Science of Logic*, "The Doctrine of Essence" (1813). Although it is quoted by Foucault, this passage does not appear in Hegel's text. Rather, it is a formula used many times by Jean-Paul Sartre in *Being and Nothingness*, trans. Hazel E. Barnes (Washington Square Press, 1992), 72, 175, 567, 638.]

[107] acquires the signification of the imaginary of interiority; it is like the skeleton whose appearance turns a body into a corpse; the past is what haunts the present from the inside.

Consequently, every presence will be ambiguous: far from being only the living sign of the present, something like its sharp point in the world, it is the secret presence of the past. Each life carries behind it its own corpse, and rather than distributing the past and the future, the present continually mixes them: all of the present's future exhausts itself in becoming its own past; all of the meaning of a life consists in being inhabited by a death that a gesture can free; and from death, too, one can return to life. There, in all likelihood, is the root of the myths through which Rudolf represents himself as the Christ resurrecting corpses, as the all-powerful master of life and death. This too can explain the ardor with which he practiced his occupation as a butcher; and if we add that love, that sexual penetration (in creating a momentary link between the interior and the exterior) bring to light, for Rudolf, this past of death that the present life encloses, we can better understand the relationship between his profession and his practice of bestiality; we can better understand that his murderous urges were particularly aimed at women with whom he had or was going to have sexual relations.

These practices of bestiality aside, Rudolf's world remains calm until his father's death. If it is true that after the death of the mother the past haunts the present in the mode of quasi-presence, a principle of spatial distribution has established itself between them: the world of the past is that of darkness, interi-

[108] ority, dream, imagination (the fantasy world or the universe of crime films that he would go to [see] up to three times in a single day); that of the present is, on the contrary, the world of active life (Rudolf is a hard worker, very interested in his occupation), it is the world of light, of the street (where he very much enjoys

strolling), it is also the world of gold, of shiny coins. But here we encounter a new point of contact between the two worlds: might the sparkle that belongs to the bright world of presence not be, like the sparkle of the dead eyes that he opened and closed on his mother's corpse, the reflection of a world of shadows where the past lies in wait? This might explain Rudolf's theft of coins when he was around twelve years old. But beyond these surfaces of contact—money, sexuality, work—the vertical temporality of the past does not yet manifestly intermix with the horizontal temporality of the present.

But the father dies, soon after having fought with Rudolf over money, as if the shiny pieces of money had abruptly exposed their hidden truth. The corpse is there, exposed in the full light of day. The morning of the funeral, the coffin leaves the house and passes into the street where, confined in school, Rudolf had envied those who could walk in the light and the sun. As a result, the two worlds of the present and the past, of life and of death, become fused: the fragile spatial partition that had been separating them is now broken, death has overrun life.

Crime finds its necessity, and its justifications find their meaning: immediately after his arrest, Rudolf had explained his act by saying that prostitutes charged too much, and that he wanted to ensure the regeneration of the world. These are reasons that can be understood only if we concede that he was seeking through his victims to get rid of all of these women who display the dark world of their sexuality in the street, in public places, in broad daylight; these women who hand over their intimacy for money, in exchange for these shiny coins that belong to the day and the present: they transform interiority into external reality; through them the past irrupts into the present. It is to reinstate their separation that murdering a prostitute became, for Rudolf, his primary task as soon as his father's death compromised their

[109]

spatial order. But in all likelihood it is also—and paradoxically—in order to take possession, to triumph over the ghostly world of the past, in order to master it in the form of a body that one can take from life to death at will.

It would thus be inadequate to say that biographical history determined the experience of lived time in its significations; and just as inadequate to give to the former the only meaning that it can borrow from that experience. In fact, through the experiences where the distinguishing mark of the past and the themes of the present intermix, we can grasp a fundamental project; it is only against the backdrop of this project, of this originary relationship to the world, that lived experiences can take on meaning. We can characterize it by saying that it is a project of conserving one's past "in the flesh," a project of maintaining what was, not at the level of essence but on the order of continuous, indefinitely prolonged presence in the almost-corporeal existence of the ghost. This project was able to escape the contradiction it contains as long as the world of fantasy and the world of reality stayed separate. But murder became necessary when they began to mix: then the child kneeling on his mother's corpse became a bringer of death, not in order to find again the same anxious turmoil but rather to make sure of his mastery of that past, where bodies lie.

Psychotherapy was precisely, through the modifications that it introduced to this project, its verification: in making memories explicit, it allowed for internalization, the "*Erinnerung*"[ff] that is the very work of memory. It opened the path to the acknowledgement of the other, not in his immediate presence but in his essential signification; his bitterness corroded memory and freed it from its corporeal concern:

[ff] ["Memory."]

I will name wilderness the temple which you were,
Night your voice, absence your face,
And when you fall back into the sterile earth
I will name nothingness the lightning which bore you.[gg]

The authenticity of time necessarily goes through the truth of the other.

NOTES

1. Foucault dedicated a very detailed reading note to the study by Gebsattel mentioned here, entitled "Phobic Psychasthenia according to Gebsattel" (BNF, Box 42b, folder 1), in which he remarks, "A patient says that the '*Weite*' [expanse] has something '*Erschreckendes*' [frightening], as if something she did not know (cars, animals, men) were going to throw themselves on her '*aus des Weite*' [from afar]. The *Weite* is experienced as something that 'holds itself before' (*Bevorstehendes*), and the living connection to it does not only consist in the lived possibility of dominating (*Bewältigen*) the world via a temporal progress (*Fortschreiten*), but also a spatial one. The *Weite* of space is not only an image of the deployed world, but also an image of destiny deploying itself (*ein Bild des sich entfaltenden Schichsals*) and it is determined by the person's attitude toward the future. Either the *Weite* promises the deployment of force—the widening (*Ausbreitung*) of personal life, success, victory—or it is threatened by domination, powerlessness, slavery; conversely, the vicinity (*die enge Nahwelt*) promises protection, secrecy (*Geborgenheit*), security. The phobic symptom is constituted through a process that is not that of *Werden* [becoming], but of *Entwerden* [unbecoming]. It represents a step in a retreat out of the *Weite* of a life that accomplishes itself (*erfüllenden*) in the narrowness of the corner of a room (*Stubenwinkel*). Sensitivity (*Empfindlichkeit*) to the phenomenon of

---

gg [Yves Bonnefoy, "Vrai nom/True Name," trans. Galway Kinnell, in *New and Selected Poems* (University of Chicago Press, 1995), 14–15. The original text reads "ce château" ("this castle") rather than "the temple."]

the *Weite* appears as a fact of expression: it expresses the fact that life is in motion, that a *Lebensbewegung* [life movement] is underway, which disentangles itself from the debate with destiny, from any attack (*Vorchuss*) in the *Weite* of the world and the future, and which inflects the direction toward the burying of the self (*Selbsteinsargung*) in an obscure proximity in which encounters are rare (*begegnesarm*). It is impossible that a personality whose *Lebensgesetz* [life norm] is a defense against the future could fully realize (*vollziehen*) the spatial *Weite*, insofar as the latter symbolizes the future. While we live the *Weite* in a modality of dynamic reaction, as *Weitergehen* [moving on], and *Weitergehen können* [ability to move on], inversely the undynamic reaction consists in the *Erlebnis* of not being able to change places (*das Nicht-von-der-Stelle-können*). The phobic person lives the *Weite* only through the elementary direction of his regressive *Lebenstendenz* [vital tendency], whose aim is the *Entwerden*, the withdrawal of the self (*Selbsteinfaltung*), the *Selbstauslöschung* [self-effacement]. In phobia, the *Weite*, instead of mobilizing force and power, mobilizes weakness and powerlessness, especially since the spatial *Umwelt* [environment], through its marked character as an expanse (free place), more violently provokes the automatic opposition to the meaning of the *Weite*. This automatic opposition has only one meaning: the *Manifestwerden* [becoming manifest] of the regressive *Lebenstendenz*. At the same time, the *Erlebnis* of the *Überwältigen* [feeling of domination] appears: there is more than the 'not being able to change places'; there is all of the weight of the inverted *Werdensrichtung* [direction of becoming]. It is not surprising that the phobic person feels dominated by the sight of the *Weite*, because he does not identify with his regressive *Lebenstendenz*, which is completely unknown to him as a bio-pathological fact, but rather with the wish to penetrate the expanse that opens up before him. This wish will be controlled by a contradiction that is incomprehensible to him: despite his desire, he cannot move. Whence the kinship between the phobic reaction and the *Zwang* [constraint]. The feeling of domination foreign to oneself (*Überwältigungserlebnis*) of the *Zwang* finds its analogue in the feeling of domination foreign to oneself which emerges from the signification of the future that the *Weite* contains. In fact, it is the call of life in the form of the spatial *Weite* that worries the phobic person, because, in perceiving this call (*Ruf*), he immediately experiences the indomitable power of his regressive *Lebenstendenz*. The *Werdenshemmung* [inhibition of becoming] is not '*erlebt*' [lived], but in the encounter between the living being and the world, it removes from the former the strength to affirm himself in the face of the world. Then the world takes on a hostile and threatening aspect, where the *Weite* is engulfing, where movements occur in disorder, where light has a painful intensity. The immediate (*selbstverständlich*) connection between man and nature is transformed into anxious alienation [*Entfremdung*]. It is the *Verlorenheit* [forlornness] of man in the world, which, brought into the present by the undynamic modalities of reaction, gains the upper hand within him, and takes possession of him in '*Angsterleben*' [lived anxiety]."

2. The phobic syndromes Foucault mentions here are treated in Viktor Emil von Gebsattel's study "Die Welt des Zwangskranken," *Monatsschrift für Psychiatrie und Neurolologie* 99 (1938): 10–74, reprinted in *Prolegomena einer medizinischen Anthropologie*, 74–128, to which Foucault also devotes a reading note (BNF, Box 42b, folder 1).

3. There is a folder dedicated to Eugène Minkowski in Foucault's archives from the 1950s that contains the following reading notes: "Lived space," "Phenomenology and pathology according to Minkowski," "Observation. Psychological and phenomenological analyses" (BNF, Box 42b, folder 1).

4. See on this topic the reading note entitled "Observation. Psychological and phenomenological analyses" (BNF, Box 42b, folder 1).

5. See, in the folder entitled "Roland Kuhn," the reading note devoted by Foucault to this clinical case study: "*Daseinsanalyse* of a case of schizophrenia. Roland Kuhn" (BNF, Box 42b, folder 1).

6. These drawings are currently conserved in the State Archives of the canton of Thurgau in Frauenfeld (Staatsarchiv Thurgau), which has held the archives of the Münsterlingen psychiatric clinic since 2005 and Roland Kuhn's personal archives since 2013. A selection of images was reproduced in Gerhard Dammann's "Roland Kuhns phänomenologische und daseinsanalytische Arbeiten zu Ästhetik und künstlerischem Schaffen," in *Auf der Seeseite der Kunst. Werke aus der Psychiatrischen Klinik Münsterlingen, 1894–1960*, ed. Katrin Luchsinger et al. (Chronos, 2015), 37-52. In his clinical work at the Münsterlingen clinic, Roland Kuhn was very attentive to his patients' artistic productions, which he understood as a kind of self-therapy. According to him, indeed, through the single act of "giving form," aesthetic expres-

sion had the function of helping the patient to find anew the movement of transformation of space and time that was at the foundation of the *Dasein*. It was the reason for which he conserved the drawings in his patients' files.

7. Inside the folder on Husserl in Foucault's archives, there is a file entitled "Consciousness of time," which contains fourteen reading notes (BNF, Box 42a, folder 3). In this same folder, moreover, a reading note is devoted to "*Zeitbewusstsein*" ("V. Vorlesung") based on Husserl's book *Die Idee der Phänomenologie. Fünf Vorlesungen*, ed. Walter Biemel (Martinus Nijhoff, 1950).

8. Alfred Storch (1888–1962): After completing his medical studies in Heidelberg and receiving accreditation as *Privatdozent* in neurology and psychiatry, he emigrated to Switzerland in 1934 and worked as an intern at the Münsingen psychiatric hospital, in the canton of Bern. In 1950, he completed his professorial accreditation in philosophy at the University of Bern. Very attentive both to the development of psychoanalysis and to Binswanger's *Daseinsanalyse*—he maintained a correspondence with Binswanger—Storch was one of the more influential representatives of the existential approach in psychopathology, to which he devoted much writing starting in the 1930s. In Foucault's archives of the 1950s, a folder dedicated to Storch's work contains many very detailed reading notes concerning, in addition to the clinical case study mentioned by Foucault here, the following studies: "Tod und Erneuerung in der schizophrenen Daseins-Umwandlung," *Archiv für Psychiatrie und Neurologie* 181 (1948): 275–93; and "Die Psychoanalyse und die menschlichen Existenzprobleme," *Schweizer Archiv für Neurologie und Psychiatrie* 44 (1939): 102–18. Also mentioned are *Das archaisch-primitive Erleben und Denken der Schizophrenen. Entwicklungspsychologisch-klinische Untersuchungen zum Schizophrenieproblem* (Springer, 1922); "Existenzphilosophisch Richtungen in der modernen Psychopathologie. Erwiderung zu R. De Rosa," *Der Nervenarzt* 23 (1952): 421–23; and "Die Welt der beginnenden Schizophrenie und die archaische Welt. Ein existential-analytischer Versuch," *Zeitschrift für die gesamte Neurologie und Psychiatrie* 127 (1930): 799–810 (BNF, Box 42b, folder 1).

9. On this topic, see the reading note entitled "The present" where Foucault remarks, "α. We must distinguish: the present as *Präsenzfeld*; the now as *Jetzt*, which is the kernel of the former. In this way the *Jetzt* is privileged: if we cut the large present into two parts, the part containing the *Jetzt* would be privileged. β. But the *Jetzt* is something abstract that cannot exist

for itself. It is not completely [*toto caelo*] different from the non-*Jetzt*, 'it is continually mediated with it.'" Here Foucault mentions Yvonne Picard's article "Le temps chez Husserl et chez Heidegger," *Deucalion*, no. 1 (1946): 93–124, as well as a passage translated by Jacques Derrida from Husserl's lectures on the intimate consciousness of time (paragraph 59): "It is evident that every temporal point has its before and after, and that the points and intervals coming before cannot be compressed in the manner of an approximation to a mathematical limit, as, let us say, the limit of intensity. If there were such a boundary-point, there would correspond to it a Present which nothing preceded, and this is obviously impossible. A Present is always and essentially the edge-point (*Randpunkt*) of an interval of time." (BNF, Box 42a, folder 3; English translation of Derrida's Husserl from Jacques Derrida, *The Problem of Genesis in Husserl's Philosophy*, trans. Marian Hobson (University of Chicago Press, 2003), 67. See also, in the same folder, a long reading note entitled "The conception of time in 'Vorlesungen zur Phänomenologie des inneren Zeitbewusstseins.'"

10. Foucault devoted a very detailed reading note to this clinical case study by Roland Kuhn (BNF, Box 42b, folder 1). This same folder ("Roland Kuhn") contains a two-part analysis of a case study that Foucault does not mention in this manuscript: "Zur Daseinsanalyse der Anorexia mentalis," *Der Nervenarzt* 22, no. 1 (1951): 11–13; and "Zur Daseinsanalyse der Anorexia mentalis. II. Studie," *Der Nervenarzt* 24 (1953): 191–98.

CHAPTER FOUR

The Experience of the Other

I. Temporality and intersubjectivity: 1. *The first explicit divergence between existential analysis and Heidegger's analytic of existence;* 2. *The experience of the other*[a] *in the psychiatric tradition, in Freud and in Husserl. II. The figure of the Other in the morbid horizon:* 1. *The other in the phenomenological domain;* 2. *The totality of the other and sexual perversions. III. Clinical case studies:* 1. *The Konrad Schwing case (Medard Boss);* 2. *The Lola Voss case (Ludwig Binswanger). IV. Daseinsanalyse's distance from Husserl's phenomenology and Heidegger's ontology:* 1. *The Jürg Zünd case (Ludwig Binswanger);* 2. *The anthropological primacy of love.*

In the method whose major ideas Binswanger has sketched out, temporality is not the ultimate foundation wherein the existential "analytic" meets the requirement that it go beyond itself in an "ontological" reflection. Time is not, for him, that from which human existence can be understood. An experience like that of mourning shows that the final meaning of temporality is not the "Being of human beings" [*l'"être de l'étant humain"*] but the existence of other humans: time does nothing but collect

---

a [Foucault uses "autre" and "autrui" throughout this chapter, and he almost always capitalizes the former. I have translated both terms as "other," indicating Foucault's use of "Autre" by capitalizing "Other"—Trans.]

the significations of coexistence; it is only ever the time of presence or of absence. The sign of transcendence that it carries does not point to the Being that opens itself and exposes itself to the human being, but rather to the Other who presents himself to him, offers him his existence in perceptual plenitude, or else deprives him of it, leaving behind the wake that absence creates. Neither, therefore, is time that through which freedom constitutes itself, but rather it is that in which freedoms confront each other; it is born from their parallelism or from their divergences: it constitutes itself as the objective time of things, as the chaotic time of movement, as the ultimate time of cosmic catastrophes, as the time of the end of times when it no longer is the encounter of freedoms. When freedoms reconnect with each other, time finds once again its originary meaning, or rather it recovers its authenticity in that which, precisely, suppresses it: it [recovers it[b]] in love, it denies itself in the form of eternity.

Time thus loses its ontological privilege twice: it does not carry the transcendence of truth, it signifies only the transcendence of the Other; it is not constitutive of freedom, because in the fulfillment of freedom's encounter with itself, freedom contests and goes beyond time. Time is only ever secondary in relation to the Other and to love.

These themes are essential. In themselves, they are the first explicit divergence between "existential analysis" and the "analytic of existence" whose programmatic themes Heidegger sketched out in the first chapters of *Sein und Zeit*.[c] It is an

---

b [Here one or many words are missing. We have added "recovers it" conjecturally.]

c [Even though Heidegger distinguishes between *existentiell* and *existential* understanding in *Being and Time*, Foucault uses only the common adjective "existentiel" in this manuscript; for example, this sentence reads, " . . . ils sont la première divergence explicite de 'l'analyse existentielle,' avec 'l'analytique existentielle' dont Heidegger avait esquissé les thèmes programmatiques dans les premiers chapitres de *Sein und Zeit*." I follow Foucault's lead in using the common adjective "existential" when he writes "existentiel/le."—Trans.]

astonishing deviation: should we primarily admire the long concern for orthodoxy, or the abrupt break? Was Heideggerian thought a method? Did it define a research style; did it constitute a language through which one could work to grasp the significations of concrete existence? In that case, it was not permissible to abandon it at the decisive moment. Even if one does not accept its implicit *theories*, a *method* has meaning only within the *totality* of the system it deploys: one cannot speak a language whose syntax one understands if one rejects its semantics. Was it, on the contrary, a theoretical foundation from which one borrowed themes? Was it only a philosophical coloring? The ease of putting it aside demonstrates the contingency of the relationships that tie it to existential analysis, and shows sufficiently that the latter could have constituted [itself] quite independently.

We will content ourselves here with taking note of this strange change of orientation.

We will return later to the problems it raises, when we have shown its implications, and also determined which imperatives it obeys. [113]

*

Since the nineteenth century, the psychiatric tradition has given ever-greater importance to the perception of the other, to "mutual recognition," and to the modalities of interhuman communication. It should suffice, in passing, to recall that Janet made of social behavior—with discursive reciprocity (speaking—being spoken) and the alternation of perspectives in tasks completed communally—both a decisive development in human evolution and one of the most fragile achievements, most easily compromised by the decrease in psychic tension;[2] that for

Blondel, morbid consciousness is characterized by the disappearance of the social and spatial references collected in the universe of language, and delusion is characterized by the emergence, in this disarticulated universe, of a "cenesthetic" world in which the fantasies of a rigorously individual space are deployed;[3] that Bleuler, finally, had described as one of the major symptoms of schizophrenia the affective retreat away from the world of others that he had named autism.[4] But in all of these analyses, the disturbance of the relationship with the other is nothing but a superficial manifestation of a deeper disorder: of a dissociation of affective structures, of a decrease in psychological energy. The pathological event is social only as a repercussion; the patient is, in some manner, in himself and in his individuality, responsible for his illness. The other and social constellations play only the role of decor.

Freud, however, had made the other into the protagonist of the pathological drama: in the form of the maternal imago, he had turned it into the major libidinal object; and in the form of the paternal imago, he had outlined it as the first moment of frustration, as the initial instance of repression. As such, the figure of the Other is doubly constitutive: it is at the starting point of structural development, and it is also at the origin of significations. If we must give to the "Oedipus complex" its broadest, perhaps best-founded meaning, we must acknowledge this essential discovery in its definition: the human figure is present at the very heart of man's development, it haunts all of his significations and is his first genetic moment; the "Oedipus complex" resolves the enigma of man and gives his mortal destiny its stamp only insofar as it illuminates man himself as the essence of man. This, undoubtedly, is where Freud's most radical effort to escape the bias of *homo natura* and detach himself from the evolutionist horizon in which he had inscribed his theory of the libido occurred. He showed that, where human reality is concerned, the succession of things is possible only starting from the coexistence of men.

But Freud's enterprise remained ambiguous.[5] In the analytical experience, the other presents itself as a point of crystallization of the libidinal investments, which is to say that the other is defined by two different systems of coherence: from one perspective, it is the stable, solid point where the most varied—even the most radically opposed—libidinal urges converge: See the figure of the mother: Melanie Klein[6] saw that it brought together, up to the point of its corporeal presence, the themes of aggressive destruction as well as those of satisfaction, and that in this way it was a theme of projection and a theme of introjection. The other is the place in the field of behavior where affective contradictions come together, yet immediately and as if under the weight of these contradictory tensions, its unity breaks down; the figure becomes polymorphous and takes on imaginary aspects that its contradictory virtualities had already sketched out. The experience of the other then develops in the unreality of fantasy: it gives itself over to the plasticity of imaginary metamorphoses and to the subtlety of delusional metempsychoses; it becomes the constant theme of phobic reincarnations. The other is therefore, in the psychoanalytic field, the moment of convergence of contradictory urges and the original theme of imaginary polymorphism; it is something like the moment of rest of psychological contradiction, but it is still and already entirely inhabited by that contradiction. And it is this meaning, perhaps, that we must give to the term "imago."

But these imaginary coordinates, taken together, are not enough to situate the other in the psychoanalytic field: it appears

[115]

as the partner of a dialogue that places it at the point of convergence of the logical significations of a language. It is the other to which this language of signs and of symptoms, the language of passion, the language of things unsaid addresses itself: the analysis of President Schreber offers an example of this immense verbal dialectic that encircles, contests, and denies the major meaning of the "I love you," but in such a way that through so many negations its immediate affirmation is always transcribed. In any case, the actual answer is never required, but always subsumed in the very thread of these contradictory affirmations: because all of this dialectic has meaning only as a parody of dialogue.

Mythic partner of a dialogue without an answer, or imaginary moment of psychological contradiction, the Other, in psychoanalysis, is essential to genesis but never constitutive of psychological experience. It is only ever grasped as a theme in a fantastical bestiary, or a figure of prosopopoeia in a rhetoric without any actual dialogue.

There too, the decisive step was taken by Husserlian thought: it was the first to uncover the constitutive character of the experience of the other as coexistence. The presence of the other, in phenomenology, does not exhaust itself in the totality of its presentations: the other is something else, and more than all of the profiles through which it is glimpsed. Objects are "constituted relatively," which is to say that the reading of their essence can happen only from a phenomenal deployment which marks its constitutive moments and forms the concrete mediation of its genesis; persons, on the contrary, are "constituted absolutely," in the sense that the other is not given through a deployment, but rather by a manifestation that designates it immediately and from the start as a totality, as an absolute origin of signification and as a possible center of reciprocity.[d] In this way, the same reflection on essence, which refers from the subject perceiving the object to the transcendental subject constituting it, will refer from the subject that recognizes the other to a transcendental intersubjectivity in whose totality each person affirms himself as a monad.[e] Henceforth "the ego is then no longer an isolated thing in a world alongside other equally isolated things in a pregiven world; the serious mutual exteriority of ego-persons, their being alongside one another, ceases in favor of an inward being-for-one-another and mutual interpenetration."[f]

We can no longer see in the disturbance of the experience of the other a derivative phenomenon, the result of a purportedly more radical alteration: it is a challenge to the most fundamental forms of existence.

*

Within the phenomenological domain, the person is thus an absolute manifestation in the form of absolute coexistence. What meaning can be given to this absolute character? How might pathological experience ignore or contest it? How can the figure of the Other, in the morbid horizon, present itself only ever as a series of fragmentary and relative apparitions?

---

d See part 3, supplement 7 of Edmund Husserl, *Ideas Pertaining to a Pure Phenomenology and to a Phenomenological Philosophy*, vol. 2, *Studies in the Phenomenology of Constitution*, trans. Richard Rojcewicz and André Schuwer, (Kluwer Academic Publishers, 1989). This volume is hereafter referred to as *Ideas II*.

e Edmund Husserl, *Cartesian Meditations: An Introduction to Phenomenology*, trans. Dorion Cairns (Martinus Nijhoff, 1960).

f Edmund Husserl, "Philosophy and the Crisis of European Humanity" [The Vienna Lecture], trans. David Carr, in *The Crisis of European Sciences and Transcendental Phenomenology*, ed. David Carr (Northwestern University Press, 1970), 298.

1. THE TOTALITY OF THE OTHER AND SEXUAL PERVERSIONS

[118] In *Ideas* II, Husserl shows how the person, as *Geist*, is founded on its corporeal presence. It is not a matter of grasping the articulation of the psychic on the physiological, or the conditioning of the soul by the body, and thereby of defining a psychosomatic causality. It is a matter of showing how the person only ever announces themself through their own body; and how this presence "in the flesh" cannot avoid referring from a field of natural determinations to a domain in which significations do not exhaust themselves in an exact essence (such as the natural significations in *mathêmata*), but rather assert themselves as a spiritual (*geistig*) reality which is em-"bodied,"[g] to "animate" them, with the perceptual contents of corporeal presence. The totality thus designated is neither the entirety of organic solidarity, nor the correlation of psycho-physical processes: it is neither a sum, nor a whole, nor a maximum, but only this minimum without which the immediate recognition of the presence of the other in the plenitude of the perceptual field would not be possible.[h]

Yet certain sexual perversions, notably fetishism, would seem to indicate an alteration in this totality, and something like a difficulty in perceiving the other as making one body, as it were, with one's own body.

Freud was first to associate perversion with the primitive forms of investment, in which certain erogenous zones are privileged and certain elements of the libidinous object valorized. And although we do not say it enough, he defines normal sexu-
[119] ality not only as the genital fixation of the erogenous zone, but

---

g [Here Foucault use the expression "fait 'corps'" (literally, "makes body"), which means to come together as one—Trans.]
h Husserl, *Ideas II*.

as the acknowledgment, as the libidinal object, of the Other in its totality, by the ego in its totality.ⁱ Perversion would thereby indicate the reactivation of the segmentary forms of libidinal relations, and in this way it would always be linked to destructive instincts whose unearthing brings forth, in a specific manner, sadomasochistic behavior.

The prestige of this concept, and the frequency with which we find, in analyses of cases of perversion, the myths of the segmented body, criminal obsessions, sadistic fantasies: all of this explains that from an anthropological perspective perversion is still considered as a behavior of dividing up the other's personality. Gebsattel, in his article on fetishism,ʲ defines the tendency that culminates there as "the desire to destroy the whole, to mutilate it and break it into pieces, to elevate an element to the status of totality, cutting off (*Ausschaltung*) the actual totality."ᵏ ⁷ But like Freud's, Gebsattel's theory stresses only the organic totality, or rather the material "moment" of perceptual presence: both imply that the erotic relationship addresses itself to the whole of the organism which is, all in all, only a segment within natural determinations, and not to this absolute totality which brings together cultural and spiritual significations.

---

i "Die Beziehungen von Liebe und Hass seien nicht für die Relationen der Triebe zu ihren Objekten verwendbar, sondern für die Relation des Gesamt-Ichs zu den Objekten reserviert"; see Sigmund Freud, *Triebe und Triebschicksale* [1915], in *Gesammelte Schriften*, vol. 5 (Vienna: Internationaler Psychoanalytischer Verlag, 1924), 462. [For the standard English translation, see *Instincts and their Vicissitudes*, in *The Standard Edition of the Complete Psychological Works of Sigmund Freud*, vol. 14, ed. and trans. James Strachey (Hogarth, 1957), 137: "the attitudes [*Bezeichnungen* (descriptions, terms) in the first edition] of love and hate cannot be made use of for the relations of *instincts* to their objects, but are reserved for the relations of the *total ego* to objects."]

j Viktor Emil von Gebsattel, "Über Fetischismus," *Der Nervenarzt* 2, no. 1 (1929): 8–20; reprinted in *Prolegomena einer medizinischen Anthropologie* (Springer, 1954), 144–51.

k [Gebsattel, "Über Fetischismus," 14. The translation is Foucault's; he borrows the quotation from the book by Medard Boss cited in the following paragraph.]

It is in these terms that Boss attempted to define the "meaning and content of sexual perversions."[1][8] Let us follow him in examining a case of fetishism.

Konrad Schwing is the eldest son of a couple living unharmoniously.

[120] The father, very retiring, appears at home only very rarely. The mother, arrogant, haughty, lives a high-society life that prevents her from taking care of her children. She has never loved her eldest son. She shows her aversion: she cannot bear for him to touch her; when social necessity compels her to kiss him, her face tenses. Sent to boarding school very early, Konrad has poor relationships with his classmates; he increasingly shuts himself away into a world of imagination and fantasy. As a little boy, he experienced great tenderness for every girl: occasionally, on the street, he would kiss a little girl he had never seen before. But at the time of puberty, only women wearing leather and animal hides sexually excite him. When he entered into contact with such objects, "the entire world was transformed,"[m] "a luminous splendor shone"[n] from the object and seemed directed at him; he stated that "the God Eros took form in these gloves."[o] A woman in herself no longer has any sexual significance for him: the more a part of the female body closely concerns sexuality, the more a representation of concrete contact with it puts him in a state of terror; he cannot think about immediate sexual contact without experiencing a feeling of guilt as intense as if he had committed a sacrilege. Conversely, gloves or boots "idealize, stylize" human forms: "a piece of leather that a woman wears erases the precise

---

1 Medard Boss, *Sinn und Gehalt der sexuellen Perversionen. Ein daseinsanalytischer Beitrag zur psychopathologie des Phänomens der Liebe* (Huber, 1947).

m [Boss, *Sinn und Gehalt*, 36.]

n [Boss, *Sinn und Gehalt*, 36.]

o [Boss, *Sinn und Gehalt*, 37.]

contours of the body; everything becomes clear and luminous; we see into the heavens, and we believe that we have before us the goddess of love."p He is thirty-one years old when he falls in love with a young woman whose similarity to Konrad's mother is undeniable; he is the only one not to notice it. With much insistence, he succeeds in marrying her, convinced that his wife will follow him into his "magic kingdom."q In fact, she practices fetishism only against her will. Konrad feels that she "lacks imagination" and that she enjoys living in "the world of ordinary things"r too much.

It is important to note that we find in Konrad many dreams of incest with the mother, but none of them are marked by fetishism; these scenes of incest are often followed by scenes of judgment in which he is sentenced to physical torture—to being quartered, for example. He also frequently sees in his dreams women's bodies in a state of decomposition, being eaten by worms; filthy animals emerge from them: these are snakes and cats that coil around or attach themselves to his legs. Here we have all of the material familiar in psychoanalysis: Oedipal themes, castration themes, theme of the virile woman. But he can only give an account of the symptom through a shaky theory of symbolism and of the "phallic" signification of gloves or of boots, that nothing in the patient's experience would justify. In fact, we must note that before school age, he manifested no sign of this narrowing of the field of eroticism manifested in his behaviors [related to] fetishism: he was, on the contrary, attracted by children of the opposite sex. But the mother, rather than facilitating this communication with the "*Mitwelt*" in the mode

[121]

---

p [Boss, *Sinn und Gehalt*, 37.]
q [Boss, *Sinn und Gehalt*, 38.]
r [Boss, *Sinn und Gehalt*, 39.]

of love, made it, little by little, impossible: the body ceased to be for him the privileged mode of affective reciprocity. Deprived of this originary experience of the corporeal connection with the mother, love and eroticism, we might say, lost their mother tongue. The body—his body and that of others—will from then on be covered in a heavy cloak of anxiety, and for a long time love will be lived by him only in the mode of a mythical relationship to a world without bodies, without weight, a universe devoid of flesh; he will imagine a whole pantheon of divinities that will be for him the only possible objects of love (the "god of love"; the "goddess of beauty"; Eros). Yet some parts of the human body still escape this originary interdiction and the mantle of anxiety that covers it; or rather it is the most superficial, the most "peripheral," the most impersonal items of clothing—those Konrad himself describes as "incorporeal" (*unleiblichen*).[s] It is these most meagre and inessential elements of the corporeal presence that continue to permit the communication of love, because there is no reason to believe that the experience Konrad describes in his naïve lyricism is not authentic. In the contact with a woman wearing gloves and shoes, he is able to find the path toward loving reciprocity, or even simply toward the experience of the other as absolute totality in the perceptual field: in this manner, he recovers what Boss calls the "*Du-Erlebnis*."[t]

Fetishism is thus founded neither on a symbolism that would reproduce, though a few formal analogies, a repressed sexual representation, nor on the fantasies of a sadism that would break up a corporeal unity. It constitutes a way of discovering, through the surface, the periphery, and the inessential, the absolute existence of the other. It is like an oblique pathway for recovering, at its

---

s [Boss, *Sinn und Gehalt*, 43.]
t [Boss, *Sinn und Gehalt*, 44 (literally, "experience of the you").]

external borders, this totality that the Other offers with his corporeal presence, but which is almost entirely blanketed by anxiety.

2. THE OTHER AS ABSOLUTE ORIGIN OF SIGNIFICATION

The field of presence in which the other appears does not only indicate the absolute manifestation of a totality, but it also reveals the origin of irreducible significations. The origin designates itself as such, insofar as the manifested significations are never already constituted in an a priori that exhausts them: whatever the points of reference may be—whether in the form of permanent features, character traits, habits—that one casts onto the surface of the Other, he remains the bearer and master of his own significations. If he presents himself as absolute totality—and not through sketches and profiles, like an object—it is characteristic of this totality never to deploy itself as definitively totalized. The other therefore always offers himself with a certain opacity. Not the opacity of things which prevents us from seeing the six faces of the die at the same time, or from perceiving the law of falling bodies immediately in a stone that falls: the opacity of things comes from their perceptual presence not exhausting the essence that animates them, and the colored plenitude with which they present themselves has meaning only through an eidetic structure that anticipates their concrete possibilities and necessarily overflows them. The opacity of others, on the contrary, comes from the fact that they are at each moment, and in each of their gestures, responsible for their own essence: things owe their obscure density to the fact that they are not at the level of their eidetic foundation, and that in starting from them it is only possible to recover them only though

[123]

the elucidation of the constitutive moments of their genesis. The other owes his density to the fact that he is in himself his own eidetic justification and that one cannot reach him through a genetic constitution, but only from an absolute position.

As we have seen, the paradox of pathological experience masks the position of the other; but at the same time absolute totality gives it a transparency that normal experience does not have. Pathological experience only ever perceives the other through significations that are already entirely deployed: it only recognizes in him a privileged moment in their genesis. The other is taken up entirely in the constitutive movement of meaning, and this is what psychiatry calls the "symbolic derealization of the other"[9] in delusion: in jealous delusion, for example, infidelity is not a theme founded on the recognition of the other's absolute position; quite the reverse, rather, the presence of the other, his existence, his behavior are only a means for the theme of infidelity to announce and deploy itself; the unfaithful partner is nothing but a constitutive moment in the genesis of a world of betrayal.[u]

This disregarding of the other as absolute origin of significations is singularly well illustrated by certain elements of one of Binswanger's observations, the Lola Voss case.[v] [10]

---

u This is the meaning we must likely give to Lagache's analysis: "Jealousy is morbid when it becomes a norm, which is to say a stable attitude, a person's permanent disposition, a constant and habitual manner of living the romantic and sexual relationship.... It grants the other only submission, not the freedom and spontaneity of attachment; it encloses the jealous person in the irreversibility of his romantic and sexual commitments." See *La jalousie amoureuse, psychologie descriptive et psychanalyse*, vol. 1, *Les états de jalousie et le problème de la conscience morbide* (PUF, 1947), 320. [Foucault's archives contain many reading notes devoted to this book by Lagache (BNF, Box 42b, folder 1).]

v Ludwig Binswanger, "The Case of Lola Voss," trans. Ernest Angel, in *Being-in-the-World: Selected Papers of Ludwig Binswanger*, ed. Jacob Needleman (Basic Books, 1963), 266–341.

Lola Voss had a pampered childhood. She was spoiled by her relatives: her mother permitted what her father forbade, and the grandmother granted what her mother refused. Raised in South America, she is sent to Germany for her studies: she shows herself to be distant and domineering; she is placed in a Catholic environment, which sets her against her Protestant father. She returns to her family, meets a Spanish physician; she would like to marry him, but the father will not consent unless the young man has a position. She takes on a defiant attitude and declares that she will enter a convent if she is not allowed to marry. Soon, she leaves for a trip to Europe with her mother. During this stay, her fiancé writes to tell her that he cannot yet consider marriage. She withdraws, becomes melancholic, erects a whole system of superstitions: umbrellas and clothing made out of rubber are unlucky; hunchbacks, conversely, are for her a sign of happiness. Her mother returns to America, entrusting Lola to an aunt. The latter probably turns her against her mother; in any case, [125] when she returns to America, her hostility against her mother has reached its peak: she no longer wants to enter her room, she refuses everything that comes from her; everything that has touched her seems bewitched, she will no longer wear clothes that have been in the same wash as her mother's; she cannot write a letter at a table where her mother has written. Finally, she is sent to Switzerland; after consulting with a first physician, she is entrusted to Binswanger.

She narrates how her superstitions began: six years earlier, one of her aunts, whom she had never seen, had just died—and Lola had told her friends she was certain that this aunt would pass away. At the same time, she had experienced the first superstitious beliefs regarding clothes: she feared that misfortune would befall her friend if she wrote to him while wearing a specific item of clothing. She hides her superstitions from everyone, especially her fiancé, but the system increasingly takes over: when she sees four pigeons, she will receive a card (the word *carta* is almost contained in the Spanish word *cuatro*). When she experiences anxiety and sees someone bringing their hands to their face, she is immediately calmed (in Spanish, hand is *mano* and face *cara*—in English *no care*; therefore the gesture means "do not worry"). All of the words that contain the syllables *ja* or *si* symbolize an affirmative response to a secret question. And this is how she describes the arrival of her hostility toward her mother: her father had bought her an umbrella; she meets a hunchback in the street, and the bad luck he carries with him transfers to the umbrella because of the affirmation *si*, which is contained in the word *Schirm*.[w] Having taken the umbrella, her mother takes on the bad luck and risks transmitting it to everything she touches. Lola tells all of these stories with great difficulty: she is afraid that the memory will allow things to reproduce themselves, and she does not allow herself to say the word *Schirm*, because of the affirmation it contains.

During her hospital stay, she takes a dislike to a nurse who leaves her umbrella lying around everywhere. The superstition spreads to all sorts of things: she will not say the nurse's name and will only call her "*jene*";[x] she refuses to drink because the glass she is given was previously in a closet in which she saw the nurse's umbrella. She turns dressing herself into a minefield: she will not wear anything red, because she wore red the previous summer—repetitions summon yet more repetitions. But at the same time, she will not buy new clothes. After fifteen months her family has her discharged from the hospital.

For some time, she writes to Binswanger: first she feels very well, she lives a normal life; yet she cannot forget the past.

---

w ["Umbrella."]

x ["That one."]

In February 1930, she shares her ideas of persecution: there are "terrible" people who enter her room or watch her from outside. She does not know them, could not name them, but she sees that they have only one goal: to kill. Her relatives, without noticing, allow these people to influence them: this is why they believe her to be ill and treat her as such. From America, she sends a final letter to Switzerland: her relatives are under the spell of a group of doctors who persecute her and prevent her from living a normal life. If she has been able to write this letter she is sending, it is because someone gave her a sign that she was free. She begs Binswanger to help her escape this conspiracy . . .

From a psychiatric point of view, a case such as this one is an example of an evolution that starts from a state of superstitious obsession and results in a manifest delusion of persecution. It is this transition that was undoubtedly grasped by a French physician whom the family consulted after Lola Voss had left her Swiss hospital. In terms clearly inspired by Janet,[y] he established his diagnosis in the following way: "obsessional doubt, phobia, superstitious ideas, worsened by hallucinations, ideas of influence, and a real delusion of persecution. This delusional psychasthenia threatens to develop into a chronic state."[z]

From the point of view of existential analysis, this evolution appears as the enrichment and development of an initial situation. It could be symbolized by saying that it is the transition from the formula "I ought to (*soll*) be cautious, since I don't know what may happen" to the formula "because everyone spies on me and plans to harm me, I must (*muss*) be cautious."[aa]

---

y This occurs between 1925 and 1930.

z [Binswanger, "Lola Voss," 281; the doctor's report is in French in the English translation—Trans.]

aa [Binswanger, "Lola Voss," 305; translation altered to correspond to Foucault's rendering.]

In the first stage, danger appears only through a system of signs that must be deciphered through more or less complicated grids: the linguistic grid of fanciful etymologies, the grid of morphological analogies, the grid of repetitions in time or of juxtapositions in space. In the second stage, perilous significations no longer need to be deciphered "through a forest of symbols," but are immediately perceptible in the behavior of relatives, in the presence of a mysterious crowd: they borrow from the presence of the other its form of absolute manifestation, while the other is no more than one of the modes of this manifestation. The meaning of things and the existence of others have switched roles: or, in other words, the peril has become persecution.

In the first phase of the illness, the symptoms of superstition constituted a defense system to escape her anxiety before the world, in this undifferentiated form that Lola called the "*Schreck-liches*," the Terrible: all of her ritualism around clothes—the care she takes to change or not change her dress, to avoid such and such an outfit in such and such a circumstance—all of this represents "surface protection" to escape the threat of the world. If she designates certain objects or people as privileged carriers of bad luck, it is to concentrate the undifferentiated origin of anxiety into easily isolatable areas. During her stay at the hospital, and maybe in accordance with a reinforcement of her defensive universe due to her psychotherapeutic sessions, all of the anxiety focuses on a single figure who becomes the sole carrier, in the world, of the "*Schreckliches*": it is the nurse Emma,[bb] last symbol of fearsome power, but also already her first personal enemy. Indeed, this concentration of superstitious terror into a single figure turns the patient's entire morbid universe upside down: the other is no longer the involuntary carrier of hostile meanings;

---

bb [In Binswanger's original text, the name of the nurse is Emmi.]

he no longer transmits them as an obscure property. He is now entirely inhabited by them, he realizes them: the other illustrates persecution as necessarily as a body that falls illustrates the law of falling bodies. The other is no longer responsible for his significations, he is possessed by them: he becomes the "*Schreckliches*" "in the flesh." It is this new form of experience that illustrates the final elements that we have on Lola Voss's delusions: we see the image of this theme—that the other is no longer the absolute origin of his own significations—expressed in the patient's belief that her relatives are led by a conspiracy of figures she recognizes, of mysterious doctors hiding behind various disguises. We encounter once again the theme of clothing, which initially appeared in the superstitious rituals—but it is no longer that superficial element protecting against evil forces: now it can potentially transmit them to people themselves; it has become the camouflage of the persecutors, the means that gives them access to their victim without being recognized. Before, clothing transmitted to people the terrible power of the "*Schreckliches*"; now it allows others to conceal the "*Schreckliches*" they possess. [129]

We might say in a general manner that delusion constitutes, beyond the concrete presence of the other, a kind of a priori of signification. There the other's autonomy is rightfully alienated; there all of the possibilities of his behavior are definitively deployed and totalized in advance. It is therefore not surprising that the delusions of persecution bring to light both themes of powerlessness and themes of clairvoyance: delivered like a prey to his enemies, the patient already knows all of their stratagems, reveals all of their plots, denounces them through each of their successive disguises; and each different face appears to him only as a new mask under which the same persecutor and the same homicidal thinking are concealed. The transcendence of the other has received new content: it was, in normal experience, that absolute presence which, while manifesting itself as totality, constantly eludes the effort to totalize; in pathological experience, it has become a sum of significations henceforth tied together, which reveal their universal evidence through the familiarity of human expressions. These expressions, in their customary variety, are now pathetic: they do not constitute what they express; they do not form, in their becoming, the dialectic of meaning that is grasped in common; they only ever betray a previous meaning. Their variety is only a diversion, and the community of meaning that they solicit is on the order of a ruse: in reality, its thread is already entirely woven.

3.[cc]

Once again, the description of lived signification refers us to an analysis of the structures of existence:[dd] if in the field of experience, the other has lost the significations that made its presence irreducible and its encounter irreplaceable, no genetic analysis can provide an account of it. We could still be tempted, on the subject of space and time, to seek in their constitution a quasi-functional disorder, to benefit from an ambiguity that is possible because spatial and temporal things always appear "against the backdrop of . . . ," and the emergence of their signification always implies the silent presence of previous genetic moments. Is space perceived as a void? Is time lived as a deployed eternity? It is always possible—although erroneous each time—to refer this pathological experience to a functional "disruption" of these moments

---

cc [Foucault has crossed out, but not replaced, the following subheading: "The other and the existential forms of community."]

dd [Foucault has crossed out "and the alteration of experience refers to an originary project."]

that, in the genesis of spatiotemporal significations, are motor coordination or vital rhythms. This abandonment of phenomenological description in favor of a functional analysis is no longer possible when it is a question of the other: the other, precisely, offers himself with a signification of the absolute that never supposes a "constitution" in the sense in which phenomenology discusses the constitutive genesis of things. The other speaks from the start the language of coexistence. And this is enough to show already that the alteration of the experience of the other implies a radically new structure of existence. For time and space, doubt was still permissible: and the path from the phenomenological description of altered experiences to the analysis of the existential structures that make them possible was perhaps not without detours, nor without possible bifurcation. With the experience of the other, the path is direct: only the existential project can rupture the style of coexistence in which the experience of the other, such as it offers itself already to phenomenological reflection, occurs. And this necessity takes on even more importance inasmuch as the pathological experiences of space and of time borrow their ultimate meaning from this experience of the other. [131]

Undoubtedly, we are now at the center of *Daseinsanalyse*, at the moment when it justifies its necessity as a method of analysis, and when it finds the fulcrum of its theoretical reflection. This is where it distances itself most decisively from Husserl's phenomenology and Heidegger's ontology: it stops developing as a genesis of significations because it now situates itself at the absolute origin of significations; it disappears as an analytic of existential structures insofar as it makes visible the absolute foundation of these structures. It situates itself outside the coordinates of a transcendental reflection, because what it is now trying to grasp is the very act of transcendence: the movement through which existence rightfully overcomes the limits of its existence in the world to weave, beyond the world, the bonds of a common existence. The "anthropological primacy" must not be granted to the *In-der-Welt-sein* as such, but to what Binswanger calls the "*In-der-Welt-über-die-Welt-hinaus-sein.*"ee 11

[132] The most authentic mode of existence is the "dual" mode: it is simultaneously the most hidden, "the most suppressed," the one that most easily compromises and alienates itself;ff it is from this mode that we must understand the world of illness.

Jürg Zünd:gg Jürg Zünd's father was a timid musician, who passed for "neurasthenic" among his family; the mother was domineering, proud, and very well educated. One of his paternal uncles was catatonic. Throughout his childhood, he is very close to his parents, who follow his every footstep, prevent him from mingling with other children, clothe him in a way that always sets him apart. He characterizes his seventh to his twelfth year as the "terrible years."hh He feels caught between his parents and his schoolmates: the latter mock him, but he feels better among them; he reproaches himself for preferring them to his parents, whom he feels he is betraying. He also feels persistently uncomfortable about the difference between his parents and his uncle and aunt, who live on an upper floor of the same house; they live a much more high-society, luxurious life; he has the feeling of having been born "on the lower level."ii At the moment of puberty, he practices masturbation, experiences reactions of guilt:

---

ee ["Being-in-the-world-beyond-and-above-the-world."]
ff Ludwig Binswanger, "The Case of Ellen West: An Anthopological-Clinical Study," trans. Werner M. Mendel and Joseph Lyons, in *Existence: A New Dimension in Psychiatry and Psychology*, ed. Rollo May, Ernest Angel, and Henri F. Ellenberger (Basic Books, 1958), 312–314.
gg Ludwig Binswanger, "Studien zu Schizophrenie Problem. Zweite Studie. Der Fall Jürg Zünd," *Schweizer Archiv für Neurologie und Psychiatrie* 56 (1946): 191–220; 58 (1947): 1–43; 59 (1947): 21–36 [all are reprinted in *Schizophrenie* (Günther Neske, 1957): 189–288].
hh [Binswanger, "Jürg Zünd," *Schweizer Archiv* 56 (1946): 193.]
ii [Binswanger, "Jürg Zünd," 193.]

he has the feeling of not being "within his rights"[jj] with regard to his parents. He is increasingly aggressive, isolated; he has the impression of attracting attention, of being the object of mockery; he feels almost undressed, penetrated by the gaze of others. For fourteen years, from ages twenty to thirty-four, he undertakes half-hearted studies: first devoted to *"Naturwissenschaften"*;[kk] then, under the impression that he is "missing something," on the advice of a psychiatrist, he turns toward *"Geistewissenschaften."*[ll] He rarely attends class: he observes that in public each of his gestures provokes laughter. Finally, he obtains the title of doctor at thirty-four. He is more and more "obsessed" and "worried."[mm] He takes large quantities of Optalidon[nn] (six to eight tablets a day). He lives at his father's house and then with a married sister. He complains of living an abnormal life. Finally, a physician who has treated him sends him to a hospital. He shows himself to be both very inhibited (unable to make a decision, to answer a letter) and very oppositional: he complains constantly about the physicians who prevent him from having sexual relationships with female patients, who are taking away from him the only possible means of healing—marriage—, who do not care about him and are not even attempting psychoanalysis. At the same time he is very querulous, he constantly needs the physicians' help: he will never heal without them, but they ask too much of him and do too little to encourage him. He has many hypochondriacal concerns. He often speaks of suicide. He is almost inactive: often he plays the piano, but they are always pieces he already knows. He refuses to give a concert.

[133]

---

jj [Binswanger, "Jürg Zünd," 194.]
kk ["Natural sciences."]
ll ["Human sciences."]
mm [Binswanger, "Jürg Zünd," *Schweizer Archiv* 56 (1946): 196.]
nn [Analgesic used to treat intense pain.]

He is sent to another hospital, where he hopes to be more active. But he is not free enough, his physician does not understand him: he has the impression of having died and of having survived his own death. He receives electroshock treatments: after the first, he feels like he has returned to a state of childhood. Afterward, he will complain that he suffered greatly from this treatment. He returns to Kreuzlingen, then leaves once again. In a third hospital, a new series of electroshock treatments seems to have helped him: he spontaneously declares that the world is more colorful, that the distance between himself and the world has narrowed. But the result does not seem to have lasted.

We can group the patient's preoccupations around several themes. First, the theme of sexual shame. He is afraid of being surprised by a woman in a state of erection. He especially experiences this anxiety around women whom he judges to be of high social rank. Spontaneously, he associates this fear with the figure of his mother, whose social ambitions were quite pronounced: "I could not find sexual satisfaction with a woman who would not have pleased my mother, who was so proud."[oo]

Then the theme of social inferiority. He is constantly preoccupied by the impression he makes on others. He is ashamed of this preoccupation, which he finds degrading, worthy only of an "informant" (*Schnüffler*). This worry is due to his lack of "virility," of *Mannlichkeit*, to his inability to assert himself; but it is also due to the fact that he "has no race," and that as a result "there is no place for him on the planet";[pp] he is a black sheep. Certain situations seem to increase this inferiority; imagining these situations is enough to provoke anxiety: for example, if in the tramway he stepped on someone's foot, or if he were suspected of

---

oo [Binswanger, "Jürg Zünd," *Schweizer Archiv* 56 (1946): 200.]
pp [Binswanger, "Jürg Zünd," 201.]

theft . . . He lives in a state of perpetual alert: "Catastrophe can occur at any moment."qq

All of these anxieties separate him from the real world, from the universe of others: others "are in a different world from him." What is more, they have plotted against him, they know the secret of good health, but do not want to give it to him; and the physicians are part of the conspiracy, which even includes the hospital porter who will not give him the secret of *joie de vivre*, of *Lebensfreude*.

To escape this persecution, and this anxiety that separates him from others, he would like to escape into anonymity. He sometimes seeks out this anonymity in enthusiasm, in a rush that would sweep him up in a movement of communion with others: if he had been in A. when the Great War broke out, if he had volunteered, he would have shared in the general elation, and he would have "escaped his own ego"; no one afterward could have pointed a finger at him. He would have been a sure thing, almost a "blue-chip commodity." And the patient finds here the second manner of escaping into anonymity: being impersonal, like a bank certificate, like a bill that passes [through] every hand; losing himself among the masses, wandering in the crowd; being like everyone else among everyone else. [135]

Across all these themes the constant unity of two contradictory terms is sketched out. It is simultaneously a matter of asserting one's virility through enthusiasm and of effacing one's individuality through anonymity; of denouncing the incessant hostility of physicians, who condemn him to illness, and of tearing [from] them the secret that will secure his health. In taking Optalidon it is a matter of establishing a barrier, a "wall" between the self and others, and at the same time of feeling a decrease

---

qq [Binswanger, "Jürg Zünd," 201.]

in the distance that separates him from humans. In short, the essential project, which he varies through his complaints or his delusional fragments, is simultaneously to escape what he calls "the prison of individuality"[rr] and to recover this individuality that he feels disappearing and dissolving under the gaze of others. He experiences himself as being in a different world than that of others, and at the same time he feels the world of others invading his own, overflowing its banks, traversing it, and definitively alienating all of his independence: a contradiction that he experiences instantaneously in abrupt explosions of shame, when he feels kept at a distance and penetrated by the other's gaze, both possessed and humiliated by this gaze.

At the level of existential structures, these contradictory experiences, and the delusional themes that develop their meaning, manifest an alteration of the forms of coexistence. The universe of the other has always been lived by the patient in the mode of opposition. Conflict between the different social milieux that constituted the nuclear experiences of his childhood: opposition between the two parts of his family, the "upstairs" part and the "downstairs" part; between his familial milieu and his school milieu. He reacts to these contradictions through aggressive moments of release: he slapped one of his schoolteachers; he was frequently violent with his father. For him the "*Mitwelt*"[ss] is no longer anything but a "*Gegenwelt.*"[tt] But when puberty and masturbation come, the opposition to the world takes on a different meaning: the search for a fight is replaced by the dread of being caught, spied on, monitored; the fear of social stigma represented by clothing is replaced by the impression of being

[136]

---

rr [Binswanger, "Jürg Zünd," 217; see also Binswanger, "Jürg Zünd," *Schweizer Archiv* 58 (1947): 2. Foucault translates the German "*Individualismus*" as "individualité" (individuality).]

ss ["World of coexistence, of being-with."]

tt ["*Gegenwelt*" literally means "the world across," the exterior world.]

undressed by the other's gaze, and denounced in one's personal inferiority; the desire to belong to a coherent group in which he would be known is replaced by the desire to disappear into a crowd where no one can recognize him. He managed to defend himself against the opposition of social groups by referring constantly to the socially privileged world of his grandparents; now, to escape all those in league against him, he can only have recourse to Optalidon, the only thing that "gives him security in his relations with the outside world."[uu] The *"Gegenwelt"* as opposition has become the *"Gegenwelt"* as persecution: the world he collided with has transformed into a world that watches him, spies on him, chases him with its inquisition, tracks him to each of his hiding spots. This explains why the world of others feels both strange and familiar to him; why he experiences, between himself and others, an insurmountable distance and a proximity he cannot bear. The other is far away because he is "against" him, and close at the same time because "up against" him. He is delivered to the hostility of the "*Mitwelt*," alienated within it.

But this "alienation" is possible only insofar as the world of the other only ever offers him "existence in the plural," or the multiplicity of simultaneous relations, and never presents itself in the form of a two-person relation: he has only ever seen his mother as the representative of a high social status; sexuality is not for him a mediation toward *another* existence, but only that about which he might have to blush before *others*; he knows nothing of the *modesty* that plays out in a couple and knows only the *shame* that is felt before a public. In short, we can say that, in Jürg Zünd, the mode of being many (*plurale Seinsmodus*) has totally eclipsed the mode of being two (*duale Seinsmodus*). In other words, the plural is never lived by him in the first person, but always in the third.

[137]

---

uu [Binswanger, "Jürg Zünd," *Schweizer Archiv* 58 (1947): 10.]

This is what we must use as a starting point in order to explain the singular forms of the experience of time and space in the patient. Time will no longer have the continuity that the project of "being-two" maintains within him: it will no longer be able to temporalize itself as aiming [*visée*] toward eternity, but will segment itself in the form of successive emergencies, which will maintain the subject in a state of perpetual alertness, under the constantly renewed threat of an unforeseen aggression. Time will no longer be lived as a continuous flux but as a jerky succession of detours, assaults, thrusts—a time of "*Druck und Stoß*,"[vv] says the patient himself—and it is both because this time is discontinuous and in order to escape its always-threatening discontinuity that he will dream of "starting everything over," of returning to a new youth whose maturation will instantiate a decisive continuity. As for space, it is no longer the familiar space of the home or of the homeland: it consists entirely of the anonymous space of the street, where one is known by no one but seen by everyone, where one is proximate to others while keeping one's distance: the space where one has neither protection nor point of support and where a threat can arise from anywhere; at his father's house the patient does not feel like he is at home; he wants to flee into the street where, by dint of being seen, one might not be noticed.

[138] In an analysis such as this one, we can thus see the idea of an "anthropological primacy" of love, and of the "being-two," verifying itself. If the descriptions we have just presented are correct, it is love that allows time to temporalize itself in its fluid continuity; space to deploy itself while carrying the immanent significations of familiarity, proximity, distance; the body to manifest its lived meaning not only on the occasion of a threat,

---

vv ["Pressure and shock"; Binswanger, "Jürg Zünd," *Schweizer Archiv* 58 (1947): 6.]

or in a reaction of shame, but in the experience of modesty. The existential structure of love therefore makes possible all of the other structures of existence to which the rigorous description of pathological experiences must refer. The origin of all significations and the foundation of all structures are located there.

We are at the center of Binswanger's existential analysis: the first pathways traced by phenomenological description within psychopathology seemed to lead there by natural inclination and by necessity. Existence must thereby not let itself be understood starting from the world of care (*Sorge*) but starting from love, and from that encounter in love (*liebende Begegnung*) of which pathological experience is specifically deprived:[ww] the fact of being oneself (*Selbstsein*) must be grasped again starting from the fact of being-we (*Wirsein*); time, starting from the instantaneous eternity of love; space, starting from the familiar homeland where the encounter continues and extends itself. And all that from which Heidegger was trying to grasp the being of existence, anxiety, dereliction, facticity—all of that Binswanger understands as the fall and descent outside of the being's security in love, and of this certainty in itself that existence finds in the encounter:[xx] in love, "existence does not understand itself starting from the world, but starting from its foundation as present, gift, or grace."[yy]

[139]

Binswanger leans on this ultimate anthropological foundation to understand simultaneously the meaning of experiences, the structures of existence that found them, and the existential project that founds them. It is there too that he sees the point of insertion of therapeutic action and the axis around which

---

ww Binswanger, *Grundformen und Erkenntnis menschlichen Daseins*, 153.
xx Binswanger, *Grundformen*, 640.
yy Binswanger, *Grundformen*, 153.

an existential development can pivot. He believes that he can also discover there the decisive dividing line between the normal and the pathological, recovering in this way at the level of anthropological foundations a distinction that phenomenological description had bracketed in order to dodge its normative implications, but to which we must, in the end, assign a meaning insofar precisely as we have unearthed the singular structures of the morbid world.^{zz}

NOTES

1. In the 1950s, Foucault dedicated many reading notes to *Sein und Zeit*. Most of them are organized by concept: "Care [*le souci*]," "The ontological," "Totality and *Dasein*," "Anxiety," "Truth," "The world," "Existentials," "Temporality," "*Dasein*," "*Existentiel* and *existential*," "The *Mitsein*," "Possibility (*Möglichsein*)." Two long notes, moreover, concern paragraph 10 ("Delimitation of the *Daseinsanalytic*, in relation to anthropology, psychology, and biology") and paragraph 38 ("*Das Verfallen und die Geworfenheit*") (BNF, Box 33a, folder 0). Foucault occasionally cites Henry Corbin's translation of Heidegger ("Extraits sur *L'Être et le Temps*," in Martin Heidegger, *Qu'est-ce que la métaphysique?* (Gallimard, 1938), 115–208).

2. See on this topic the folder that Foucault dedicated to Janet, which contains, among other reading notes, one entitled "Psychological tension" (BNF, Box 38, folder 3).

3. Foucault drafted various reading notes on Charles Blondel's book *La conscience morbide. Essai de psychologie générale*, 2nd ed. (Félix Alcan, 1928 [1914]) (BNF, Box 38, folder 1).

4. One of Foucault's reading notes from the 1950s is dedicated precisely to "autistic thought according to Bleuler," in which he cites the latter: "One of the most important symptoms of schizophrenia is the preponderance of inner life (*Binnenleben*) with an active turning-away from the external

---

zz [Blank page.]

world. The most severe cases withdraw completely (*ziehen sich ganz zurück*) and live in a dream world; the milder cases withdraw to a lesser degree. I call this symptom autism" (BNF, Box 38, folder 1). The English translation of this quotation is from Eugen Bleuler, "Autistic Thinking," in *Organization and Pathology of Thought: Selected sources*, ed. and trans. David Rapaport (Columbia University Press, 1951), 399–437. Another reading note is dedicated to Binswanger's essay "Über Phänomenologie," *Zeitschrift für die gesamte Neurologie und Psychiatrie* 82, no. 1 (1923): 10–45, reprinted in *Ausgewählte Vorträge und Aufsätze*, vol. 1, *Zur phänomenologischen Anthropologie* (Francke, 1947), 13–49. In this note, Foucault writes, "Example of autism. Bleuler defines it: "This detachment (*Loslösung*) from *Wirklichkeit* [reality], together with the relative and absolute predominance of the *Binnenleben* (inner life), we term autism" (*Lehrbuch*). We could accumulate the characters of autism" (BNF, Box 38, folder 1). The English translation of the quotation is from Eugen Bleuler, *Dementia Praecox; or, the Group of Schizophrenias*, trans. Joseph Zinkin (International Universities Press, 1950), 63.

5. The idea that there is an ambiguity at the heart of Freudian doctrine between the genetic moment of the signification of the pathological experience—the "drama"—and the evolutionist perspective in which it is inscribed is central to Georges Politzer's book *Critique of the Foundations of Psychology*, trans. Maurice Apprey (Duquesne University Press, 1994 [1928]), and was taken up by various authors in France starting in the 1930s. Lacan, while recognizing that the concepts of complex, drama, and conflict contain Freudianism's important "phenomenologically acquired knowledge," nevertheless reproaches Freudian psychology for its "claims to move from interpersonal relations . . . to the biological function that is taken to be their substratum"; see "Beyond the "Reality Principle,"" in *Écrits*, trans. Bruce Fink (W. W. Norton, 2006), 73. In his *Sketch for a Theory of the Emotions*, Jean-Paul Sartre recognizes "psychoanalytic psychology" as having been "the first to lay the emphasis upon the signification of psychic facts," but he also complains about the contradiction between its "understanding" of these facts and the underlying causal theory. See Sartre, *Sketch for a Theory of the Emotions*, trans. Philip Mairet (Routledge, 2002), 29–33. In the *Phenomenology of Perception*, when he lays out his thesis about "the body in its sexual being," Maurice Merleau-Ponty asserts with Politzer that "whatever the theoretical declarations of Freud may have been . . . the

significance of psychoanalysis is less to make psychology biological than to discover a dialectical process in functions thought of as "purely bodily," and to reintegrate sexuality into the human being." See Merleau-Ponty, *Phenomenology of Perception*, trans. Colin Smith (Routledge & Kegan Paul, 1962), 157–58. Similarly, Eugène Minkowski underscores "the great wretchedness of psychoanalysis, despite the critically important facts that it was able to bring to light" in "Le contact humain," *Revue de métaphysique et de morale* 55, no. 2 (1950): 126.

6. In a reading note entitled "M. Klein—Lagache," Foucault summarizes the lecture Melanie Klein (1882–1960) gave in 1951 at the 17th International Congress of Psychoanalysis entitled "The Origins of Transference." It was published in English in *The International Journal of Psychoanalysis* 33 (1952): 433–38 and translated into French by Daniel Lagache and published as "Les origines du transfert," *Revue française de psychanalyse* 16, nos. 1–2 (1952): 204–14 (BNF, Box 38, folder 4).

7. In a reading note about Gebsattel's article "Über Fetischismus," Foucault writes: "while the normal urge directs itself toward the whole, in the instant of its present, "the tendency—culminating in fetishism—of the sexual desires separated from eroticism directs itself toward the dispersal (*Zerstörung*) of this whole, toward its segmentation and its fragmentation, [toward] the elevation of a part to the whole, bracketing the true whole." See Gebsattel, "Über Fetischismus," *Der Nervenarzt* 2, no. 1 (1929): 14 (BNF, Box 42b, folder 1).

8. Medard Boss's book *Sinn und Gehalt der sexuellen Perversionen* is mentioned by Roland Kuhn in his analysis of the Rudolf R. case titled "The Attempted Murder of a Prostitute," trans. Ernest Angel, in *Existence: A New Dimension in Psychiatry and Psychology*, ed. Rollo May, Ernest Angel, and Henri F. Ellenberger (Basic Books, 1958), 365–425. Inside a file entitled "Boss" in the Foucault archives, a reading note summarizes the Konrad Schwing case (BNF, Box 42b, folder 1). Boss's book also appears, in this same box, in a bibliographic note drafted by Foucault on the theme of the "pathology of space," as well as in a note devoted to Gebsattel's study "Die Welt des Zwangskranken," *Monatsschrift für Psychiatrie und Neurolologie* 99 (1938): 10–74.

9. Foucault describes this phenomenon in chapter 4 of *Maladie mentale et personnalité*: "It is to this radical alteration that the frequent syndrome of "symbolic derealization of others" refers: the feeling of strangeness

before language, the system of expression, the other's body; the difficulty of obtaining even certainty about the other's existence; the heaviness and distance of an interhuman universe in which things freeze when expressed, in which significations have the massive indifference of things, and in which symbols assume the gravity of enigmas: this is the rigid world of the psychasthenic and of most schizophrenics" (65; a version of this sentence appears on pp. 52–53 of *Mental Illness and Psychology*).

10. See the file entitled "Lola Voss" in the Foucault archives, where Foucault collected his notes during his first reading of Binswanger's study (BNF, Box 42b, folder 1, consisting of 11 double-sided sheets of paper).

11. Binswanger theorizes this idea in his book *Grundformen und Erkenntnis menschlichen Daseins* (Niehans, 1942) and takes it up again in the Ellen West case. In a reading note entitled "Eternity and love," Foucault notes, "When we speak of eternity we no longer speak of the *In-der-Welt-sein* but rather of the *In-der-Welt-über-die-Welt-hinaus-sein*, of the *"duale modus"* of the human being, and of the *we* that constitutes itself in love starting with the I and the Thou. We must no longer speak of *Selbstsein* [being oneself], of *Zeit* [time] and of *Raum* [space]; but of *Wirsein* [being we], of *Einigkeit* [union, agreement], and of *Heimat* [homeland]. The present no longer defines itself by *Entschlossenheit* [resolution], but by the encounter (*Begegnung*) of the I and the Thou in the eternal moment of love. It is no longer a matter of a *Seinkönnen* [being able to be], but of a *Seindürfen* [having the right to be]. Because this is the authentic mode of the *Menschsein* [being-human], it is the most hidden, the most suppressed (*erdrückteste*). It was necessary in the history of humanity to wait for Christianity as the religion of love for it to break through, likewise for the individual *Dasein*." Foucault is loosely quoting Binswanger, "Der Fall Ellen West: Daseinsanalyse und Psychoanalyse," *Schweizer Archiv für Neurologie und Psychiatrie*, vol. 54 (1944): 115–16. For the English translation, see "The Case of Ellen West: An Anthopological-Clinical Study," trans. Werner M. Mendel and Joseph Lyons, in *Existence: A New Dimension in Psychiatry and Psychology*, ed. Rollo May, Ernest Angel, and Henri F. Ellenberger (Basic Books, 1958), 312.

CHAPTER FIVE

Existential Anthropology

I. Daseinsanalyse *in relation to phenomenological psychology and to Sartre's existential psychoanalysis: 1. The reflection on existence; 2. The patient and the forms of his freedom. II.* Daseinsanalyse's *therapeutic vocation: the physician-patient relationship. III. Signification and expression: 1. "Existenzerhellung"; 2. The Lina case (Roland Kuhn). IV.* Daseinsanalyse *between metaphysics and objective analysis.*

[. . .]ª and breaks itself in her.^{b 1} To simplify, let us say that phenomenological psychology and psychopathology are not two modes of reading human reality, each of which concerns one of the faces of its duality; rather, both of them only have meaning through a reflection on existence, because the first, phenomenological psychology, reads the manner in which this existence announces itself, the other defines the manner in which this existence obscures and eliminates itself.

The second remark we wanted to make concerns Sartre and existential psychoanalysis, at least in the way he sketches it out at the end of *L'Être et le Néant*.^c The difference with Binswanger

---

a [The beginning of the chapter has not been found.]
b This is the process that Binswanger calls *"Verweltlichung"* ["mundanization"; see note 1].
c [Jean-Paul Sartre, *Being and Nothingness*, trans. Hazel E. Barnes (Washington Square Press, 1992), part 4, chapter 2, § I, "Existential Psychoanalysis."]

jumps out immediately: it is already there at the beginning of the reflection, and in the manner in which the urgency of a new reflection on man is asserted. For Binswanger, the point of rupture with comprehensive psychology is situated precisely at the limit when comprehension no longer comprehends, when it comes up against its own impossibility. In Sartre, the necessity, for an existential reflection, of abandoning phenomenological description appears in that this description risks comprehending too much, risks welcoming, in the infinity of intelligible relations, all forms of eventuality, and thereby shutting itself up in a universe of possibles, where the equivalence of essential connections strips existence of its necessary oneness. Comprehension, in Jaspers's sense, "remains a grasp of general connections. For example we will realize the link between chastity and mysticism, between weakness and hypocrisy. But we are ignorant always of the concrete relation between *this* chastity (*this* abstinence in relation to a particular woman, this struggle against a definite temptation), and the individual content of the mysticism; exactly like psychiatry . . ."[d] It thus becomes necessary to set aside the general relations wherein analysis dissipates the reality of existence, in order to grasp anew the "individual plenitude" defined both by the "totality of one's impulse toward being," through the "original relation to oneself, to the world, and to others," and finally, at the heart of these relations of existence, by the "unity of the original project."[e] We will return to the differences between Sartre's existential analysis and the "*Daseinsanalyse*" of the school of Binswanger; for now, it is sufficient [to see] what such different points of departure imply. What Sartre refuses is

---

d Sartre, *Being and Nothingness*, 715 [translation slightly modified].
e Sartre, *Being and Nothingness*, 719 [translation modified; in particular, Sartre writes "the Other" rather than "others" and a "fundamental" project rather than an "original" one—Trans.].

a certain kind of psychological abstraction which attempts to find, in the concrete modes of existence, essential significations that are both immanent to this concrete plenitude and something like offering themselves in it, yet going beyond it insofar as they confer upon it a meaning and make it possible. The point at which we must denounce abstraction is when essence begins to appear and to assert itself. Conversely, Binswanger's initial refusal denounces an abstraction that separates and detaches from man any part of his total existence: for him it is necessary to abandon a complete reliance on phenomenological description not at the moment when it aims at [*vise*] essence but at the moment when, renouncing the search for essence, it sets its own limits, and recognizes in human existence two regions, one of which, being inaccessible to it, relies entirely on a naturalist explanation. The same concern for a concrete understanding of man breaks off, in Sartre and in Binswanger, toward two very different horizons: haunted by Politzer's genius, Sartre begins his search for the concrete with a denunciation of an essence that abstracts man from his conditions of existence and alienates him in a metaphysical cosmos; trained in the school of the psychiatrists who, since Bleuler, have sought to return the meaning of illness to the totality of the sick person, Binswanger starts his analysis by excluding anything that can fragment the whole of human reality and by denouncing, for example, this "cancer" (*Krebsübel*) of psychology, which is the opposition between subject and object, the man and his world, the self and the non-self.[f] The psychological abstraction from which phenomenological description did not free itself consists, for Sartre, in superimposition; for Binswanger in juxtaposition. But already, through this

[143]

---

[f] Ludwig Binswanger, "The Existential Analysis School of Thought," trans. Ernest Angel, in *Existence: A New Dimension in Psychiatry and Psychology*, ed. Rollo May, Ernest Angel, and Henri F. Ellenberger (Basic Books, 1958), 193–94.

[144] critique of abstraction, two philosophical universes are sketched out; for Sartre, it will be a matter of setting aside anything that can separate man from himself, anything that can tear him from his concrete existence, in order to find what can render him entirely present to the least of his actions, the free choice he makes for himself;[2] for Binswanger, it is a matter of finding the unity in which all of the dimensions of his presence in the world are founded, the root of his being. Sartre's existential analysis will question freedom on what it does; *Daseinsanalyse* interrogates the being on what he is.

This assertion of human unity could yield ambiguity: since the end of the nineteenth century it has been formulated too often, and in terms that are too different, to avoid appearing now as a rhetorical theme or an abstract requirement. These days, the idea of human totality in psychology seems like little more than a formulaic nod to its tradition. But Binswanger is careful to set aside empty or hybrid conceptions, mythic images, prudent syntheses which are often the only content given to human totality.[3] We must, he explains in *Ideenflucht*,[g] "free each theme from the purely clinical framework, in order to examine it starting from the totality of this theme which is man."[4] [Yet] this idea of man [145] must not be a guiding myth, but a concept rigorous enough to allow a transition from a descriptive and still prescientific apprehension of the human being ("*Menschsein*") to a rigorously scientific anthropology. This is to say that in Binswanger human totality is not one of those themes that pertain to the preliminary

---

g Ludwig Binswanger, "Über Ideenflucht," *Schweizer Archiv für Neurologie und Psychiatrie* 27, no. 2 (1932): 203–17; as well as vol. 28, nos. 1–2 (1932): 183–202; vol. 29, no. 1 (1932): 1–37 and 193–252; and vol. 30, no. 1 (1933): 68–85; reprinted in *Über Ideenflucht* (Orel Füssli, 1933), here 188 [reprinted in *Ausgewählte Werke*, vol. 1, *Formen missglückten Daseins*, ed. Max Herzog (Asanger, 1992), 2–231. The [French] translation is Foucault's (and the English translation mine—Trans.)].

prudence of prefaces, through which the gods of critique are conjured, or that serve to boost the enthusiasm of conclusions by repairing the conceptual insufficiencies of the analysis. But it is a theme that must serve as a foundation for a scientific reflection on man: it is a radical requirement insofar as it targets man at his root, and must be at the root of any understanding of man.

Man must therefore not be considered as a unity after the fact of provisional syntheses: he is not a hierarchy of interlocking structures (in the style of the traditional "*leiblich-seelisch-geistig*"[h] pyramid), but the radical unity of all of the empirical forms of his existence; the unity of man must be sought and located at the level of his existence, which is to say of his being-in-the-world.[5]

But there too, existential comprehension must be torn away from an insufficiently radical conception of the "*In-der-Welt-sein.*" In his biological research, Uexküll showed that it is not possible to study the functional structures of a living organism as a whole (*Funktionskreis*[i] [6]) without considering it inside a behavioral milieu (an *Umwelt*) within which its functions are deployed. But this *Umwelt* is not the natural objective world, articulated according to the rational figures imagined by the positive spirit: in reality, there are as many *Umwelten* as there are organisms, because each organism constitutes a behavioral milieu for itself from a blueprint characteristic of its species. But Binswanger refuses to follow Uexküll when he applies this idea to the analysis of human behavior, and sets aside any assimilation between being-in-the-world and the organism's unity with its behavioral milieu. It is that the animal is indeed linked to its *Bauplan*, to its blueprint, while human existence involves innumerable possibilities of being, and the essence of man lies precisely in this

[146]

---

h ["Corporeal-spiritual-intellectual."]
i ["Functional cycle."]

radical freedom. This freedom implies (and this is essential for pathology) first that each possible way of being envelops, beyond the project of a world, a project of the self—which is to say that freedom is not only constitutive of [the subject's] universe but also of the subject itself of this universe and of this freedom; the animal organism is given to itself in the unicity of its blueprint; the human subject must always give himself to himself in the infinity of his possible ways of being. And it is this freedom, additionally, which opens man to truth, [which] makes possible for him this openness to being through which, according to Heidegger, the access to what is true is defined.[j] While the animal, as an organism enclosed in its structures, only ever constitutes the world in relation to its functional categories, man as existence can journey toward and in a world unveiled in its truth.[7]

The goal of constituting an existential psychopathology is precisely to tear the reflection on man away from all of these "fallback positions of the understanding" (as Häberlin has it)[8] through which human existence is subsumed by the modes of organic substance.[9] To give human totality a radically different meaning from that which we give, at the level of naturalist reflection, to reflexes, behaviors, conduct; to conceive of it as an absolute foundation that makes possible a freedom open to truth: this is to move definitively past the naturalist horizon, and for Binswanger, to return to the foundation of any understanding of man.

Putting aside any theoretical discussion for the moment, we must recognize that this is a radical change in the norms for understanding mental illness. Since the eighteenth century, or more precisely, since the time when the mentally ill person ceased

---

j See Martin Heidegger, "On the Essence of Truth," in *Pathmarks*, ed. and trans. William McNeil (Cambridge University Press, 1998), 136–54.

to be inscribed by religious thought into the absolute universe of Good and Evil, and to have—insofar as he was possessed—his episodic but significant place in Satan's battle against God, psychopathology had become, by natural necessity, both deterministic and relativistic. Deterministic, because it was precisely the abolition of freedom that was seen in alienation, as the faculty of human nature that was the highest, but also the most exposed, the most precarious, and as the patient was sick precisely inasmuch as his vanished freedom abandoned him to a determinism from which any human signification had faded away: the sickness lay in having lost one's freedom, which no doubt explains why it was so easy to take away the patient's real freedom, and why it was impossible to imagine a psychopathology from any point of view other than that of triumphant determinism.[k] Relativistic, insofar as madness appeared as the manifest proof that the access to truth depends on psychological conditions that vary according to the individual: already the *Encyclopédie* asserted that madmen are little more than a variation on the great theme of human errors and passions;[l] and the idea that the problem of mental pathology cannot be framed in terms of truth but must instead be defined in terms of "mentality" became more and more pervasive. The psychology of mentality plays the same role of screening in relation to the philosophical notion of truth that the psychology of determinism plays in relation to the philosophical notion of freedom.

[148]

Yet, in a surprising revolution, Binswanger, starting from the classical horizon of psychiatry, ended up repositioning

---

k This is undoubtedly one of the roots of the old prejudice that normal psychology must use pathological psychology as a "natural experiment."

l [See the entry "Folie (Morale)" in Diderot and d'Alembert's *Encyclopédie*, vol. 7 (1757), 42b-44a. A collaborative critical digital edition of the *Encyclopédie* is available at http://enccre.academie-sciences.fr/encyclopedie/article/v7-22-0.]

[149] psychopathology entirely within the perspective of freedom and of truth. The patient's pathological universe will be considered from the point of view of the forms of his freedom and of the way in which his radical freedom projects itself into one form of existence or another; and the world onto which the existing subject opens will be put in place in relation to the world of objective plenitude onto which the interhuman community of subjects opens.

But might this not amount to returning, in psychiatry, to a metaphysical point of view that indexes man's concrete reality to transcendental abstractions? Is the effort to return a sick manner of thinking, a demented reason, a senseless behavior to the calm universe of a freedom that asserts itself and a truth that is constituted not, in some way, an attempt to stifle what has always been metaphysically scandalous in them? In wanting to restore to the sick man what is most essentially human in man, does Binswanger not condemn himself to a quasi-theological detour through a truth and a freedom whose content goes beyond human existence, and whose origin precedes it? We will no doubt need to return to the question of what belongs to theology in phenomenological thought and in existential analyses. For the moment, while we consider not the idea in its objective content as much as the concepts in their methodological articulations, and insofar as we must always credit a method in order to be able show rigor with regard to the idea, we could respond to these objections from Binswanger's perspective.

[150] First we would observe that the philosophical concepts that subtend our consideration of pathological facts are not metaphysical abstractions, but on the contrary that they imply a movement beyond metaphysics, precisely insofar as they are thought from the foundation that is human existence (*Dasein*); freedom does not deploy itself as a choice between instantiated

possibles, before any existence, by the eventualities of essence, but rather freedom is the fundamental mode of being of human existence as such.[m] And it is moreover this freedom that "possesses the human being so originarily that only *it* secures for humanity that distinctive relatedness to being as a whole [and] as such."[n] The recourse to a Heideggerian conception of existence therefore does not result in exiling man in the ethereal universe of metaphysical reflection, but of taking up any reflection on man at the level of that foundation that is man himself in his existence.

But we must further note that *Daseinsanalyse*, as Binswanger understands it, is not situated at the level of this ontological foundation. The first section of the first part of *Sein und Zeit* has as its title the "fundamental analysis of *Dasein*" and as its theme the determination of the ontological characteristics of *Dasein*: these "*Seinscharaktere*" are the "existentials" that have their foundation in the being of *Dasein*, while the categories are also "*Seinscharaktere*," although their foundation lies in the being of what is not human reality.[o]

But these are ontological modes of interrogation that orient themselves explicitly toward the *Seinsproblem*.[p] Existential psychopathology's mode of interrogation is not ontological and cannot be insofar as, as a reflection on the sick man, it can only ever concern man's modes of being rather than, in a general manner, his being as human reality. Undoubtedly this problem of the being of *Dasein* must remain on the horizon; but ontological

[151]

---

m [In the margin: "quotation from Heidegger."]
n Heidegger, "On the Essence of Truth," 145–46 ["and" has been added to the quotation to reflect Foucault's phrasing—Trans.].
o Martin Heidegger, *Being and Time*, trans. John Macquarrie and Edward Robinson (Blackwell, 1962), § 44–45.
p ["Problem of being."]

reflection in the manner of Heidegger can only ever be referential.[10] This is undoubtedly what Binswanger intended to underscore in his work on the *Ideenflucht* by stressing that, for him, it was not a matter of analyzing "the fundamental structures of human existence," but the "existential possibilities that *Dasein* has in fact chosen."[q][11] And taking up the same theme in one of his final texts: *Daseinsanalyse* "does not propose an ontological thesis . . . but makes ontic statements on the subject of factual findings about actually appearing forms and structures of human existence."[r] In avoiding the deterministic and relativistic postulates of classical psychiatry, we do not tear *Daseinsanalyse* away from the sphere of concrete experience.[12] On the contrary, we bring it back to that sphere, underscoring that human reality does not have the same ontological status as the reality of "nature," and that its concrete plenitude therefore cannot have the same signification and cannot be subject to the same kind of analysis. But [that which] human reality [requires] is no less scientific and no less in need of a foundation in concrete experience: "*Daseinsanalyse* is a science of experience . . . with the method and the ideal of exactness of the *Erfahrungswissenschaften*."[s] [t]

One might say that this adds up to many detours and philosophical pirouettes just to end up landing on one's feet, and not very steadily. That the human sciences must develop according to a specific style, without ceasing to be sciences of experience—this is undoubtedly a commonplace whose banality does not

---

q Binswanger, *Über Ideenflucht*, 188–89.

r Ludwig Binswanger, "The Existential Analysis School of Thought," 192 [translation modified to reflect Foucault's phrasing].

s ["Sciences of experience."]

t Ludwig Binswanger, "The Existential Analysis School of Thought," 192. [The English translation reads "existential analysis is an empirical science . . . with the method and the ideal of exactness of the *phenomenological* empirical sciences"—Trans.]

justify the long methodological journey we have just undertaken. It should suffice to note for now, still in favor of Binswanger, that a proposition that is so general, and which appears as mainstream as this one, has methodological importance only because of all the processes that justify and elucidate it. Human science must be a science of experience without being a natural science—this is an empty proposition that can designate and encompass the most diverse forms of anthropological speculation: a science of the spirit in the manner of Dilthey; an eidetic psychology such as Husserl defines it; a cultural anthropology such as it is practiced by Margaret Mead or Abram Kardiner[13] . . . and so on. But if we specify the meaning of "experience" and that of "natural science," then the methodological options necessarily take shape; should we push these notions as far as they will go, and endeavor to trace them to their roots, then the banality of the commonplace fades, and forms of analysis impose themselves which may be subject to many criticisms, but which certainly stand up to charges of banality.

All of the preceding analyses must seem long and drawn-out to someone accustomed to the evidently livelier rhythm of shock therapies: we must acknowledge that with these, we have the twofold advantage of a quite thin theoretical foundation and, in some cases, of real healing.[u] It is very tempting to acknowledge validity in a reflection on illness only insofar as it offers, at the same time, the means of eliminating it. [153]

However, this temptation is not without danger. Psychiatrists do not have so many means of healing at their disposal; they are attached to those they have, and we understand them; we also understand them when they assert that what is true for

---

u See generally Jean Delay, and in particular his *L'électrochoc et la psychophysiologie* (Masson, 1946).

understanding the sick man must be effective for restoring him to the plenitude of health. But it is difficult to follow them when they seek to define the truth of illness from the process that suppresses it. This is for two reasons.

When a psychiatrist claims that a schizophrenia or manic-depressive episode constitutes a mood dysregulation (the first in the form of a weakening qualified as "hypothymic," the second as an exaggeration qualified as "hyperthymic"), his only essential proof is one fact: the electroshock, which has caused the symptoms to subside, has provoked a disruption in the functioning of the third ventricle, and in the hormonal and vegetative regulation it oversees.[v] But this reasoning is only valid if considered as a postulate: we must admit that the truth of the illness exhausts itself in this mood disturbance, and that the sick man is nothing other than a man, with the addition of a poorly functioning third ventricle; pathology is returned to the limits of functional disorders, and illness remains on the order of functionality. Who can fail to see that this means abstracting the illness from the patient himself, turning it into a separate being that exists or does not exist, that appears or disappears according to the avatars of a determined function? On the pretext of staying concrete, and of defining illness only with the real means we have of eliminating it, in the end we commit the worst abstraction, which lies in forgetting the man himself.

But we also expose ourselves to an even worse sophism, which lies in confusing understanding illness with understanding the means of acting on it: it is to blur, through a curious illusion, what makes it be and what makes it disappear. For many long years the "viscous" mentality of epileptics has been discussed, and there has been an attempt to make it the fundamental

---

v Jean Delay, *Les dérèglements de l'humeur* (PUF, 1946).

psychological trait not only of epileptics themselves but also of a whole series of individuals of similar "types":ʷ in the end, the epileptic's viscosity is probably due to the barbiturates with which, since the end of the last century, we have developed the habit of saturating him from the first seizure. We would not find a single mention of epileptic "viscosity" in the observations prior to these forms of therapy. But there is an even richer example of a confusion of this kind. Babinski—who can be credited with having defined the differential signs of hysterical paralysis—believed he could identify its nature from the suggestion that put an end to it: before a patient who had collapsed, he would repeat, parodically, the biblical phrase "rise up and walk," and from his patient actually rising up and walking he thought he could deduce that her illness was as feigned as the thaumaturgy that healed it. My theory is true because I heal; but the illness is false, because I heal it . . . Illness, however, does not have the same nature as all of the processes through which it disappears: if they reduce it, it is not because it is reducible to them; it is that they have dominated it in the course of a shared dialectic.ˣ

[155]

We could thus emphasize arguments of this kind in order to free a reflection on illness from any therapeutic engagement. Yet the problem of healing does pose itself in relation to existential analysis. But it does so outside of any pragmatic horizon: in other words, healing, which is rejected as a criterion in the analysis, is nevertheless recognized to be its vocation. In order to fully

---

w This is what Mme Minkowska called the "mentalité '*glyschroïdique*'" (!). [See "Charakterologische Probleme im Lichte psychiatrischer und genealogischer Hereditätsforschung (mit besonderer Berücksichtigung der Epileptoidie)," *Zeitschrift für die gesamte Neurologie und Psychiatrie* 82, no. 1 (1923): 199–211.]

x It would be interesting to see how psychoanalysis has always oscillated between these two conceptions: that of a dialectic of illness and therapy (resistance, defense mechanisms), and that of an identity between the illness's content and the process of healing (abreaction).

illuminate this problem of therapeutics in relation to theory, and of the physician in relation to the patient, we would undoubtedly need to recall Max Weber's analysis of the role of vocation, of "*Beruf*," in science:[y] perhaps this is where Binswanger, after Jaspers, drew his conception of medical science, both as a theory of man and as a practical action on man.[14] It is indeed as a theory of man, and within its analysis, that existential reflection finds both the possibility and the necessity of therapeutic action. Among the existential structures—or what we would rigorously need to call existentials—we encounter the modes of interhuman existence: the existence of any man necessarily opens onto this human milieu that the Germans call the "*Mitwelt*"; and if this milieu, in its historical forms, in its current content, does not belong to the very necessity of this existence, it belongs to necessity that existence open onto this milieu. In the preceding chapter, we saw the forms that this milieu, or rather this existence in the "*Mitwelt*" can take in the course of an illness; but as a fundamental structure of existence, this "*mitweltich*" existence cannot disappear without existence itself disappearing, and in this measure therapeutic action, insofar as it implies, at its root, a copresence, a relationship of man to man, must always be possible. By elucidating the interhuman horizon of any existence, *Daseinsanalyse* thereby discovers the basis upon which therapeutic action can and must be effected.

Here the therapy is not a blind practice that discovers its truth in whatever successes may occur;[15] it is the very truth of the analysis that clears up the path toward healing.

---

y [In German, "*Beruf*" simultaneously means the "occupation," the "profession," and the "vocation." Here Foucault is referring to Max Weber's 1917 Munich lecture entitled "Wissenschaft als Beruf," published in English as "Science as a Vocation," trans. Rodney Livingston, in *The Vocation Lectures*, ed. David Owen and Tracy B. Strong (Hackett, 2004), 1–31).]

In these still speculative remarks, there is more than an optimism that already satisfies itself, before any challenge. There is enough to exorcise certain medical attitudes that are affective crystallizations just as much as they are theoretical biases and ethical prejudices. Indeed, if we do not accept that the existence of any man entails as a fundamental characteristic this being-with, this "*Mitsein*," in which any relationship to the other is rooted—and ultimately any physician-patient relationship—the physician can only ever see the patient in the abstract form of an undifferentiated man, of an individual representative of a species, and the concrete presence of a man face to face with a man erases itself in the recourse to the generality of the human being. In this way the real rapport is lost in what Hegel would call "bad infinity," that of a diffuse pity in which "it is never an individual, never an absolute" that is aimed at [*visé*],[z] but in which the individual is concerned only as an allusion to the species, as a momentary and precarious example of a generality. Everything that is serious goes to humanity and leaves the man on the sidelines; the human encounter is avoided through the humanitarianism of a "pity for humanity" that Jaspers designates and condemns as "*Menschenliebe*."[aa][16] At the same time as it is a methodological revision, it is an affective conversion, a reversal of attitude that Jaspers, and after him, Binswanger, require of the physician: and they know that the root of evil lies in the old medical positivism of the end of the nineteenth century which, on the basis of evolutionism, places the human species before human existence, the humanitarian postulate before the

---

z Karl Jaspers, *Psychologie der Weltanschauungen* (Springer, 1919), 112. [Foucault borrows this reference from Binswanger's "Karl Jaspers und die Psychiatrie," which he cites below (see the following note).]

aa Ludwig Binswanger, "Karl Jaspers und die Psychiatrie," *Schweizer Archiv für Neurologie und Psychiatrie* 51, no. 1 (1943): 1–13.

encounter with man, universal pity before individuated understanding; and which, in its stated concern for realism and fidelity to experience, succumbs to the worst of idealisms, since finally, if it attaches such importance to the abstract generality of the species, it is in order to avoid seeing the patient's actual reality, to avoid taking seriously the concrete contradiction of his existence, the real meaning of his mad life—for fear, as Breton would put it, "of shattering its kernel of darkness."[bb]

If the physician avoids the sick man out of "pity for long-suffering humanity," it is indeed for fear of the patient himself, and what would suffice to prove it is that other attitude, which is implied by the first and which, even more than it, organizes theoretical perspectives: that attitude that consists, says Binswanger, in taking the other "by his weak point"[cc]—in other words, with regard to the physician's relationship to the patient, seeking the ways in which he "is not like the others," emphasizing the disturbances that are designated as such in relation to an ideal erected as a norm, exhausting the essence of the illness in the sum of the patient's deficits—a negative conception of illness that is like the "cordon sanitaire" wrapped around the sick man by the physician, the security measure he takes to separate, in radical fashion, the normal from the pathological. Conversely, it is clear that if, instead of taking the patient by his "weak point," we truly credit his possibilities, and if we seek to determine which of these are not yet closed off in him, then an entire recasting of the old concepts is necessary, and a new therapeutic attitude is also essential.

[159]

---

bb [André Breton, "Introduction to Achim von Arnim's *Strange Tales*," in *Break of Day*, trans. Mark Polizzotti and Mary Ann Caws (University of Nebraska Press, 1999), 88–110: "These days, the sexual world, despite the memorable explorations made in the modern age by Sade and Freud, has never, as far as I can see, stopped countering our will to penetrate the universe with its unshatterable kernel of *darkness*" (109).]

cc Binswanger, *Grundformen und Erkenntnis menschlichen Daseins* (Niehans, 1942), 308.

It is no longer a matter of eliminating illness, as one might remedy a deficit, by allowing for the return of suppressed functions, but rather of opening new possibilities: it is no longer a matter so much of erasing the past as it is of preparing a future.

At no moment are Binswanger's ideas closer to Goldstein's than in these perspectives on therapy[dd] [17] and on the rapport that must, in the medical situation, establish itself between the physician and the patient. The Goldsteinian idea that a segmentary disturbance, such as a reflex that has stopped functioning, can have meaning only within a totality that makes it appear to be not so much a disposition as it is a positive mode of response has, indeed, a practical consequence: the physician-patient situation must not have the primary goal of highlighting the series of specific deficits and abstracting them from the overall conduct, but rather of showing what new style of behavior emerges over the course of the illness, which original norms it obeys, what are the types of "realization" (*Leistung*) to which it is still susceptible. One might say that this idea is not new and that, since Jackson, we know how to show positive aspects within illness, which are like the correlatives of its negative aspects:[18] there would [160] be in illness a process of dissolution which, in suppressing the superior functions and structures (negative phenomena of illness), might make room for the inferior functions and structures which the more primitive stages of evolution had deposited at the very foundation of the organism. This reappearance of the most ancient, the simplest and most stable structures, constitutes the entirety of the positive phenomena of illness. But this is only an apparent positivity, since it has been made possible only by the negative process that eliminates the superior instances and

---

dd To my knowledge, Goldstein is never cited by Binswanger and his school, except in rare bibliographic notes.

since it is unlikely to instantiate any new behaviors outside of segmentary and primitive conduct. The positive content of illness is not taken seriously within evolutionism, because evolutionism makes it nothing but the result of a subtraction. On the contrary, Goldstein and Binswanger grant importance to this positive signification of illness, and even if they base it on different fulcrums (the organism's normativity for Goldstein; the ontological meaning of existence for Binswanger), both of them end up with a radical transformation of the physician-patient relationship, with a reinvention of the physician's approach to the question of the patient.

*

[161] We must therefore give an originary meaning once more to the physician-patient relationship, insofar as it is the foundation of any therapeutic action. And in order to find [it], we must go beyond all of the alterations through which it has been assimilated to other kinds of relationships in which existence as such is not called into question. In psychotherapy, two people encounter each other, and this is the originary situation (even if it obviously does not encompass all of the possible relations between the physician and the patient, taken as such): this is a truth that we are constantly tempted to obscure, as if to trivialize its unmatched importance. For the sake of technical security, we like to reduce one of the partners to a scientific abstraction, who would deploy his processes in analyzable elements: the patient is turned into a psyche, where personal conduct is projected according to the dimensions of impersonal realities, such as the Freudian unconscious, which is a kind of third figure in which the physician's knowledge attempts to connect to the patient's suffering, and in which, in response, the patient projects himself in the objective, solid, almost palpable form of a petrified past. It is also

undoubtedly to mask the danger and the radically "com-promising" character of this dual presence in the therapeutic relationship that we only ever call into question a single direction of this relationship: that which goes from the physician toward the patient—and that we interpret as real intervention, as effective, transcendent action of the former on the latter—and never that which goes [from the patient toward the physician]. Undoubtedly psychoanalysis uncovered, in the essential notion of transference, the reality of a relationship oriented in the inverse direction, from the patient toward the physician. But this is only a pseudo-relationship insofar as its being addressed to the physician is contingent: transference onto the psychoanalyst—and this is what, according to Freud, makes it effective—is nothing but repetition, and more precisely one of the repetitions of a primitive relationship of the child with his father or his mother; what gives therapeutic transference its value is that at one and the same time it reiterates a primitive situation and is directed, from the outside, by the physician; its value in no way inheres in its being a current movement of the patient toward this particular person who is his physician. Insofar as it goes from the patient toward the physician, the relationship of transference is not current, but primitive, and it does not address itself to the physician but to an anterior imago; insofar as it is a current relationship, which plays a current role in neurosis and in its solution, then it does not go from the patient toward the physician, but only from the physician who directs it toward the patient who experiences it. At the core of every therapeutic attitude, there is finally an even more radical forgetting of this confrontation between two existences: because in its classic forms, and we must include psychoanalysis in this, therapy presents itself above all as being "at the service of one thing" (*Dienst an einer Sache*),[ee] and the physician-patient

---

ee [See Ludwig Binswanger, "Psychotherapie als Beruf," *Der Nervenarzt* 1 (1927): 138–39.]

relationship appears as an episode against the backdrop of a more real, and more general, debate between illness and health, reason and unreason, social adaptation and maladaptation, the instances of order and repression and those anarchic instances of unregulated passion. Insofar as [the physician] forgets that he is in the presence of the patient's concrete existence, and that the patient is in the presence of his concrete existence as a physician, he cannot help but put himself at the service of one of these "things," he cannot avoid aligning himself with health, reason, order, while trying to bring his patient over to them; and instead of wanting to base his action on the patient's own existence, he contents himself with justifying it through those realities that he believes he is serving. But is he not committing the twofold error of missing his patient in his concrete existence and of accepting, without giving an account of them, these "abstract things" that he has made a duty of serving? Does he not run afoul of the old Platonic question: can a physician heal if he does not know what health is?[ff] A question that Jaspers echoes in *General Psychopathology*, when he writes that "the physician must be able to give a philosophical account of what he means by health."[gg]

We must therefore return, beyond all this forgetting, beyond these lapses into natural objectivity, to the originary encounter between the physician and the patient. Jaspers had already defined it in its purity—both as total void and absolute plenitude: "The doctor is neither a technician nor a savior, but an existence for another existence."[hh] But the originary character of this

---

ff Plato, *Republic*. [Foucault is probably referring to the passage in *The Republic* where medicine is defined as an art whose proper effect is health (Book I, 346a-346e).]

gg Karl Jaspers, *Allgemeine Psychopathologie. Für Studierende, Ärzte und Psychologen*, 3rd ed. (Springer, 1923 [1913]), 439. [This sentence does not seem to appear in the English translation, which is of the seventh edition—Trans.] [Foucault borrows the quotation from Binswanger's "Karl Jaspers und die Psychiatrie," 4.]

hh Karl Jaspers, *Philosophy*, vol. 1, trans. E. B. Ashton (University of Chicago Press, 1969), 155. [The same quotation also appears in Binswanger's "Karl Jaspers und die Psychiatrie," 3.]

relationship does not imply its simplicity, since it is this interhuman relationship (*mitmenschlich*) that is both on the order of "being one with the other" (*miteinandersein*) and on the order of "being one outside the other" (*auseinandersein*): copresence entails exclusion; confrontation opens onto the possibility of conflict. And for this reason psychotherapy rests on the same fundamental situation as any action exercised by man on man, whether it be on the order of suggestion, pedagogy, or communication. But in which way precisely is psychotherapy a specific action? How does the fact that one of the partners is a physician specify the "*Mitmenschensein*" that characterizes any encounter?[ii] It is this precise question that Binswanger and R. Kuhn sought in succession to answer, because it was in the answer that they expected to discover the foundation for their psychotherapeutic action.

[164]

In an article published in *Nervenartz* in 1935, Binswanger returns to the theme of a distinction—almost a contrast—between lived history (*Lebensgeschichte*) and vital function (*Lebensfunktion*).[jj] The physician's singular situation face to face with the patient is promoted by a dialectic inherent to his concrete situation: on one hand, he is invested by the patient with an entire lived history which culminates in him, and of which he holds, in the eyes of the patient, the mysterious meaning; there is something like a "maternal foundation" (*Mutterboden*) in any psychotherapy—already quite often highlighted by psychoanalysis—which carries the physician to the heart of the lived history (*Lebensgeschichte*). But at the same time, through his understanding of the psyche, of its unique mechanisms and fundamental processes, the psychiatrist can confront all of the vital functions, by which we mean not only all of the organic functions but also all of the psychological functions, with this lived history. "Existential communication and the action

---

ii ["Being-with."]
jj See above [p. 5].

whose goal is the liberation of biologico-psychological forces constitute the two dialectical poles of medical psychotherapy."[kk] Here [165] the physician appears as a dialectical mediator, as a reconciler of concepts; he is the opposition surmounted, the dialectic unknotted, we could almost say the "end of history": which is to say that his position is still defined, as in classical psychiatry, as in classical psychoanalysis, by a status of transcendence.

We no longer find this theme in Binswanger's more recent writings (nor do we find the fundamental and ultimate character of the opposition between *Lebensgeschichte* and *Lebensfunktion*): and the idea of a dialectical reconciliation as the essence of therapy has given way to the idea of an existential elucidation.[19] This elucidation, too, must start from the significative contents of lived history, such as can be opened up to us by a descriptive comprehension in the manner of Jaspers, but these contents in themselves cannot allow for elucidation, insofar as "they are not their own light"; [insofar] as they can be lived as much in the mode of reflective consciousness as in that of a marginal or diffuse consciousness. The child's attachment to his mother is not significant in itself unless we take into account the manner in which it is lived, accepted as a passion or mutely enveloped as a need: lived experience can neither give an account of itself *nor, especially, of the person living it*. This is why we must go beyond it toward the existential analysis which will make it fully significant, as the expression of a fundamental mode of existence. Psychotherapeutic action goes from the comprehension of lived contents to the analysis of the existential structure that expresses itself through them: it does not consist in reconciling the two

---

kk Ludwig Binswanger, "Über Psychotherapie," *Der Nervenarzt* 8 (1935): 113–21, 180–89; reprinted in *Ausgewählte Vorträge und Aufsätze*, vol. 1, *Zur phänomenologischen Anthropologie* (Francke, 1947), here 135. [Foucault dedicated a lengthy reading note to this article (BNF, Box 38, folder 1).]

terms of an opposition, as Binswanger's early writings seemed to indicate; *it consists in finding in signification an expression.*²⁰

At least this is the meaning that seems to emerge from Binswanger's and R. Kuhn's most recent writings.ˡˡ

[166]

*

How can this elucidation of meaning as expression, this "*Existenzerhellung*,"²¹ have therapeutic efficacy?

Here is an example of neurosis and of psychotherapeutic action analyzed by R. Kuhn.ᵐᵐ

Lina belongs to a Catholic family of Swiss farmers who live in isolation, in the middle of the countryside. She got a job in town. When she is twenty-three years old, she meets a young Protestant: she enjoys going out with him and brings him home one day; her parents do not like him and the father orders [her] to cut off relations because of the religious difference. She thinks her father is right, especially since her friend threatened to kill himself if she abandoned him: this threat made an unpleasant impression on her. She shares her decision with her friend: he sets a time to meet with her; she does not go. At the end of the following week, he disappears, and at the edge of the forest, near the farm where Lina was raised, his corpse is found. At the same time, Lina receives a letter he had written to her a few moments before killing himself: he reproaches her for not having kept her word, for liking to "play with men," for having robbed him of his

---

ll Roland Kuhn, "Daseinsanalyse im psychotherapeutischen Gespräch," *Schweizer Archiv für Neurologie und Psychiatrie* 67, no. 1 (1951): 52–60. [See Foucault's reading note on this article in the archives (BNF, Box 42b, folder 1).]

mm [Roland Kuhn, "Zur Daseinsstruktur einer Neurose," *Jahrbuch für Psychologie und Psychotherapie* 1, no. 2 (1953): 207–22. See Foucault's reading note on this clinical case analysis in the archives (BNF, Box 42b, folder 1).]

joie de vivre, for having "a stone heart to treat a man so cruelly"; but he still loves her and his "last word is Lina."[nn]

[167]   For the first few days Lina is devastated: she can neither eat nor sleep. When she learns how the corpse was discovered, her affliction increases: she no longer has tears to cry; she has anxious dreams.

Two weeks later the picture changes: she is sleeping once more, without dreaming. But upon awakening each morning, she feels wound up, "worried inside";[oo] she can no longer find any rest and cannot bear anything. She relates this worry to her guilt, she feels as if she is being stalked, and throughout the day she has the feeling of "arriving too late."[pp] She returns home and goes [to] the place where her friend's body was found. At night, she dreams that she sees this body stretched out on the road. She then feels that she is getting better. She attempts to distract herself, goes out frequently, dances, wears makeup, plucks her eyebrows, wears gaudily elegant outfits. For the first time, she begins to spend time with flighty women. Several men are taken with her, but she does not let them get close, and they move on. After each of these affairs, she feels herself getting worse. She can no longer bear to be alone; she is afraid in the dark. She can speak only of ordinary trivialities. When she is with others and wants to laugh, she feels held back by "something in particular":[qq] she feels herself becoming pale; she begins to feel cold; she experiences something like a rigidity in her face that spreads over her body little by little; she feels like she can no longer move; she is seized by anxiety.

---

nn   [Kuhn, "Zur Daseinsstruktur einer Neurose," 208.]
oo   [Kuhn, "Zur Daseinsstruktur," 208.]
pp   [Kuhn, "Zur Daseinsstruktur," 208.]
qq   [Kuhn, "Zur Daseinsstruktur," 209.]

She then confides in a priest, begins to go to church regularly and performs her religious duties scrupulously. But she is not getting better—on the contrary. She goes out less and less, does not know what to do, and repents—always more bitterly—having missed that momentous night, the appointed meeting: if she had gone, the calamity would not have occurred; she is entirely responsible for it. She begins to wander; her face is pale, it has the rigid mimicry of a mask; sleep has disappeared. She is finally taken to the physician whose help she had declined immediately after the death of her friend; two and a half years have now gone by. She explains that she had thought she could get over it on her own, but now sees that she cannot go any further without someone's help. Yet her unhappiness seems to her to be beyond any human succor. The physician discusses this impression with her during the first hours of psychotherapy. In order to be helped, she would need something completely unexpected, undreamt of, a miracle. Her despair is therefore not entirely meaningless, if she is still hoping for a miracle. But miracles do not occur if we do nothing but wait for them. Perhaps speech, a meeting, a dialogue could elicit such a miracle, and the wonder of healing. [168]

This is the point at which psychotherapeutic action inserts itself. At a basic level, it appears plainly as a recovery of the past. In the first dream that follows the beginning of the treatment, she sees her friend's soul among the flames of hell. She explains to the physician the rancor she feels against the Church, against the Catholic priests, whom she sees as accomplices in the tragedy: four years earlier, she had loved a young man, also a Protestant; her love had [been] as deep at the time as it was superficial with her second friend; but her father, leaning on a priest's authority, had from that moment on refused the marriage. She harbored deep resentment about it. The physician easily helps her accept that she often had a conduct of compromise: if she had actually yielded to her father, she would not have wanted, a second time, to marry a Protestant whom she did not seem to love very much; her obedience was mixed with stubbornness and rebellion. In a later dream, she sees a man driving a horse-drawn cart laden with wood to the middle of a forest that she does not remember having seen before: the horses swerve; the man falls between the wheels; he is crushed. When she wakes, the patient feels great anxiety. In the associations that follow the retelling of this dream, Lina recounts that she always accompanied her father into the woods; her father would bring back huge wood carts that he drove very imprudently; each time she was very afraid. She immediately adds that she has always hated her father: she had to help him in the fields and in the stable, and, since she was twelve, he had forced her to play the part of a farm-hand. She detested this occupation, and noticing it, her father beat her. Even when she was sixteen, he continued to slap her. Soon afterward, she has a new dream: she is in a strange house that is in flames. Her father and a neighbor, outside, try to put out the fire: they do not succeed; at the moment where she will be taken by the flames, she manages to escape through a little door. In reporting this dream, she thinks that she must have set the fire herself, but she is surprised that it is not her father's house that burns. When she was ten, she had wanted, despite her father's interdiction, to light a kerosene lamp; an explosion had occurred and she was left with facial burns whose traces were visible for a long time. Her father had reprimanded her very violently. She remembers suddenly that she was very attached to her father and that she accompanied him everywhere. But abruptly everything had changed, when her father mistreated her so badly in relation to the accident. She was also indignant that he had a new child each year, and that she herself had to leave school during all the periods when her mother could not take care of the house.

Across all of this dream material, and the associations that enhance it, we see some important lines of this "lived history" emerging. It does seem that the work of psychotherapeutic elucidation develops in keeping with methods and opens onto results that are themselves psychoanalytic: reappearance, through the veil of a symbolic world, of memories long buried; discovery of classic themes of attachment to the paternal imago, which in girls is specific to the oedipal situation. However a fact immediately presents itself: in this example the return to the most primitive situations is not systematically sought after; the past reappears in an obvious connection to the present, without the psychiatrist ever seeking to resurrect, as the absolute principle of the entire story, the originary situation, the initial situation, what Freud called the primal scene. And yet I think that no psychoanalyst would have failed, with regard to the dream of the fire and the memory of the explosion, to speak here of a "screen memory": one of those reminiscences that are privileged by memory and singularly valorized among other memories only insofar as [they] are a way of masking a more ancient and more important event, to [which] [they] are only a symbolic allusion and also a blocking mechanism: the symbolism of the lamp, of the fire, of the explosion, the ease with which the patient went from this memory to that of her brothers and sisters being born each year, and of her mother letting her do her work as housewife, lady of the house, mother, all of this allows us to wager, without hesitation, that a psychoanalyst would not have curbed his curiosity there and instead would have asked what more specific oedipal relationship, or even what violently intense libidinal scene might be hiding behind the anecdotal memory of a lamp that explodes and the dream of a house on fire. Roland Kuhn does not seem to have this curiosity, and the effort of existential analysis to elucidate the past seems to have a very short range compared to the

[171]

"long cycles" of psychoanalysis, which does not hesitate to go back to rigorously primal events. Why this difference?

In psychoanalysis, recovery takes the form of repeating the event or the affect, and therapeutic efficacy, which is not associated with even exact memories that can be reconstituted by means of an intellectual archaeology, is conferred upon the memories that are instead experienced with the vividness of primary emotion (this is abreaction) and the intensity of the feelings at their origin (transference). Healing occurs through a sort of ruse, in that the inertia of the unconscious—what Freud [calls] the principle of repetition—which provokes the stereotypical iteration of symptoms, the cyclical return to primal situations, the constant eruption of the same anxiety, this inertia that "makes the illness" is used in the psychoanalytic situation as a tool for healing: paradoxically, what encloses the illness in the cycle of these repetitions must allow the patient to find an exit. How does this paradox manifest in reality? And why is this wager, which consists in wanting to heal via the very events that made one sick, effective?

It is that the repetition of the trauma and of the anxiety produces itself in this scripted situation that the psychoanalytic decor imposes: the rules that go from the obligation that the patient lie on the couch to the psychanalyst's obligation to maintain a neutral attitude, not to mention the principle of free association for the patient, and that of free-floating attention on the physician's part—all of these prescriptions create an analytic situation in brutal rupture with the patient's real situation. They erect an abstract, unreal environment around the patient, and it is as a result of this isolation that the memory's reappearance can take on an absolute value: the present then becomes unreal, while the past presents itself as the reality and the very truth of the current illness. The patient externalizes his memories in the present: which is only a manner of internalizing—by the grace of the analytic situation and of its fundamental abstraction—through the past, his illness. If the first step in the treatment is the restoration of the past beyond the fringes of the unconscious, it is to give the present the signification of the past. But this is not yet sufficient to justify the efficacy of a treatment that presents itself as the elucidation of the past: at the moment when the past lives again, it is necessary that the other figure involved in this repetition not be the ordinary other, whose familiar reactions respond immediately to the patient's feelings. On the contrary, it is necessary that he be a major other, locked into a silence that, precisely, tears him out of that repetition in which the patient's ever-solicitous attitude wants to implicate him; what is required is a figure who, [as] the bearer at least virtually of the truth about the patient, demonstrates via his scientific serenity and his occupational indifference that no one can answer [the patient's] calls, since they are only ever addressed to the phantoms of his past, and that the dialogue for which he seeks an interlocutor has been carried out and is still being carried out with the fantastical figures of his childhood. In bringing memories back to life, the present assumes the signification of the past; via transference, both together acquire the definitive status of pastness. [173]

The therapeutic motives of existential analysis are profoundly different.

Contrary to psychoanalysis, the elucidation of the past has the goal of giving to the past the living meaning of the present: its goal is not to re-actualize it but rather to make it unreal. Let us return to the example of Lina, such as it was analyzed by Roland Kuhn. There is something contradictory about the symptoms: on the one hand, Lina feels responsible for her friend not being there; and at the same time, she feels his presence everywhere and experiences it in the mode of anxiety, as the always-threatening appearance of a face filled with reproach. But each term of this contradiction is not simple in itself. When she reproaches herself for the absence of her friend, she experiences a kind of worry, accompanied by flushing and a thumping heart, which has the same affective quality as what she experienced in the presence of her first friend, and thereafter of all men who approached her. Yet she never experienced this impression—whose erotic components she readily acknowledges—in the presence of her second friend. A certain coldness had always kept her at a remove from this friend, whose attachment to her she had enjoyed without ever becoming aware of truly loving him. And now she finds herself experiencing this romantic emotion, but tinged with anxiety, each time she feels the enigmatic presence of the dead friend, each time his face threatens her in daydreams or in dreams; and this worry dissipates only in the presence of a real man, or during the erotic contacts she sought with the first men to come along after her friend's suicide: there, in this carnal presence, no more romantic emotion, never the malaise that makes her heart thump and her face flush. Everything occurs as if the emotion of love could no longer be addressed to the real presence of a man, as if one could no longer imply the other, but rather as if they were mutually exclusive. The real presence hides and silences the emotion of love; and the emotion of love can now only concern an imagined presence against a backdrop of absence. There is thus a whole interlacing of presence and absence taking place: the departed person is still mixed into the presence of things; he is more present than at the time of his presence; and the present, inversely, is lived only from a remote distance, with the indifference into which, ordinarily, the past slips.

What therefore will the therapy consist of? Giving to the past the status of absence, resituating it in relation to the open-ended plenitude of the present, making empty space for an encounter with reality. The elucidation of the past must not have another meaning than this one. Through this elucidation, Lina discovers that the troubling face she sees in her anxious dreams is that of her friend only in its broad strokes, but the impression of reproach and anger is that of her father, when earlier, and still recently, he reprimanded her. She also discovers that her guilt has not crystallized around the missed appointment so much as around the flirtatiousness with which she played at awakening in a man a hope that she then disappointed. She finally discovers that her casualness in her relations with her friend echoes the disappointment she previously experienced with her father: all her childhood, she had believed that he felt a tender affection for her; after the incident with the lamp, she feels disappointed, betrayed; her own love received no response. She "withdrew" (her mother confirms that her personality changed completely after this episode): she closed herself off from the love of others, or rather she experiences the love that others show her as an opportunity to toy with them, and to disappoint them. She also closed herself off from this past that is now for her stripped of signification; she forgets the affection she once felt for her father, and later she will forget the real but hidden feelings she had for her friend. And in this universe, which is closed off and fragmented into these successive presents, it is understandable [176] that memory would not have the status of memory, but rather the impure and mixed status of the present fantasy of what is absent; that regret would not have the progressively attenuated meaning of the past, but rather the always current, always freshly renewed meaning of anxiety. But it is also understandable that the reopening of the universe that has passed, the discovery of its now outdated significations, restores to the patient her authentic temporality, opens her to the plenitude of the present and the urgency of what is to come. In existential psychotherapy, the past is not invoked to give a meaning to pathological absurdity and a content to its always empty present; it is elucidated only so that the present, by putting the past back into the distance, by considering it as authentically past, might go beyond it into the future.

We find something like the concrete image of this slipping of the past toward its actual anteriority in the fantasies developed by dreams over the course of the psychotherapy. The first dream after the beginning of the treatment had shown to the patient her dead friend's face appearing suddenly in the middle of a house in flames. In a later dream, the setting of the fire was replaced by a winter landscape, of glacial harshness: Lina is in a car that stops; a man gets in; the car turns onto a steep road; it races downhill at breakneck speed; at the moment when Lina arrives at the peak of her anxiety, the road changes and the car continues on its way at a much slower pace. This transition from dreams of fire to dreams of ice, this transformation of anxiety in the face of burning life into anxiety in the face of cold death are the echo in her imaginary life of her healing in real life. Death is taken seriously, a cold and obscure thing, vertiginous descent; and from now on, it will no longer be denied in the fantasies of a survival that is elusive but burning. The work of mourning in the survivor thus does not consist in detaching the libido from its vanished object, as Freud had it, but rather, as Binswanger observes, in totally modifying the existential modalities, in assuming in life the existence of the dead person, not in an imaginary and paradoxical persistence but as an absence populated by memories that accumulate little by little in the depths of the past.[rr]

But this backward movement of death into the past, which is for Lina the path of healing, can only occur if temporality has found once again its authentic root, its essential openness onto

---

rr Binswanger, *Grundformen und Erkenntnis*, 167–85.

the future. And it is in the living, concrete, current relationship of the patient to the physician that this originary orientation is found anew. In psychoanalysis, the figure of the physician is experienced by the patient in a paradoxical mode: he is simultaneously that absolute figure that the abstraction of the psychoanalytic décor removes from any insertion into real life and that relative, transitory, polymorphous figure to which transference gives in succession the faces of old childish myths. If the patient's relationship with the physician is challenged and elucidated by the analysis, it is insofar as it [is] haunted by previous fantasies, for which it is the chosen milieu; it is therefore insofar as it is taken by the patient to be what, in reality, it is not; but insofar as it is a relationship between a physician—taken in his medical capacity—and a patient who, as a patient, comes to ask him for help and succor, then it constitutes an absolute situation in which both protagonists are caught, without any opportunity ever arising to illuminate, develop, or transform it. [178]

In existential analysis the physician-patient relationship is experienced entirely differently. For the patient, the physician is not the figure that incarnates the past, but rather the figure that opens the future, the figure that can make the impossible possible once again. Undoubtedly, in existential psychotherapy we find transference phenomena in the most classic psychoanalytic sense. Once Lina lost all trust in her father, she locked herself up in an attitude of secrecy that she replicated, on several occasions, with her physician. During psychotherapy she had met a young man, Catholic like her, with whom she went out very regularly; for many weeks she hides this friendship from the physician; but she frequently has anxious dreams (she is with two of her sisters on a glacier; suddenly she finds herself alone, it is very dark; she loses her balance, slips and then sinks. In another dream, she is pursued by a monkey that transforms into a devil). She then decides to tell her psychiatrist about her new relationship: and soon after, she describes the hatred she feels for her father. We can see the process: first she acted with the physician by showing him the same mistrust she shows her father. But then the physician can no longer offer the help she was seeking: she makes this "miracle" that she was awaiting—without entirely believing in it—at the beginning of her treatment impossible. It is once she has abandoned her attitude of secrecy that she can express and relive all of her hatred for her father. It is not because the transference occurred that the elucidation of the past was made possible; on the contrary, [it was possible] because it was not able to occur, because the physician imposed his figure as a real, living man whose well-meaning help was required, in whom one does not find the past because, in reality, one awaits the future. The psychotherapeutic relationship is effective not insofar as it restores former relationships, but insofar as it creates new ones: it constitutes, as Binswanger puts it, a new *Mitmenschensein*.[ss] And this is how we must interpret Binswanger's healing of a hysterical woman.

It was a patient who presented with compulsive movements of the torso and the neck which were so violent that it was necessary to administer chloroform when they occurred in close succession. Despite the excellent connection between the physician and the patient, it had not been possible to relate these phenomena to the subject's biography. And, during a particularly violent attack, Binswanger approaches the patient and squeezes her throat: in order to be able to breathe, she makes a swallowing movement, and the series of compulsive movements interrupts itself. From this gesture the psychotherapy was made possible, a new relation with the other established itself, through the intervention of the

---

ss ["Being-with."] Binswanger, "Über Psychotherapie."

medical figure, bursting into her concrete reality in the middle of the pathological universe.

And we grasp the second difference between the figure of the Freudian analyst and that of the psychotherapist as Ludwig Binswanger or Roland Kuhn conceives it: [the psychotherapist] is not the absolute figure we were discussing in relation to psychoanalysis, but on the contrary a real figure who really intervenes—in other words, who takes risks in the patient's world and who, on the basis of the elucidation of existential structures, acts according to the patient's real possibilities. Binswanger's gesture, as a physician's real, brutal intervention, was effective—or rather was executed by the physician—only insofar as the analysis had revealed enough potential for it to be well received by the patient such that its violence would elicit no reaction of hatred and crystallize no masochistic symptom. The physician abandons the mask of indifference prescribed by analysis: he intervenes directly, concretely, in the illness; he presents himself to the patient as a figure of dialogue, and not as the mirror in which, in psychoanalysis, the patient's monologue is reflected. [180]

The physician's role in existential psychoanalysis is thus more important and lesser than in psychoanalysis: lesser because he is no longer the absolute figure, imaginary dialectician of silence; more important because the patient, on the path that leads him once again to the springtime of the world, encounters the well-meaning and familiar figure of the physician.

*

Psychoanalysis could debate all of this and—sticking only to the facts—highlight certain recent trends in the therapeutic method among the analysts themselves: it could show in the works of

Karen Horney[tt] [22] or in those of Alexander[uu] [23] an effort, parallel to that of existential analysis, to orient the treatment less toward the total recovery of the past than toward the opening of future possibilities; to transform the psychoanalyst from the thaumaturge he was in the Freudian tradition into a real partner in a real situation, into a concrete interlocutor in a dialogue that continues and extends the problems of concrete existence. Existential analysis would thereby not be so opposed to Freudian psychoanalysis as it might like to be: the former might simply be taking up the looser methods that the latter has now been practicing for some time.

One day, these convergences might appear highly significant, and history can give them the solemnity and gravity of necessity. But if, by methodological probity, we stay within the perspective of existential anthropology, it must be recognized that they are only superficial and contingent. Because the methods of psychoanalysis, even loosened, still postulate that the patient's relationship to the physician is on the order of libidinal investment: the physician's attitude still expresses itself in terms of frustration and satisfaction, and healing still takes the form of an economic reorganization; the affective charges have [been] displaced, the inhibitions have been lifted, the system of satisfactions has been adapted to the subject's situation.

We find no trace of this in existential analysis: for it, the essential aspect of the encounter between the physician and the patient is not its libidinal innuendos and that which gives it its signification in the patient's biography, but rather it is the encounter's anthropological foundation, and that which makes it possible as a confrontation and conjunction of two existences.

---

tt Karen Horney, *New Ways in Psychoanalysis* (New York: W. W. Norton, 1939).
uu [The note is missing; Foucault does not provide any reference.]

The final foundation of therapy is also the foundation of the encounter. Therapy must no longer seek its model in the sexual relationship, but rather elucidate its foundation as an existential relationship.

No doubt this is where *Daseinsanalyse* finds itself confronted with its central problem: it is at this point that, no longer guided by its polemical intention and its critique of other forms of reflection on man and on illness, it is constrained to assume its own choice.

Indeed, in order to elucidate this problem of the encounter, it must choose between a return to the problem of expression, to the analysis of language,[24] to an investigation of this objective sphere in which meaning acquires the compact solidity that allows for understanding and recognition, and a metaphysical recourse to the classic theme of love as a fundamental possibility of forging a relationship between existences that roots itself in them but at the same time goes beyond them.

[182]

This second solution would require many modifications to the conceptual apparatus put into place by existential analysis so far: to Heideggerian themes, it would be necessary to add an old metaphysics of love, now paired with a Plato who had been converted, baptised, and sanctified by the Church Fathers; it would be necessary to accept, for existence, the possibility of going beyond [the] facticity of being-in-the-world, and this inside the world itself; it would be necessary to suppose an "*In-der-Welt-über-die-Welt-hinaus-sein*"; it would be necessary to establish, above existence, the *Dasein*, a *Wirsein*, an ontological "we"; it would be necessary to confer specific existential structures upon it, and to substitute the unity of the eternal instant to the temporal ecstasies of the past, present, and future.[vv] Finally, it

---

vv Binswanger, *Grundformen und Erkenntnis*, 84.

would be necessary to analyze in this going-beyond not an existential possibility that opens itself up, but an existential obligation that imposes itself (not a *Seinkönnen*,[ww] but a *Seindürfen*[xx]),[yy] or in other words, to superimpose an ethical reflection onto ontological and anthropological reflection. So many themes that are rejected in Heideggerian thought, and which seem to express the bad religious conscience of a school of thought that does not have the courage of its own thinking; so many themes that engage the reflection on man in a metaphysical impasse.

[183]

Conversely, the first solution—the rigorous analysis of the phenomenon of expression—could lead quite far: it would be, indeed, a matter of studying language inasmuch as it heals, which is to say inasmuch as it is a language of dialogue, an objective language; it is not, indeed, a matter of studying incoherent expression, where meaning undoubtedly emerges, but does so only at the moment when it is expressed, it would be necessary to study this language of man to man that is understood in the moment when it is spoken, and which nevertheless continues to contain a meaning when the conversations have ended or the books are closed. It would be necessary to consider the objective forms of expression, and the historical contents it encloses: these real relations between men that make it possible give it at each moment its appearance and its style, and they are the concrete condition of a concrete relationship between the physician and his patient. But such considerations, it is too obvious, would make the framework of existential analysis explode: it would

---

ww ["Ability to be" in the sense of a capacity (Mendel and Lyons translate this as "being-able-to-be"; see note below—Trans.)]

xx ["Ability to be" in the sense of having the right (Mendel and Lyons translate this as "being-allowed-to-be"—Trans.)]

yy Binswanger, "The Case of Ellen West: An Anthopological-Clinical Study," trans. Werner M. Mendel and Joseph Lyons, in *Existence: A New Dimension in Psychiatry and Psychology*, ed. Rollo May, Ernest Angel, and Henri F. Ellenberger (Basic Books, 1958), 312.

entail the reduction all of the idealism it contains to concrete historical problems.

In any case, what lies before *Daseinsanalyse*, at the end of its speculation on its therapeutics, is a choice that will require it to abandon its initial horizon. It is a matter of choosing between history and eternity, between the concrete communication of [184] men and the metaphysical communion of consciousnesses, between immanence and transcendence; in short, between a philosophy of love and an analysis of the phenomena of expression, between metaphysical speculation and objective reflection.[25]

Binswanger opted for speculation and the philosophy of love.[26] In his great theoretical work, *Grundformen der Existenz*,[zz][27] he devoted a great many pages to love: his good intentions manifest themselves in and are authenticated by the boredom they evince; like everything that is made to be moving, they do not go far, and if they have another goal, they miss it.[28]

But it is more interesting to see the opposition between the analysis of expression and the philosophy of love in relation to a special case: the problem of art and aesthetic phenomena. There more than elsewhere the reality of this opposition is affirmed, and *Daseinsanalyse*'s choice is made clear.

NOTES

1. The concept of *"Verweltlichung"* [mundanization] is discussed by Binswanger in his studies on schizophrenia, especially in "The Case of Lola Voss," trans. Ernest Angel, in *Being-in-the-World: Selected Papers of Ludwig Binswanger*, ed. Jacob Needleman (Basic Books, 1963), 266–341. In a reading note dedicated to this clinical case study and the ones preceding it, Foucault remarks, "In the case of Lola Voss, as in the others, there

---

zz [Foucault is referring to *Grundformen und Erkenntnis menschlichen Daseins*.]

is *Verweltlichung*: i.e., the *Dasein* falls out of its "*eigentlichen, freien Selbstseinkönnen*" [its authentic, free power of being oneself] and becomes prey (*anheimfallen*) to a specific *Weltentwurf* [world-project]; it is overwhelmed (*Überwaltigen*) by it. It is the *Geworfenheit* [thrownness], characterized by Heidegger as the omnipotence of the *On* (*Gereden* [gossip]; *Neugier* [curiosity]; *Zweideutigkeit* [equivocation]). (But here, in the case of Lola Voss, it is a *Geworfenheit* of the mythical *Dasein*.) In this *Verweltlichung*, the *Idealbildung* [ideal image] plays a principal role: indeed, far from widening or deepening the *Selbstseinkönnen* [power to be oneself], this presumptuous (*verstiegene*) *Idealbildung* limits it to the vise (*Schraubstock*) of a *Weltentwurf*. This lack of agreement (*Einklang*) between the Ideal and the *Wirklichkeit* [reality] is what we call schizophrenia" (BNF, Box 42b, folder 1). Furthermore, in a reading note entitled "*Daseinsanalyse* and psychopathology," Foucault writes in reference to the Jürg Zünd case: "What is interesting in psychopathology starts here: it speaks of symptoms, of *Krankheitserscheinungen*, of stereotypical behavior, of dissociation of personality, of autism, etc. These are categories applied to man from the exterior: they serve to classify, to diagnose. All this is interesting when the "*Verweltlichung des Selbst*" [mundanization of the self] occurs, there were it is no longer possible to speak of existence and of love; when patients have ceased to be free *Selbst*. It is the patients themselves who come to engage in the psychopathological dialectic that reduces them to the *naturwissenschaftlich* [of the natural sciences] level" (BNF, Box 38, folder 1). See Ludwig Binswanger, "Studien zu Schizophrenie Problem. Zweite Studie. Der Fall Jürg Zünd," *Schweizer Archiv für Neurologie und Psychiatrie* 59 (1947): 21–36.

2. Here Foucault refers quite explicitly to Sartre's study of Baudelaire, in which he claims specifically that "the free choice which a man makes of himself is completely identified with what is called his destiny." See Jean-Paul Sartre, *Baudelaire*, trans. Martin Turnell (New Directions, 1950 [1947]), 192. In a manuscript from the 1950s entitled "L'agressivité, l'angoisse et la magie" [Aggressiveness, Anxiety, and Magic], Foucault analyzes the paradoxical relations between psychology and philosophy: "phenomenology," he notes, "was born and nourished by a critique of psychology." He goes on to say that "contemporary existentialism—Sartre in his *Baudelaire*—played the same game with freedom: by protecting pure freedom from any objective determination, it can assert it in the most concrete existence, and call

on psychoanalysis, or psychopathology, to discover freedom and its project in advance of any psychological constitution" (BNF, Box 46, folder 4).

3. See on this topic Foucault's critique of the notion of totality in *Maladie mentale et personnalité* (PUF, 1954), 11–12: "In all these recent forms of medical analysis, therefore, one can read a single meaning: the more one regards the unity of the human being as a whole, the more the reality of an illness as a specific unity disappears and the more the description of the individual reacting to his situation in a pathological way replaces the analysis of the natural forms of the illness. By means of the unity that it provides and the problems that it eliminates, this notion of totality is well adapted to introduce into pathology an atmosphere of conceptual euphoria. It was from this atmosphere that those who had to any extent been inspired by Goldstein wished to benefit. But, unfortunately, the euphoria was not matched by an equal rigor." This passage is unchanged in *Mental Illness and Psychology*, trans. Alan Sheridan (University of California Press, 1987), 9. In a preparatory typescript for this book, Foucault added to this passage a footnote in which he mentions Merleau-Ponty's *The Structure of Behavior*, trans. Alden L. Fisher (Beacon Press, 1963) and Canguilhem's *Essay on Some Problems Concerning the Normal and the Pathological*, Section One of *The Normal and the Pathological*, trans. Carolyn R. Fawcett with Robert S. Cohen (Zone Books, 1991) (BNF, call number 28803). This footnote does not appear in the final version of *Maladie mentale et personnalité*.

4. This same passage appears in a reading note Foucault drafted during this time, which takes its title from one of the final paragraphs of Binswanger's *Über Ideenflucht*: "The *Daseinanalytic* method" (BNF, Box 42b, folder 1). This reading note is a part of a series of eight double-sided sheets of paper devoted precisely to this work. Lacan was the first in France to mention this study, in "The Problem of Style and the Psychiatric Conception of Paranoiac Forms of Experience," trans. Jon Anderson, *Critical Texts* 5, no. 3 (1988): "The phenomenologically inspired work on these mental states (for example the most recent work of a Ludwig Binswanger on the state called 'flight of ideas' that one observes in manic-depressive psychosis, or my own work on *Paranoiac Psychosis in Relation to Personality*) does not detach the local reaction, which is most often noticeable only through some pragmatic discordance, specifiable as mental disorder, from

the totality of the patient's lived experience, which such work tries to define in its originality. This experience . . . can be validly described as the coherent structure of an immediate noumenal apprehension of oneself and of the world" (translation modified). Lacan refers to "Binswanger's great study on *Ideenflucht*" in 1935 in his review of Minkowski's *Le temps vécu* in *Recherches Philosophiques*, no. 5 (1935–36): 428.

5. See on this topic Foucault's reading note about Binswanger's *Über Ideenflucht*, entitled "The *Daseinsanalytic* method," in which he writes: "1. Starting from a clinical and psychiatric point of view, to liberate each theme from the purely clinical framework, so as to consider it from the totality of the theme that is man. It is a matter of understanding it as a proper and *eigentümlicher* [singular] mode of the human *Dasein*, as a proper and *eigentümlicher* existential possibility. It is the anthropological method, which consists in considering a particular domain of the human *Sein* apart from the totality of the theme of *man*. It is the idea of *man* that operates the transition—through deduction, in depth study, and the drawing of connections—from a prescientific phenomenon of the *Menschsein* to an anthropological scientific phenomenon (such as nature, or life for the facts of the natural or biological sciences). 2. In this idea of agglomeration, it is not a matter of a unity of "*lieblich-seelisch-geistig*," but rather of the idea of *Existentialität* [existentiality], as of a link between the ontological structures that constitute existence. Therefore the anthropology in question will be existential anthropology" (BNF, Box 42b, folder 1).

6. Jakob von Uexküll develops this concept especially in his 1909 book *Umwelt und Innenwelt der Tiere* (Springer, 1909).

7. Here Foucault picks up on arguments made by Binswanger in his article "The Existential Analysis School of Thought," especially in Section II, "The Differentiation Between Human Existence and Animal Being: "World" in Its Existential Analytical, and "World Around" (*Umwelt*) in Its Biological Meaning," 195–200.

8. Paul Häberlin (1878–1960): He taught philosophy and pedagogy, first in Bern from 1914 to 1922, then in Basel until 1947. He had a strong influence on Binswanger, who always considered him one of the most noteworthy philosophical figures in his training. His voluminous correspondence with Binswanger is a testament to their personal and intellectual relationship; through it we can trace the evolution of *Daseinsanalyse* from

its founding. See *Briefwechsel. 1908–1960*, ed. Jeannine Luczak (Schwabe, 1997). Foucault's archives from the 1950s contain a folder on Häberlin, which holds reading notes about the following works by the philosopher: *Der Gegenstand der Psychologie. Eine Einführung in das Wesen der empirischen Wissenschaft* (Springer, 1921) and *Der Mensch. Eine philosophische Anthropologie* (Schweizer Spiegel, 1941) (BNF, Box 42b, folder 1). In addition, other reading notes are devoted to the following studies: "Der Gegenstand der Psychiatrie," *Schweizer Archiv für Neurologie und Psychiatrie* 60, nos. 1–2 (1947):132–44; and *Der Charakter* (Kober, 1925) (BNF, Box 33a, folder 0; Box 38, folder 1). Häberlin's anthropological studies *Der Mensch* and *Der Charakter* are also mentioned by Foucault in the manuscripts of the lectures that he gave on anthropology at Lille and at the École normale supérieure in the early 1950s (see BNF, Box 46, folder 1). A modified version of *Der Mensch* had been published in French in 1943 in a translation by the Swiss philosopher Pierre Thévenaz; see Paul Haeberlin, *Anthropologie philosophique*, trans. Pierre Thévenaz (PUF, 1943). Thévenaz was very active in the French phenomenological debates of the 1950s: in 1951, he gave a talk alongside Maurice Merleau-Ponty, Paul Ricoeur, and Jean Wahl at the International Phenomenology Colloquium organized at the Husserl Archives in Louvain; see *Problèmes actuels de la phénoménologie*, ed. H. L. Van Breda (Desclée de Brouwer, 1952). He had also written an article on Häberlin's thought in 1940: "Remarques sur l'être, l'individu et le concret," *Revue de théologie et de philosophie* 28, no. 117 (1940): 350–58.

9. In a reading note dedicated to Häberlin's book *Der Gegenstand der Psychologie*, Foucault observes: "Psychology, as a science with its proper object, and its *Erkenntnisprinzip* [principle of understanding], tries to liberate itself as much as possible from the natural sciences to become a "psychological psychology." This is what Freud tried to do from the natural sciences; Dilthey and Spranger attempted the same thing in taking the *Geisteswissenschaften* [human sciences] as a foundation; Jaspers aims at a "*verstehende Psychologie*" [comprehensive psychology] for itself. All have the same goal: a psychology that is empirical without being "*naturwissenschaftlich*" [based on the natural sciences] (this is different from Natorp whose psychology does not seek to be empirical). Now this psychology lacks a philosophical foundation. It is like a man who seeks his path without having a clear consciousness of it. This is why it uses concepts borrowed

from the natural sciences like so much residue. Häberlin's task is: the philosophical foundation of a *"verstehenden Psychologie"* freed from the natural sciences. But Häberlin also wants it to be a psychology" (BNF, Box 42b, folder 1). On this topic, see the similar observation that Foucault makes in a footnote of his introduction to "Dream and Existence," when he cites the preface of Häberlin's study *Der Mensch* as an important example of how it might be possible to circumscribe "the working dimensions of anthropology . . . [in opposition] to any type of psychological positivism claiming to exhaust the significant content of man by the reductive concept of *homo natura.*" See Michel Foucault, "Dream, Imagination and Existence," trans. Forrest Williams, in *Dream and Existence*, ed. Keith Hoeller (Humanities Press, 1993), 31.

10. In a reading note entitled "Ontology and anthropology," Foucault observes, quoting Binswanger, that "Heidegger's analytic concerns *Dasein überhaupt* [in general]. "Insofar as we limit our research to human *Dasein*, and that we do not consider *Dasein überhaupt*, our research distinguishes itself as anthropological from Heidegger's ontological perspective. On the other hand, in the course of our research it will become ever more obvious that any research that must be termed anthropological is not possible without the *Berücksichtigung* [taking into consideration] of the ontological method.'" See Ludwig Binswanger, *Grundformen und Erkenntnis menschlichen Daseins*, 33 (BNF, Box 33a, folder 0).

11. See on this topic the reading note entitled "The *Daseinsanalytic* method," where Foucault remarks, "While fundamental ontology has the goal of analyzing the *Grundstrukturen* [fundamental structures] of *Dasein*, by orienting themselves specifically toward the *Seinsproblem* [problem of being], existential anthropology [Foucault writes "l'anthropologie existentielle/ale"] has the goal of studying "false" existential possibilities, which the *Dasein* has chosen itself, into which it has sunk, or in which it has awakened (*hineingeratenaufgewachsen*) [engaged itself-grew]" (BNF, Box 42b, folder 1).

12. On the theme of the link between *Daseinsanalyse* and "experience," see Foucault's reading note about Wilhelm Szilasi's article on the experiential foundation of *Daseinsanalyse*: "Die Erfahrungsgrundlage der Daseinsanalyse Binswangers," *Schweizer Archiv für Neurologie und Psychiatrie* 67, no. 1 (1951): 64–82. Foucault writes: "1st question: what sort of experience is

the study of human *Daseinsformen*? *Daseinsanalyse* is a descriptive empirical discipline. To that extent, it concerns everything that determines our place inside being. Taken scientifically, this place must be characterised as "*die Welt*" and, in its transcendental form, as "*das In-der-Welt-sein*." But no transcendental reflection or reflection about fundamental ontology can be carried out successfully if it does not find a sufficiently large basis in natural experience. . . . 2nd question: what is this phenomenologico-empirical discipline's relation to transcendental reflection's forms of experience (*Erfahrungsweise*)? In the natural explanation (*Verstandigung*) that expresses itself, there is an *Anleitung* [directive] for natural ontology. Binswanger's empirical knowledge seeks a transcendental foundation: not a fundamental ontology, but a *Zwischenlage* [intermediary position] in transcendental experience. "This experience is not an anthropology, nor is it a phenomenological anthropology; it is an experience with its own depth and its own objectivity; in this objectivity that the psychological is elucidated." . . . 3rd question: in what way does *Daseinsanalyse* designate the framework of transcendental objective experience possible in the *Daseinsverlauf* [existential trajectory]? By "nature," we must not understand objective and mechanical nature, but rather the Greek meaning of *phusis*: "*das in jedem gegenständlichen erfahrene zum Vorschein-kommen-lassen*" [the letting-come-to-appear that we experience in every objective thing]. In the same way we must understand *Leben* as *bios*, not in the sense of biology but in that of biography" (BNF, Box 42b, folder 1).

13. In the early 1950s, Foucault dedicated many reading notes to Margaret Mead (1901–1978) (BNF, Box 44b, folder 4) and Abram Kardiner (1891–1981) (BNF, Box 38, folder 4). On the young Foucault's interest in cultural anthropology, see Jean-François Bert's "Michel Foucault défenseur de l'ethnologie. 'La magie—le fait social total,' une leçon inédite des années 1950" (*Zilsel* 2, no. 2 (2017), 281–303).

14. Here Foucault is referring to the article "Psychotherapie als Beruf," *Der Nervenarzt* 1 (1927): 138–45 and 206–15, which he mentions in a reading note about the distinction between "*Lebensfunktion*" and "*innere Lebensgeschichte*" (see Binswanger's "Lebensfunktion und innere Lebensgeschichte," *Monatsschrift für Psychiatrie und Neurologie* 68 (1928): 52–79; reprinted in *Ausgewählte Vorträge und Aufsätze*, vol. 1, *Zur phänomenologischen Anthropologie* (Francke, 1947), 50–73) (BNF, Box 38, folder 1).

15. On this point, see a manuscript fragment from the 1950s entitled "An Example of Psychoanalysis: The Wolf Man. The Notion of a Psychoanalytic Milieu" (BNF, Box 46, folder 4), where Foucault writes: "*Introduction.* Classic distinction between Freudian practice and theory. In reality, the practice is *intervention* and the analysis of the intervention must clarify:
- The explicit meaning, wanted by the person intervening;
- The *real* meaning of what has *actually* intervened.

There will thus be:
- The facts: the consciousness of the illness, the healing;
- Between them, the process, and in this process, there is simultaneously:
  - That on which one intervenes;
  - That which actually intervenes.

Hence: to dissociate the unity of Freudian practice; to free it from the dogmatism of healing. Healing is a fact, not a proof. Problem of blind practices, in which success precedes the truth of this success, where the truth anticipates the truth; there the intention is exceeded by the real meaning, but it ceaselessly tends to make it unreal.

. . . *Conclusion:*

1. Psychoanalytic practice is not a homogeneous whole. There is no need to accept or refuse it as a block. It belongs to those blind practices in which:
- There is a positivity, which is the reason for their progress; there is a certain "*Wirklichkeit*" [reality];
- But this positivity is not yet for itself its own light: it is lit only from the exterior. The practice never has the obviousness of a fact.

2. The paradox of these blind practices is that the progress of their effectiveness, of their positivity, is not always a measure of the progress of their rationality.
- Example of alchemy: its irrationality grew alongside its positivity (von Helmholtz); [example] of pedagogy: in Weimar Germany.
- Similarly, psychoanalysis sees its positivity develop, but without its rationality increasing as a result.

   1. Psychoanalysis is now in a position to think itself in the mode of interaction with the milieu: whence its pedagogical character. But there is enough to make a sociology of policing out of it.

2. At the same time, it knows its imaginary character: it knows the relativity of the concept of illness. But these concepts and these methods can be perverted. While in Freud's errors, there was maybe a certain rationalism that, as erroneous as it was in relation to the truth of its practice, was a guarantee of its use:
  - A certain idea of man's biological needs;
  - [a certain idea] of the rationality of man's normal development...

3. But reflection on psychoanalytic practice, in its positive aspects, can undoubtedly show where the rationality will come from that will transform this blind practice into a practice that is sure of itself.
  - We have seen it result in pedagogical problems, either through the notion of illness, or through that of relearning, or through that of the reactive milieu;
  - And in the end it is to a science of real development and of the conditions of this development that psychoanalysis should refer:
    • The science sketched out in the *Three Essays* is in reality founded only on a false interpretation of practice (on the myths of this practice);
    • This science will need to constitute itself in the mode of a real analysis of the requirements and conditions of life."

16. In his reading notes of the 1950s, Foucault devotes two double-sided sheets of paper to Binswanger's article "Karl Jaspers und die Psychiatrie": "—Constant preoccupation of a respect in the face of the "*Unendlichkeit* [infinity] of the individual"; which in psychopathology excludes both idealism and positivism: positivism because it takes mental illness as a *Naturprozess* [natural process]; idealism because it disdains (*verwerfet*) mental illness as foreign to reality in its false representations (*Philosophy* I, 243). It is beyond idealism and positivism that human connections and debates with the patient are instantiated. Which does not mean pity (*Mitleid*). "Spreading oneself out in pity, in general *Menschenliebe* [love for humans], where there is suffering in general, is the extreme opposite of love: in that case one never aims at an individual, at the absolute; one aims only at oneself" (Karl Jaspers, *Psychologie der Weltanschauungen*, 112)" (BNF, Box 38, folder 1). A file entitled "Binswanger (texts)" holds another reading note on the topic

of "*Trieb* and *Geist*" [drive and spirit] that mentions this article (BNF, Box 38, folder 1).

17. In reality, Binswanger cites Goldstein quite frequently and explicitly in his works: see especially *Über Ideenflucht*, which Foucault knew, but also the essay "The Existential Analysis School of Thought," which is also cited by Foucault in this manuscript. It is therefore strange that Foucault reproaches Binswanger for not citing Goldstein, especially since in a reading note he observes, summarizing this article in Binswanger's words: "Man is thrown into his being—and to this extent he also has an *Umwelt* like the animal—, and yet he has the possibility of transcending this *Sein* which is his, i.e., of climbing beyond it (*übersteigen*) in care and of swinging beyond it (*überschwingen*) in love. Von Weizsäcker's conception is still closer. Similarly with Goldstein's" (BNF, Box 38, folder 1; the passage Foucault is paraphrasing appears on pp. 198–99 of "The Existential Analysis School of Thought"). The relationship between Binswanger and Goldstein goes back to the 1920s, as a voluminous correspondence between 1925 and 1960 attests; it is conserved in the Binswanger archives at the University of Tübingen in Germany. Goldstein was among the many visitors who went to Kreuzlingen to visit the sanatorium during Ludwig Binswanger's tenure as its director; see Max Herzog, *Weltentwürfe. Ludwig Binswangers phänomenologische Psychologie* (De Gruyter, 1994), 19. It is thanks to Binswanger, moreover, that Roland Kuhn also became familiar with Goldstein's theories, to which he dedicated training courses for physicians in Münsterlingen in the early 1960s; see Roland Kuhn, *Münsterlinger Kolloquien*, vol. 4, *Kurt Goldstein. Aufbau des Organismus (1963–1965)* (Königshausen & Neumann, 2014). See also Heinrich G. Müldner, "Roland Kuhn: Zum Problem der ganzheitlichen Betrachtung in der Medizin. Ein Beitrag zum 50. Todestag Kurt Goldsteins," *Neurologie & Rehabilitation* 21, no. 6 (2015): 311–16.

18. Here too, Foucault follows Binswanger closely. Binswanger notes in *Über Ideenflucht*, "K. Goldstein was the first neurologist to see—and only against the backdrop of the empirical view of things—that a "pathological" behavior can only be understood from its new "being in the world" and that it is only starting from this being that the rupture can be sensibly comprehensible. Jackson, von Monakow, Head had recognized that the destruction of a function, for example in aphasia, does not unfold without rules but that it seems to regulate itself according to a determined norm. . . . In this way,

the concept of the pathological effectively took a new turn. Now it was no longer the expression for something purely negative, in other words the contrary of the norm, but it also allowed itself to be conceived positively, precisely starting from the norm." See *Schweizer Archiv fur Neurologie und Psychiatrie* 28 (1932): 201.

19. On dialectical reconciliation understood as the essence of therapy, see Foucault's reading note on Binswanger's essay "Über Psychotherapie": "*In which manner* can a psychotherapy act *in actuality* (*tatsächlich*)? The "*Arztsein*" [being a physician] adds something to the *Mitmenschensein* [being-with]: what? This something new depends on medico-psychological knowledge, and on the action consistent with this knowledge. *Arztsein* and *Mitmenschensein* are in a dialectical relationship to each other. The dialectic between the maternal foundation (*Mutterboden*) of any psychotherapy (point of view of the *Lebensgeschichte*) and the understanding of the psyche as an *Organismus* (point of view of the *Lebensfunktion*) constitutes psychotherapy's dialectic. "Communication within existence, and the action that has as its goal the liberation of biologico-psychological forms, constitute the two dialectical poles of medical psychotherapy." This is why the psychotherapist can neither be purely the patient's friend nor the person at the service of a cause (135)" (BNF, Box 38, folder 1). The concept of existential elucidation (*Existenzerhellung*) such as Binswanger uses it is mentioned by Foucault in his discussion of Binswanger's article "Karl Jaspers und die Psychiatrie." See the reading note entitled "Jaspers and psychiatry," in which he observes, "The highest aim of psychotherapeutic action is the call to personality: helping the man become more *durchsichtig* [transparent] to himself. Whence the themes of *Existenzerhellung*, and of existential communication. Becoming more *durchsichtig* does not mean knowing oneself better; neither is it what one can attain through psychoanalysis; it is what can be done only in the *Geist* and by (*durch*) the *Geist* (Jaspers, *Philosophy* I, 239); and which is possible only in *geschichtlich* [historic] communication with another existence. "The physician is neither a technician nor a savior (*Heiland*), but an existence for an existence, a transitory *Menschenwesen* [being of man] with another" (Jaspers, *Philosophy* I, 155 [the last phrase is rendered as "mortal like the other" in the English translation]). The psychiatrist must have a *Weltanschauung* [vision of the world], but this does not mean that the physician must impose his *Weltanschauung* on the patient; in

reality, it is on the contrary the broadness of the horizon, the aptitude to be temporarily "*Wertungsfrei*" [neutral], to be "*vorurteilslos*" [without prejudice], aptitude which is found only in men who have, furthermore, strong originary *Wertungen* [appreciations] and a well-minted (*ausgeprägte*) *Weltanschauung*. The physician must be able to give a philosophical account of what he means by health (*Gesundheit*)." See Karl Jaspers, *Allgemeine Psychopathologie*, 439 (BNF, Box 42b, folder 1).

20. This is precisely the argument that Foucault develops in his introduction to *Dream and Existence*, when he pleads for a theory which "reinstates in its necessity the immanence of the meaning to the image" ("Dream, Imagination and Existence," 38).

21. The concept of "*Existenzerhellung*"—which Foucault translates as "élucidation de l'existence"—is the object of a series of reading notes devoted to Jaspers's philosophical work. The second volume of Jaspers's three-volume *Philosophie* (Springer, 1932) was precisely entitled *Existenzerhellung*; for the English translation, see *Philosophy*, vol. 2, *Existential Elucidation*, trans. E. B. Ashton (University of Chicago Press, 1970). See especially the note entitled "*Daseinsanalyse* and *Existenzerhellung*," in which Foucault reproduces the following quotations: "In reverting from each distinct being to *Dasein* as the all-encompassing consciousness (*allumfassenden*) . . . philosophy brought to mind the rudiments of a *Daseinsanalyse* [analysis of existence]. In reverting from the being in general, as *Objektsein* [object-being] in the world to Existence, it determines the task of an *Existenzerhellung*. . . . *Daseinsanalyse* as such is not obligatory from the point of view of existence (*existenziell unverbindlich* [in the English translation, "is existentially noncommittal"]) . . . it shows "*das Allgemeine des Daseins*" [the general of *Dasein*; in the English translation, "the universal of existence"]. In existential analysis everyone will recognize himself, not as this individual (*Einzelne*) but as an *Ich überhaupt* [I at large or in general]. . . . *Existenzerhellung*, on the other hand, involves commitment. It "*Sprache des Einzelnen zum Einzelnen*" [speaks from the individual to the individual]. Instead of general intuitions (*Einsichten*) about possible elucidations (*Erhellungen*), it shows the potential of the individual (*Einzelne*) in his unconditional roots and ends" (Jaspers, *Philosophy* I, 71; translation has been modified to reflect Foucault's French). "The clearer the *Daseinsanalyse*, the greater the possible *Existenzerhellung*. For the clarity of *Daseinsanalyse* will make me feel that

consciousness in its immanence flatly excludes myself, the self of which I am conscious. *Daseinsanalyse* becomes a *Grenzkonstruktion* [boundary construction] against *Existenzerhellung*" (Jaspers, *Philosophy* I, 71; BNF, Box 42b, folder 1). The concept of *Existenzerhellung* also appears in Hans Kunz's *Die anthropologische Bedeutung der Phantasie*, vol. 2, *Die anthropologische Deutung der Phantasie und ihre Voraussetzungen* (Recht und Gesellschaft, 1946), about which Foucault wrote a reading note entitled "Anthropological interpretation of the imagination"; he observes, "H. Heimsoeth said that there could not "be a closed system for a process that cannot be completed." The essence of man cannot be established once and for all, since man, as a free man, is not predetermined in his possibilities and his decisions, and therefore is inexhaustible. But it is false and untenable to deny, with the [exaggerations] of a speculative and transcendental apriorism, any constancy in the essential structures of the actual *Selbst*, in favor of an absolutely irrational flow (*Fliessen*). Philosophical anthropology refutes the pretense of allowing the satisfaction of the *Weltanschauung*'s security needs (*weltanschauungliches Sekuritätsbedürfnissen*). Andersen (*Das Existenzbegriff und das existenzielle Denken in der neueren Philosophie und Theologie* (Thienemann, 1940, 175)) says that existential elucidation (*Existenzerhellung*) does not lead to a point "of eternal validity," and that "we are still in the domain of validity of sin and instability (*Vergänglichkeit*), from which we cannot liberate ourselves"—Not only must anthropology recognize this, but it must persist in this renunciation . . ." (BNF, Box 42b, folder 1).

22. In one of the boxes in Foucault's archives containing his notes from the 1950s, there is a file dedicated to Karen Horney, which contains a reading note precisely entitled "Horney. New ways in psychoanalysis" (BNF, Box 38, folder 4). Many pages, moreover, discuss "Self-analysis" (See Karen Horney, *Self-Analysis* (W. W. Norton & Co., 1942)). The same box also contains a file entitled "Karen Horney. *New Ways in Psychoanalysis*—1934" [the English title here is Foucault's; the earlier reading note's title is translated from French—Trans.].

23. Franz G. Alexander (1891–1964) and Karen Horney (1885–1952) were both members of the Berlin Psychoanalytic Institute during the 1920s, before emigrating to the United States after the National Socialists' rise to power. Alexander founded the Chicago Institute for Psychoanalysis, which he co-directed with Horney for three years. In 1950, he presided

over the session of the Paris International Congress dedicated to "The Evolution and Present Trends of Psychoanalysis"; see *Congrès international de psychiatrie, Paris 1950*, vol. V: *Psychothérapie—Psychanalyse—Médecine psychosomatique* (Hermann, 1950), 1–28. In Foucault's archives from the 1950s dealing with psychoanalysis, there is a file devoted to Franz Alexander which contains a reading note entitled "New orientation of psychoanalysis." There Foucault remarks, "Psychoanalysis has great difficulty detaching itself from its origin—cathartic hypnosis—in order to give itself over entirely to the task it has now discovered for itself: emotional re-education. 1. It is still considered to be a "therapeutic act" on the patient that concerns only his past (as in the hypnosis session). In fact, analytic sessions must be considered as catalytic agents that make new experiences possible . . . ; to a certain extent the patient's daily life must be guided; the sessions must be considered as "shadow plays" of real life. In short, it is a question of forming or of reconstituting the ego's functional capacity. 2. Becoming conscious of memories is considered to be the determining factor, and the presence of unconscious memories is considered to be the cause of neurosis. Yet it has been shown that becoming conscious is only the result and not the cause of healing (see Rank, Ferenczi; Alexander, "Zur Genese des Kastrationskomplexes," *Internationale Zeitschrift für Psychanalyse* 16 (1930): 349–52): true therapeutic success occurs when the patient can master an unbearable emotional conflict in the transference relationship. Then, he becomes more permeable to memory. Under these conditions, memory is: α. the barometer of the ego's force in the face of emotional situations; β. It helps the patient discriminate between the present and the past. There can, however, be good therapeutic methods without becoming conscious of the past (*Psychoanalytic Therapy. Principles and Application* (The Ronald Press Company, 1946: 18–22)" (BNF, Box 38, folder 2). In another reading note from the same period, Foucault also mentions Alexander's book *Psychosomatic Medicine: Its Principles and Applications* (W. W. Norton, 1950), which he cites in its French translation (BNF, Box 44a).

24. The problem of expression, or rather of the expressive act, and of the analysis of the "structure of language, which dream experience, like every expressive fact, necessarily envelops" is at the heart of Foucault's introduction to "Dream and Existence" ("Dream, Imagination and Existence," 35).

25. Psychiatry's need to choose between metaphysical speculation and objective reflection had been illuminated in the early 1950s by the journal *La Raison. Cahiers de psychopathologie scientifique*. After the International Congress of Psychiatry in 1950, an editorial in the journal, while underscoring the "crisis in contemporary psychiatry," criticized the inaugural speech by Jean Delay, President of the Congress, for having put on the same level "the modern forms of speculative metaphysics" represented by "phenomenology and existential analysis" and the "most objective experimental scientific methods." See "Éditorial. Le Congrès international de psychiatrie et la crise de la psychiatrie contemporaine," *La Raison. Cahiers de psychopathologie scientifique* 2 (1951): 7.

26. Among the reading notes in the folder on Binswanger (BNF, Box 38, folder 1), Foucault dedicates two in particular to the theme of "love." In one of them, Foucault quotes: "Existence is already, in itself, a loving encounter, revelation of *you* for *me*, and of *me* for *you* in the *we*. It is only because things are so that I can find you and choose you reciprocally. The person who does not notice this, who does not see that those who love each other can find each other, that the plenitude and duration of their love are possible only on the basis of this originary possibility of the loving encounter, will be able to understand neither the supra-spatial nor the supra-temporal meaning of the "being together in love," nor the difference of this world in relation to that of care" (Binswanger, *Grundformen und Erkenntnis menschlichen Daseins*, 84). "In love, the body is transparence, transparence of you; the corporeal form belongs to the essential image and all partial corporeal forms are forms of love" (*Grundformen*, 448). In love, "existence does not understand itself starting from the world (of care), but starting from its foundation as gift, present, or grace" (*Grundformen*, 153). The "anthropological *Vorrang* [priority] goes by right to the *dualen Seinsmodus* [mode of being-two] of love, before all other modes of being in the world, before all the *Weltorientierungen* [orientations in the world] (Jaspers), all of the *Verzweckungen* [constraints] (Häberlin), and all anxious cares . . . inasmuch as love is not to be understood starting from anxiety on the one hand and intentionality on the other. On the contrary anxiety is to be understood starting from the *Zurückgeworfensein* [being-thrown-back] of the *Dasein* outside of the *liebenden Seinsicherheit* [security of being in love] and of the *Seinsverbundenheit* [connectedness of being] in the

necessity and heroism of existence, and intentionality is to be understood starting from the *Hineingeworfensein* [being-thrown-in] of the *Dasein* outside of the full *Bedeutsamkeit* [significance] of the being in the worldly *Einzelbedeutung* [univocity] of the object" (*Grundformen*, 640). In the other reading note, Foucault continues to quote: "The exact *Wirheit* [we-ness] is always masculine-feminine (*männlich-weiblich*) in the double sense that it itself is so, and that each of its members is so," since each member is "*schöpferischproduktiv*" [creative-productive] and "*schöpferisch-rezeptiv*" [creative-receptive]. "What is inconceivable, ungraspable in love represents a twofold wonder (*Wunder*): in addition to that of loving, that of being loved, and it is not that virile love encompasses the first, and feminine love the second; but each of the two particular forms of love has its own manner of living both wonders. In the highest love, the difference between masculine love and feminine love is *aufgehoben* [surmounted] in the twofold Hegelian sense of the term" (*Grundformen*, 683 and 115). "[The] dialectic of the world and of love . . . is balanced (*ausgeglichen*) where the loving beings have the power to grant to the [lightness] and occupation of care the weight and rest of love, to the seriousness of the *Weltarbeit* [work of the world] the happiness of its *Humor* [humor], and to the pride in success according to the world (*Welterfolge*) the knowledge of infinitude and the fact of holding oneself firmly in the mode of belief in eternity (*das gläubige Feststehen in der Ewigkeit*)" (*Grundformen*, 97). Foucault also devotes a reading note to "Love according to Jaspers" (BNF, Box 42b, folder 1), where he remarks that in love, "the object . . . , as indefinitely multiple as it can be in the concrete, is given in a specific manner: it is immediately plunged into the totality of the world, illuminated by a *Lichtstrahl* of the absolute, and linked to it. According to the Christian expression: the object is seen in God and not isolated (*vereinzelt*). It is not grasped as something finite, but as drowned (*eingebettet*) in the infinite. The *Einstellung* [attitude] goes toward the Everything. Since this everything as such can never be an object (*Gegenstand*) for the human spiritual structure, we reach toward it (*intendiert*) through a finite object that thereby holds itself in a particular glimmer (*Schimmer*), or rather it is itself the glimmer of the absolute"; see Karl Jaspers, *Psychologie der Weltanschauungen*, 3rd ed. (Springer, 1925 [1919]), 118).

27. This work is often mentioned by Foucault in the texts he published during the 1950s, as well as in his reading notes from that period. In a

reading note entitled "Binswanger, *Grundformen und Erkenntnis menschlichen Daseins*" (BNF, Box 38, folder 1), he writes, "Analysis according to Ellenberger," referring to Ellenberger's presentation of this book in a series of articles published in *L'Évolution psychiatrique* on the topic of "Swiss psychiatry"; see especially vol. 17, no. 2 (1952): 374–77. Another of Foucault's reading notes has the topic "R. Kuhn. Review of Binswanger, *Grundformen*," and Foucault notes, "In the *Grundformen*, Binswanger wants to grasp man in all of his *Dasein*. In addition to the "*Zu sich selber Sein*" [being beside oneself], there are the *mit-menschlichen* relationships (the *duale* and the *plurale Daseinsmodus*). The first accomplishes itself in love; the second, in the "*Nehmen des Andern bei etwas*" [taking the other as something]. In the me-you relationship, Binswanger sees the "*Ürphänomen des Menschseins*" [originary phenomenon of being human]: it is fundamental in relation to the *Daseinsweisen räumlichen* [spatial and temporal modes of being]. Binswanger writes, "We can see that the loving *Miteinandersein* [being one with the other], love holds itself '*frierend*' [frozen] outside the door of this project of being" (about Heidegger). Binswanger does not seek to constitute a philosophical ontology like Heidegger, "he does not talk about *Dasein* as such, but about human *Dasein*; he seeks to make an anthropology, for that matter in the phenomenological sense of the word" (289)" (BNF, Box 42b, folder 1).

28. In a bibliographical folder dedicated to phenomenological psychopathology, there is a reading note entitled "Against *Daseinsanalyse*," which records references to studies by two psychiatrists who had critiqued Binswanger's project. The two articles in question are: Karl Friedrich Scheid, "Existenziale Analytik und Psychopathologie," *Der Nervenarzt* 5, no. 12 (1932): 617–25; and Renato De Rosa's "Existenzphilosophische Richtungen in der modernen Psychopathologie," *Der Nervenarzt* 23, no. 7 (1952): 256–61. About the first, Foucault writes, "*Daseinsanalyse* misunderstands the limit between a philosophical *Seinslehre* [doctrine of being] (ontology) and a psychological science of beings." About De Rosa's article, Foucault observes, "Critique from a Jaspersian point of view: impossibility of taking for *Gegenstand* [object] the totality and the *Ursprung* [origin] of the *Menschsein*" (BNF, Box 42b, folder 1). It is interesting to note that these authors, although writing from different perspectives, both reproach *Daseinsanalyse* for leading psychopathology to sink into speculation. A critique of this

kind had also been addressed to Binswanger's "doctrine" by the Dutch psychiatrist Henricus Cornelius Rümke during the first International Congress of Psychiatry, held in Paris in 1950, in which Binswanger participated. In a paper given in a session on the psychopathology of delusions, Rümke had stated that, in his opinion, "much of what Binswanger says should be stripped of its philosophical baggage, and many things of great value would remain"; see "Signification de la phénoménologie dans l'étude clinique des délirants," in *Congrès international de psychiatrie. Paris, 1950*, vol. 1, *Psychopathologie générale. Psychopathologie des délires* (Hermann, 1950), 134–35.

MANUSCRIPT CONTEXT
Elisabetta Basso

The Research Projects of the 1950s: Between Philosophy and Psychology[1]

Michel Foucault drafted the manuscript that we have entitled *Binswanger and Existential Analysis* in the early 1950s, when he was teaching in the Faculty of Letters at the University of Lille. Having earned his *agrégation* in philosophy in 1951, he was recruited to an assistant lectureship in psychology by Lille, which he held from the beginning of the school year in 1952 to the fall of 1955. He then left France for Sweden, where he was appointed lecturer and Director of the Maison de France in Uppsala.[2] In the archives, this manuscript is filed next to two other handwritten manuscripts entitled, respectively, *La question anthropologique* and *Phénoménologie et psychologie*.[3] It is difficult to make a definitive pronouncement on these documents: while the first reproduces the typical structure of course lecture notes, the other two appear to be more polished texts. In all likelihood Foucault used each of these manuscripts for his teaching, but *Binswanger and Existential Analysis* in particular presents itself as a finished work. Indeed, in a list of "works in progress" published in 1953 in the *Annales de l'Université de Lille*, we see a book entitled *Psychiatrie et analyse existentielle*. Foucault specifies that this is his secondary thesis, and moreover indicates that it is already "complete" and "in press" with Desclée de Brouwer.[4]

However, this book was never published. It is therefore possible that our present manuscript corresponds to this publication project, announced and then abandoned by Foucault.

The thesis and book projects undertaken by the philosopher during this period are as numerous as they are diverse. For example, if we are to rely on a letter that Jacqueline Verdeaux sent to Ludwig Binswanger in 1954, Foucault was intending at the time to prepare a "work on delusions."[5] Indeed, in 1952 the young philosopher had obtained a diploma in psychopathology at the Institute of Psychology in Paris. The following year, he also earned a diploma in experimental psychology. From October 1951 to the spring of 1955, thanks to the support of Louis Althusser, he was also a lecturer in psychology at the École normale supérieure (ENS). The philosopher and historian of science Gérard Simon, who attended his courses in 1953–1954, preserved many notes on the sessions Foucault devoted to "causality in psychology": the arc he traces runs from Leibniz, La Mettrie, and Cabanis, through Gestalt theory ("psychology of form"), Husserl, and Freud, and culminates with Binswanger and Merleau-Ponty.[6]

At the same time, Foucault worked as a psychologist in Georges Verdeaux's and André Ombredane's Parisian laboratory, created in 1947 at the Hôpital Sainte-Anne within Professor Jean Delay's department. There Foucault assisted the neuropsychiatrist Georges Verdeaux and his wife Jacqueline with their experiments on the clinical use of electroencephalograms, performed on patients at the hospital. He also familiarized himself with the Rorschach psychodiagnostic test, which he found particularly intriguing.[7] In Georges Verdeaux's archives, a 1952 report about an experiment with polygraph techniques mentions a young "M. Foucault, holding an *agrégation* from the University, lecturer at the École normale supérieure," who was perfecting a tachistoscopic test "targeting the mentally ill, delinquents, and normal subjects."[8] At the time, the Verdeaux directed the EEG unit at the Centre National d'Orientation created by the administration of the Fresnes penitentiary. Foucault would accompany Jacqueline Verdeaux there every week in order to perform medico-psychological exams on prisoners.[9]

At the beginning of the 1950s, then, Foucault seems to have turned toward psychology, to the point that—while wishing to create a psychology laboratory at ENS[10]—he even considered a career in psychiatry. It was Daniel Lagache, whom Foucault had known since finishing his *licence* (undergraduate studies) in psychology at the Sorbonne in 1949, who dissuaded him from choosing this path. Indeed, Foucault's interest in psychology was inextricably linked to his training in philosophy. In a French tradition going back to the nineteenth century, with Théodule-Armand Ribot, Georges Dumas, Pierre Janet, Paul Guillaume, Henri Piéron, or even Daniel Lagache, the most influential professors in the history of psychology have been philosophers. The study of psychology formed an integral part of the undergraduate degree in philosophy; it was only at the end of the 1940s that psychology was institutionally recognized as its own discipline in France. The first diploma in psychology was created by Lagache at the Sorbonne in 1947, and it was as chair of child psychology that Merleau-Ponty, appointed at the Sorbonne in 1949, articulated his phenomenological project. In his article "La recherche scientifique et la psychologie," which Foucault drafted in the early 1950s and which was published in 1957, he described precisely this paradoxical situation, in which "medical, scientific, or even philosophical training served as guarantors for the recruitment of researchers interested in doing experimental psychology."[11]

At the time, in France, philosophers did not think highly of psychology. This situation was highlighted explicitly by Jean

Piaget, who succeeded Maurice Merleau-Ponty at the Sorbonne from 1952 to 1963:

> French psychology has only been able to develop in the fringe of official institutions and in constant struggle with the powers that be of academic philosophy. . . . There is certainly a *licence* in psychology of recent date, . . . but practically this *licence* leads to very little, for from the point of view of a teaching career there is no *agrégation* in psychology, and from the point of view of a practical career it remains insufficient without the Diplomas of the Institute of Psychology, originating in the no-man's land between official chairs and not having the same official status as the Faculties.[12]

At the Sorbonne, moreover, Georges Canguilhem—who had offered a polemical answer to the question "What is psychology?" in his famous lecture of 1956 at the Collège philosophique[13]— devoted a course to the history of scientific psychology, in which he asserted that "instead of worrying about the existence of the 'human sciences,' philosophy must examine what is at stake in this psychology, what its titles are."[14]

At the very beginning of the 1950s, like most philosophy students interested in psychology, Foucault regularly attended Merleau-Ponty's lectures at the Sorbonne.[15] More than simply an autonomous science, psychology was presented there as a mode of reflection which, beyond its "express declarations,"[16] was destined to "[outrun] itself through its own momentum"[17] toward phenomenology. The numerous reading notes preserved in the archives of the Bibliothèque nationale de France (BNF)[18] reveal that Foucault was well-acquainted with the two works that Merleau-Ponty had published in the mid-1940s, *The Structure of Behavior* and *Phenomenology of Perception*. Among the documents that Foucault drafted as he prepared his courses at the beginning of the 1950s, there is a manuscript entitled "Les thèmes psychologiques de la phénoménologie de Husserl et de Merleau-Ponty" [Psychological Themes in Husserl's and Merleau-Ponty's Phenomenology];[19] during this period, he also mentioned to Jean-Paul Aron that he was working on an article on Merleau-Ponty.[20] It is also likely that Merleau-Ponty's 1947–1948 course at ENS on Malebranche, Maine de Biran and Bergson—about which the archives have returned to us a twenty-one year old Foucault's notes[21]—led him to further study the post-Cartesians, especially Malebranche and Bayle, while completing his diploma in psychopathology.

In 1951, with Georges Canguilhem's support, Foucault was admitted to the Fondation Thiers, a residential research foundation; the research topics he proposed ran the gamut from "the problem of the human sciences in post-Cartesian philosophers" to "the notion of culture in contemporary psychology."[22] One of the first doctoral thesis projects considered by Foucault, who asked the Sorbonne's Henri Gouhier to direct his secondary thesis on "Malebranche psychologue,"[23] dates back precisely to this period.

When Raymond Polin, chair of the department of philosophy at the University of Lille, recruited the young Foucault to teach psychology—on Jules Vuillemin's recommendation—he was looking for a philosopher, not a psychologist. At the time of their meeting in 1952, Foucault explained that he was writing a thesis on the "philosophy of psychology."[24] He was relatively free to choose the topics of his courses. In a letter to Jean-Paul Aron, while complaining about the medical doctors teaching psychology at the university, he stated that he intended to "organize a 'seminar' in theoretical psychoanalysis," since "no one else dared to risk such 'indecencies.'"[25] Indeed, many lecture notes preserved in Foucault's archives at the BNF are focused on psychoanalysis; these are lectures he could have delivered either at Lille or at ENS. Their titles include "L'angoisse chez Freud" [Anxiety in Freud], "Maladie et personnalité chez Freud" [Illness and Personality in Freud], "Freud et la psychologie de la genèse" [Freud and the Psychology of Genesis], "La théorie psychanalytique" [Psychoanalytic Theory], "L'inconscient en psychanalyse" [The Unconscious in Psychoanalysis], "Un exemple de psychanalyse: l'homme aux loups. La notion de milieu psychanalytique" [An Example of Psychoanalysis: The Wolf Man. The Notion of a Psychoanalytic Milieu].[26]

Foucault's interest in Freudian theory during this period was always intertwined with a theoretical reflection on classic philosophical subjects, such as experience, signification, expression, and language. The very many reading notes and lecture notes that Foucault devoted to psychoanalysis are coeval with his equally rich and detailed notes on Husserl's phenomenology.[27] Transcendental phenomenology particularly interested him, to the point that—as specified in a curriculum vitae appended to a letter addressed to Georges Dumézil in October 1954—he was planning a thesis on the "notion of "World" in phenomenology and its importance for the human sciences." His secondary thesis, on the other hand, bore the title "A Study of the Psychophysics of Signals and the Statistical Interpretation of Perception."[28]

"CONCRETE REFLECTION ON MAN"

The archives from this period are extremely dense and show us a young Foucault active on many fronts: beyond psychology (social psychology, animal psychology, cybernetics, reflexology, etc.)[29] and phenomenology (he dedicated many reading notes not only to Max Scheler, but also to Paul Ricoeur and Tran Duc Thao[30]), many reading notes are focused on philosophical anthropology, cultural anthropology, and sociology.[31] Moreover, while Hegel had been omnipresent in Foucault's notes since the 1940s, it was only in the 1950s that Foucault began to read Heidegger and Nietzsche assiduously. His curiosity with regard to Heidegger is observable in his very rich notes on "Anaximander's Saying,"[32] on the *Letter on Humanism*,[33] on some key concepts of *Sein und Zeit*, and on the anthropological question exposed in the study *Kant and the Problem of Metaphysics*, whose French translation by Alphonse de Waelhens and Walter Biemel was published by Gallimard in 1953.[34] Foucault's reading of Nietzsche, which he dated roughly to 1953,[35] might have been spurred by his reading of Karl Jaspers, in relation to Foucault's interest in the subject of mental illness.[36] This hypothesis seems to be confirmed by the archives from this period, which attest that Foucault was studying both the thought of the German psychiatrist and philosopher and the works of Nietzsche.[37] Indeed, Jaspers's book on Nietzsche appeared in French translation at the very beginning of the 1950s;[38] Jules Vuillemin wrote one of its first reviews.[39]

Despite this bountiful philosophical panorama, the only work that Foucault published in the 1950s was devoted to mental illness. *Maladie mentale et personnalité* came out in 1954 as part of the Presses Universitaires de France's "Initiation philosophique" series, which was edited by Jean Lacroix and whose editorial board included Gaston Bachelard, Georges Bastide, and Paul Ricoeur. In his correspondence with the young philosopher, Jean Lacroix explains that he wishes to publish "short volumes that are *simple*, clear, easy," whose goal would be to "examine in broad strokes the various questions covered by the program of the *baccalauréat* [high school leaving exam] and establish a basic classroom library."[40] In his study, Foucault presents and compares the principal psychological and psychiatric approaches to mental illness, from evolutionism to psychoanalysis, from existential analysis to Pavlovian materialism. The work had been solicited by Louis Althusser, whom Foucault had known since he was a student at ENS. Although Foucault had left the French Communist Party in October 1952—he had become a member in 1950, precisely through Althusser, but more as a sympathizer than a true militant—*Maladie mentale et personnalité* mostly reveals his commitment to a materialist perspective that was associated, at the time, with the Marxist journal *La Raison: Cahiers de psychopathologie scientifique* [Reason: Journal of Scientific Psychopathology], which had been founded in 1951 by Henri Wallon, who remained its editor.[41] In the first section of this text, which tackles the "psychological dimensions of illness," Foucault surveys some of the recurrent themes in the contemporary critical landscape, such as the centrality of the problem of "signification" in psychology, and Freudian theory's ambiguity in relation to evolutionism, on the one hand, and the historicity of forms of experience, on the other. However, in the second section, which deals with the "real conditions of illness," he is clearly echoing the *Cahiers*' main arguments. In this way, he asserts that a person with a mental illness is nothing but an extreme expression of the conflicts of bourgeois society. He explains that such a society mythologizes "mental alienation" while simultaneously pushing it to the outer limits of the city; this dynamic is nothing but a translation of the scandal of an alienation whose true nature is social and historical.[42] Also in keeping with the *Cahiers*' perspective, Foucault writes about Pavlovian theory in glowing terms, describing it as the only viable perspective for "an experimental study of conflict."[43]

While the reference to Pavlov would disappear from Foucault's later works, other elements of this text would remain central to his thinking. Among them, we observe especially the necessity of referring any definition of mental alienation back to the society characterizing it as such. His praise of the investigative report on the "wretchedness of psychiatry" led in 1952 par Albert Béguin in the journal *Esprit*—where psychiatrists such as François Tosquelles, Henri Ey, Louis Le Guillant, Lucien Bonnafé, and Georges Daumézon deplored the condition of the "madmen" in hospitals[44]—calls to mind the tone of *History of Madness*. The critique of the existential approach to psychology that finally emerges from *Maladie mentale et personnalité* is another subject that would find echo in Foucault's critique of the human sciences during the 1960s. This theme recurred throughout Foucault's handwritten notes from the mid-1950s. For example, in one manuscript from the Lille period, Foucault explains that phenomenological anthropology's refusal of any "scientific and real analysis of human conduct" had the result of discovering an "essence of man that uncovers itself only in the negative modality":

> It is the human sciences that are charged with saying that the essence of man cannot be fully captured by an objective analysis, their mission is to show, in man, something other than his own conditions, something other than his own manifestations, something other than his own companions in humanity; in short, that it is incorrect to say that "man is the very root of man." Under the pretext of showing man in his totality, contemporary sciences seek to show that man is something other than man.[45]

In this way, Foucault critiques the school of "concrete psychology" which, on the basis of the groundwork laid by Georges Politzer at the end of the 1920s, had influenced both the materialist perspective and the various phenomenological approaches.[46]

In a brief comment appended in pencil to the end of the same manuscript fragment, Foucault concludes:

> Psychology, under the pretext of analyzing the concrete—phenomenology, under the pretext of returning to things—both converge toward the most abstract thing: toward an essence of man valid only in the realm of anthropological speculation.[47]

It is precisely this "inflection of phenomenology toward anthropology" that Foucault attempted to study further during this period, in order to analyze "what foundations have been proposed for concrete reflection on man."[48] At least this was the project announced in his other publication of 1954, the introduction to the French translation of Ludwig Binswanger's article "Traum und Existenz." It is important to underscore that, as he was writing *Binswanger and Existential Analysis*, Foucault was giving courses on anthropology at Lille and ENS (*La question anthropologique*) and studying Husserl assiduously. On this topic, Philippe Sabot has suggested that Foucault's manuscript on *Phenomenology and Psychology* from the Lille era might correspond to the thesis he announces in his 1954 letter to Dumézil: "the notion of 'World' in phenomenology and its importance for the human sciences." We will only truly be able to assess the scope of Foucault's interest in Binswanger's existential anthropology when we have considered these works as a whole; they will all be published in the coming years in the *Foucault's Early Lectures and Manuscripts* series.

BINSWANGER IN FRANCE

Among the few "dates in the history of psychiatry" that Foucault cites in his appendix to *Maladie mentale et personnalité*, Ludwig Binswanger's work is listed alongside classics by Philippe Pinel,

Pierre Bayle, Emil Kraepelin, Sigmund Freud, Ivan Petrovič Pavlov, and Eugen Bleuler. This shows Binswanger's importance in Foucault's estimation, despite the latter's skepticism about existential analysis in this text.[49] Foucault was not alone, at the time, in deeming Binswanger's program to be one of the most significant within the landscape of psychiatric research. In the mid-1950s, Binswanger was well-known in the European psychiatric milieu. During the first International Congress of Psychiatry, held in Paris in 1950, the Dutch psychiatrist Henricus Cornelius Rümke presented *Daseinsanalyse* as the "method which is all the rage";[50] in the treatise on psychiatry published in the same year by Paul Guiraud, the phenomenological school is analyzed alongside psychoanalysis, the Zurich school, and organo-dynamism.[51] In 1955, Henri F. Ellenberger, in his *Traité de psychiatrie* within the *Encyclopédie médico-chirurgicale* edited par Henri Ey, described existential analysis as one of the "great innovations of modern psychiatry" and as "one of its most promising disciplines."[52]

French psychiatrists and philosophers had access to Binswanger's ideas not only through Sartre and Merleau-Ponty, who began to cite him in their writings in the 1940s, but especially because of the coverage he received in *L'Évolution psychiatrique*. The journal had been founded in 1925 around a group of psychiatrists and psychoanalysts that included René Allendy, Angelo Hesnard, René Laforgue, and Eugène Minkowski; its goal was to promote "a practical, new, fundamentally clinical psychology,"[53] using "the method imagined by Professor S. Freud and expanded by numerous foreign physicians and psychologists."[54] Binswanger's name appears in the very first issue of the journal, in a contribution by Minkowski on the subject of schizophrenia;[55] in 1938, one of Binswanger's articles on Freud and philosophical anthropology would launch a series of French translations of his work.[56]

If Binswanger principally owes his introduction in France in the early 1920s to Minkowski, we should not underestimate Jacques Lacan's influence. He discovered Binswanger's writings in the early 1930s,[57] and at the end of the 1940s played an important role as a relay between Swiss psychiatry and the French philosophers he had rubbed shoulders with as a young psychiatrist—whether at Alexandre Kojève's Hegelian seminar at the École Pratique des Hautes Études (EPHE) or through the intermediary of the *Évolution psychiatrique* group and of the Société Psychanalytique de Paris. In 1953, when the Swiss psychiatrist Roland Kuhn attempted (without success) to meet Merleau-Ponty in Paris, it was Lacan he asked for help. This missed opportunity would lead another enthusiast of *Daseinsanalyse*, the philosopher Henri Maldiney, to complain about French phenomenology's "intellectual protectionism."[58]

It was precisely because he was distancing himself from the phenomenological model associated with Merleau-Ponty that Georges Gusdorf, Althusser's predecessor at ENS, decided in 1946–1947 to open "the doors of the world of madness in its intrinsic reality" to the École normale's philosophy students.[59] Due to his friendship with Georges Daumézon, he brought Foucault and his fellow students to the psychiatric hospital in Fleury-les-Aubrais, near Orléans, and to Sainte-Anne, where Paul Guiraud was organizing presentations of patients. Binswanger himself deeply admired Merleau-Ponty's work; he often cited it in his writings, surprised to see "how open the French have always been to phenomenology."[60] During his visit to Paris for the International Congress of Psychiatry in 1950, he had a long meeting with Jean Wahl,[61] and in his presentation at the Sorbonne, he stressed the distance between *Daseinsanalyse* and Sartre's positions.[62]

The "lack of interest, among philosophers, in direct contact with human reality"[63] which Georges Gusdorf complained about also led Gaston Bachelard to contact the Swiss psychiatrists during this period.[64] In the book he had just finished, *La terre et les rêveries du repos* [Earth and Reveries of Repose], he advocated for a "psychology of the imagination of matter" which made considerable use of Hermann Rorschach's test based on the perception of shapes. The foremost specialist of the "psychodiagnostic" was Roland Kuhn at the Münsterlingen hospital, in the Canton of Thurgau, a few kilometers away from the clinic directed by Binswanger in Kreuzlingen. The Rorschach test was precisely one of the reasons why Georges and Jacqueline Verdeaux became acquainted with him after the war.[65] It was during one of Kuhn's visits to Paris that Bachelard had the opportunity to meet the psychiatrist, who later helped him contact Binswanger.[66] The latter had already manifested his approval of Bachelard's writings on the imagination in an article on the "The Existential Analysis School of Thought."[67] Foucault knew this essay well and recalled it in his introduction to "Dream and Existence," observing in a section about Binswanger's conception of dreams that "no one has better understood the dynamic work of the imagination and the incessantly vectorial nature of its movement" than Bachelard.[68]

In letters from 1948 and 1949, Bachelard announced to Binswanger that he intended to hold "a series of in-depth lectures on [these] problems."[69] Moreover, in 1951, he told the psychiatrist that he had discussed his work with his daughter, who had the *agrégation* and was a lecturer at the École normale supérieure de Sèvres, and that "she would speak about it with her candidates for the *agrégation*."[70] Through this correspondence, we discover the French philosophical networks in which Binswanger's work circulated during the late 1940s and early 1950s, when the young Foucault made his own discovery of *Daseinsanalyse*. When Merleau-Ponty cited "the Swiss psychologist and psychiatrist" in his 1951–1952 course at the Sorbonne on the "Human Sciences and Phenomenology," he was far from being the only philosopher interested in Binswanger.[71] As for the psychiatrists, Henri Ey and Eugène Minkowski had taken over the editorship of *L'Évolution psychiatrique* after the war, and increased the journal's coverage of the phenomenological approach. In 1948, Henri Ey launched his book series at Desclée de Brouwer, the *Bibliothèque neuro-psychiatrique de langue française*, which, throughout the 1950s, would promote important works in psychiatry, phenomenological psychopathology, and psychoanalysis. It was within this series that in 1954 a new edition of Minkowski's seminal work from 1927, *La schizophrénie*, was published. Minkowski emphasized the value to be found in translating Binswanger's work and introducing *Daseinsanalyse* in more concrete terms to the French psychiatric scene.[72] In so doing, he was paving the way for the translation and introduction of "Dream and Existence."

BINSWANGER'S EXISTENTIAL ANTHROPOLOGY

The hundreds of reading notes that Foucault devoted to existential psychopathology in the first half of the 1950s are far from being limited to "Traum und Existenz." The archives at the Bibliothèque nationale de France reveal that he had already read not only all of the work by Binswanger that was then available, but also the writings of most of the German-language psychiatrists, physicians, philosophers, and anthropologists linked to the development of phenomenological psychopathology. If we scan the various bibliographical inventories that Foucault drafted in those years, we get the impression that he had considered writing a thesis on existential psychiatry.

When, in 1953, Jacqueline Verdeaux suggested to Foucault that he help her with the translation of "Traum und Existenz," he already had an advanced understanding of phenomenological psychopathology. Moreover, his collaboration with both Verdeaux at Saint-Anne had reinforced Foucault's interest in existential analysis at a time when he was studying Husserl's and Heidegger's phenomenology. The work on existential analysis was also announced in the introduction to "Dream and Existence," where Foucault stated that he would undertake the task of "situat[ing] existential analysis" in "another work."[73] The manuscript *Binswanger and Existential Analysis* could therefore correspond to this thesis and publication project. Finally, Foucault's intention to publish a study that would constitute a "theoretical and general introduction to *Daseinsanalyse*" is confirmed by a letter that he wrote to Ludwig Binswanger on April 27, 1954, at a moment when he was immersed in the translation of "Dream and Existence." In reference to the introduction that he had just completed, he asserted that "for the moment [he had] had only two preoccupations: to show the importance of the dream in existential analysis, and to show how [Binswanger's] conception of the dream entails a complete reworking of analyses of the imagination." As for the rest, he added, he intended "to pursue it in a broader study of anthropology and ontology."[74]

It is difficult to establish with certainty the order in which Foucault drafted his two works on Binswanger. In any case, *Binswanger and Existential Analysis* concludes precisely on the topic which forms the focus of the introduction to "Dream and Existence": the problem of expression. Indeed, in his introduction, Foucault seems to want to redeem *Daseinsanalyse* from the speculative drift he accuses it of in his manuscript. Through his analysis of the experience of dreaming, he offers *Daseinsanalyse* the path of analyzing the "objective forms of expression."[75] Even if he affirms that Binswanger's theme of the "encounter with concrete existence" and the "status that is finally to be assigned to the ontological conditions of existence pose problems,"[76] Foucault's judgment of existential analysis in his introduction is rather favorable. Still, in response to these problems, which he contents himself with mentioning, he announces, "we leave that issue to another time."[77] Could this be an allusion to *Binswanger and Existential Analysis*?

The experience of having met Binswanger personally in March 1954, through the intermediary of the Verdeaux,[78] is one of the reasons that might have led Foucault to abandon the project of publishing a text whose conclusion might seem very severe in regard to *Daseinsanalyse*. In addition, meeting with the psychiatrist gave Foucault the opportunity to ask him directly about the problems which, although barely sketched out in the introduction, are at the heart of the manuscript. In a letter written to Binswanger in May 1954, after their meeting in Kreuzlingen, Foucault states that he would be very happy, during their next discussion, "to ask you a few questions on this problem of facticity, transcendence, and love."[79] Unfortunately, while there are several documents that bear witness to Foucault's first visit to Münsterlingen and Kreuzlingen, there are none that could inform us about the second meeting with the Swiss psychiatrists, which took place in Brissago in September 1954.

In any case, *Binswanger and Existential Analysis* now allows us to establish a significant link between Foucault's early publications. Even if Pavlov's theory is not at issue in this manuscript, the alternatives Foucault places before *Daseinsanalyse* at the end of his text—when he observes that it must choose "between metaphysical speculation and objective reflection"[80]—recalls the two approaches to psychopathology explored in *Maladie mentale et personnalité*. Foucault goes one step further than that book in *Binswanger and Existential Analysis*: now the alternative between metaphysical speculation and objective reflection is situated within a more radical interrogation of the legitimacy of the anthropological discourse prompted by phenomenology. Indeed, here Foucault introduces existential analysis only after having presented, in a general manner, Husserl's program, from eidetic psychology to transcendental phenomenology:

> We will try to reproduce this movement by which any phenomenological analysis is called, especially when it addresses pathological experiences, to go beyond itself and to seek its foundation in a form of reflection that defines itself as anthropological.[81]

We do see here the "other work" Foucault had announced in his introduction to "Dream and Existence," a work which "shall try to situate existential analysis within the development of contemporary reflection on man."[82] On the one hand, Foucault finds Binswanger's perspective attractive because, unlike the various naturalist approaches to psychopathology, it considers the illness not as an accident external to the subject but as the subject's own "project." On the other, *Daseinsanalyse* allows him to uncover the anthropological drift that he sees as inevitable in Husserl's phenomenology. Foucault's interest in Binswanger's project thus comes from the fact that his method, while situating itself in the lineage of phenomenology, has the merit of confronting phenomenology on its major obstacle, illness. Indeed, the critique of phenomenology in relation to the limit represented by pathological experience is a central element in various work notes Foucault drafted during this period. In a preparatory manuscript entitled "La recherche scientifique et la psychologie," for example, he writes:

> Phenomenology, in its critique of psychologism . . . remained . . . haunted by the problem of knowing how truth

could emerge within understanding, and the accusation of naturalism leveled against psychological objectivities, the requirement of an analysis of the constitutive sphere, transcendental subjectivity's recourse to the ground of experience resolutely maintain philosophical interrogation in a clarified space from which the shadows of not-knowing, the night of truth, and the decay of man have been swept away. It is therefore not surprising, this adventure of phenomenology, which, after having gotten rid of psychologism, finds in psychology or the reflection on psychology the starting point for its radical deepening.[83]

This is why, Foucault concludes, "Husserl has certainly deserved his Merleau-Pontys and his Binswangers."[84]

In other handwritten notes from the 1950s, Foucault expands on the link between the phenomenological perspective, psychology, and anthropology. He observes that if, on the one hand, man's "decay," represented by pathological experience, leads phenomenologists toward a reflection on psychology, on the other, this reflection can only lead to an anthropology:

> The evolution of Husserl's thought from the idealist rationalism of the *Logische Untersuchungen* [*Logical Investigations*] to the descriptive and genetic idealism of the writings on History or the genealogy of logic is nothing but the progressive discovery of the ever-more pressing necessity of an anthropology. Husserl's successors did not err: anthropology in Scheler, in Heidegger, in Sartre.[85]

Certainly, this anthropology is the foundation of the psychology that brought it into being, but it also contests psychology's pretention to constitute itself as a scientific understanding of man:

Indeed, in defining anthropology as the kind of analysis of human existence that inscribes the real conditions of this existence at the level of its ideal essence, we see that anthropology cannot be anything but the radical contestation of any scientific or dialectic analysis of the relationship of man to his environment. What anthropology denies psychology is its scientific ambitions.[86]

From this point of view, we can understand the manner in which Foucault describes the anthropological project that subtends *Daseinsanalyse* in his introduction to "Dream and Existence," a project that defines, alongside it, "the working dimensions of anthropology"; this project, Foucault writes, "opposes anthropology to any type of psychological positivism."[87] Now, in the manuscript from which we have been quoting, Foucault expands precisely on this "passage from a psychology to an anthropology that it perpetually calls upon and requires, but which also perpetually contests it and always refuses it any definitive guarantee or validation."[88] In this respect, he mentions the work of Merleau-Ponty, which he deems to be the "most lucid and measured reflection on this passage,"[89] and schematically describes

> His book [*The Phenomenology of Perception*] as tackling the theme: phenomenological reduction takes place within psychology, such that psychology is called into question by the reflection on man that it has itself sparked; this book is in this way simultaneously the most lucid and the most naïve.[90]

If the transition from psychology to anthropology prompted by phenomenology is "naïve," it is not only because it calls into question the very psychology that gave rise to it. It is mostly because the anthropology that is constituted by attributing an ideal essence to man ends up lacking any anchoring in the real conditions of man's existence. In another manuscript from this period, Foucault interprets this operation as a kind of reinvestment of the "idealist capital" that had previously been attached to theology:

> The meaning of phenomenology is to ensure a reutilization of this idealist capital. Anthropology is the vicar of theology, as the Pope is to Christ. Yet the paradox of this story is that psychology, which had previously played the antitheological role of a reduction to a determinism of affections, a theory of knowledge, of value, and of liberty, has made itself complicit in this theological maneuver. It allows itself to be led into error by the *here and now* claimed by anthropology, against the *there and then* of theology, and sees in this refusal of any beyond the guarantee of its positivity. We thereby see the movement of a psychology which purports to find its guarantee in an anthropology which recuperates the fundamental concepts of a theology through which the validity of psychology is contested. . . . Man has become the natural site of theology—and its point of application. And its scope. Whence the allure of the human sciences.[91]

Faced with a psychology that ends up "basing itself on an anthropology that evades objectivity"[92]—a trap to which *Daseinsanalyse* also falls victim—Foucault invites *Daseinsanalyse* to return to "objective reflection." However, the naturalist approach that anchors the arguments of *Maladie mentale et personnalité* is absent in the manuscript on Binswanger, and the "materialist approach" that Foucault claims for psychology—as he asserts in one of the texts I have just cited—becomes more complicated here:

> Materialism must be methodological in the human sciences. Loosening phenomenology's grasp on psychology is

the only means of returning to psychology its materialist signification.[93]

In *Binswanger and Existential Analysis*, this "methodological" materialism toward which Foucault attempts to push *Daseinsanalyse* takes the form of humans' concrete communication and of the analysis of phenomena of expression; these formulas bear witness to Foucault's attempt to give content to this notion of the "concrete" that had been deployed so insistently by French philosophers, psychologists, and psychiatrists since the 1930s.

"FROM PSYCHOLOGY TO HISTORY"

At the end of his life, returning to the early stages of his intellectual trajectory, Foucault acknowledged that he had wanted to escape the then dominant "dilemma of a philosophical anthropology and a social history,"[94] before he finally "understood that the subject would have to be defined in other terms than Marxism or phenomenology."[95] In the fall of 1955, as his departure for Sweden was fast approaching, we learn from the correspondence between Jacqueline Verdeaux and Ludwig Binswanger that she had the project of working with Foucault on a "kind of dictionary of *daseinsanalytic* terms" to accompany her translation of the Suzanne Urban clinical case study.[96] This text, however, would appear in 1957 without Foucault's name or any appended dictionary. In Uppsala, Foucault worked simultaneously on a translation of Viktor von Weizsäcker's *Der Gestaltkreis*[97] and on one of the volumes he had under contract with the publisher Les Éditions de la Table ronde. The contract, which bears the provisional title *Histoire de la folie*, was signed by Michel Foucault and Jacqueline Verdeaux.[98] In reality, this book would become Foucault's principal thesis, defended at the Sorbonne in 1961 under the direction of Georges Canguilhem. As for Jacqueline Verdeaux, she continued to explore *Daseinsanalyse*. In 1955, she translated Jakob Wyrsch's *La personne du schizophrène* and worked on the French version of one of Roland Kuhn's books on the Rorschach test, *Phénoménologie du masque*, which appeared in 1957 with a preface by Gaston Bachelard.[99] Foucault agreed to read the proofs of her translations, which he asked her to send to Uppsala. But he asked himself, "am I still competent?"[100]

In 1961, in the first edition of *History of Madness*, Foucault presented himself as "an author [who] is by profession a philosopher who turned to psychology, and from psychology to history."[101] This "history without dates or chronology," as he described it during his thesis defense on May 20, 1961,[102] has raised numerous questions among historians;[103] nonetheless, it was precisely the need to historicize the experience of mental illness that pushed Foucault to abandon existential psychiatry. The extensive modifications he made to *Maladie mentale et personnalité* in 1962, in the new version of the book entitled *Mental Illness and Psychology*, illustrate this change in orientation very explicitly. In the final chapter, indeed, Foucault observes,

> To be sure, mental illness may be situated in relation to human genesis, in relation to individual, psychological history, in relation to the forms of existence. But, if one is to avoid resorting to such mythical explanation as the evolution of psychological structures, the theory of instincts, or an existential anthropology, one must not regard these various aspects of mental illness as ontological forms. In fact, it is only in history that one can discover the sole concrete a priori from which mental illness draws, with the empty opening up of its possibility, its necessary figures.[104]

In 1984, in the preface he drafted for the American edition of *The History of Sexuality*, Foucault returned to his interest in existential analysis, specifying that it ultimately left him dissatisfied because of "its theoretical weakness in elaborating the notion of experience, and its ambiguous link with a psychiatric practice, which it simultaneously ignored and took for granted."[105] However, the phenomenological approach still profoundly marked the next step in Foucault's trajectory, *History of Madness*. Recalling the period when he was writing that book, Foucault admitted that he continued to feel "divided between existential psychology and phenomenology" and that his "research was an attempt to discover the extent to which these could be defined in historical terms."[106] Indeed, even as it opens onto a movement beyond existential psychiatry, *History of Madness* is a book that owes much to its approach to mental illness. Foucault's project of thinking a history not of psychiatry but rather of madness, before any psychopathological conceptualization, is not far from that of the psychiatrist-phenomenologists who attempted to approach mental illness first as an extra-scientific phenomenon, independent of any clinical classification. Indeed, for Foucault, the task was not to retrace the history of a truth of mental illness that could eventually be accessed, but rather to identify the "degree zero of the history of madness, when it was undifferentiated experience,"[107] which "still remains for us the mode of access to the natural truth of man."[108] In this perspective, there is no place for any kind of psychiatry:

> Carried back to its roots, the psychology of madness would appear to be not the mastery of mental illness and hence the possibility of its disappearance, but the destruction of psychology itself and the discovery of that essential, non-psychological because nonmoralizable relation that is the relation between Reason and Unreason.[109]

On the one hand, as Georges Canguilhem observed in the report he drafted in 1960 about Foucault's thesis, *History of Madness* has the merit of "reviv[ing] a fruitful dialogue between psychology and philosophy at a time when many psychologists are willing to separate their techniques from an interrogation of the origins and the meaning of these techniques."[110] But on the other, this philosophical reflection entails some difficulties. As Pierre Macherey insightfully puts it, "by moving beyond the idea of a psychological truth of mental illness toward that of an ontological truth of madness," the historical "rectification" toward which Foucault oriented his research at the very beginning of the 1960s ended up "leaving intact the presupposition of a human nature"[111] for which Foucault had critiqued philosophical anthropology throughout the 1950s. Once again, the question of man and anthropology remained central to Foucault's preoccupations. It was precisely this question that he worked to refine and deepen in the 1960s with the development of his "archaeological" program.

*

I wish to thank all of the members of the editorial board of the "Cours et travaux de Michel Foucault avant le Collège de France" series for their attentive readings of the manuscript and for their advice, as well as the team working on the French National Research Agency's "Foucault Fiches de Lecture / Foucault Reading Notes" (FFL) project (ENS de Lyon, Triangle—UMR 5206, CAPHÉS-UMS 3610, ENS-PSL and BNF) for the computing tools they developed to consult Foucault's reading notes. I would also like to thank Mireille Delbraccio and Claude Erdélyi for their rereading of the manuscript, as well as Bruno Verdeaux, Regula Kuhn, Liselotte Rutishauser, and the Ludwig Binswanger Archives at the University of Tübingen for the documents they made available to me.

E.B.

NOTES

1. For an elaboration of this material, see Elisabetta Basso, *Young Foucault: The Lille Manuscripts on Psychopathology, Phenomenology, and Anthropology, 1952–1955*, trans. Marie Satya McDonough (Columbia University Press, 2022).

2. For a detailed chronology of Foucault's formative years, see Daniel Defert, "Chronologie (1926–1967)," in Michel Foucault, *Oeuvres*, vol. 1, ed. Frédéric Gros (Gallimard, 2015).

3. BNF, Fonds Michel Foucault, Box 46, folders 1 to 3 (call number NAF 28730).

4. "Travaux et publications des professeurs en 1952–1953," *Annales de l'université de Lille. Rapport annuel du Conseil de l'université (1952–1953)* (G. Sautai et fils, 1954); quoted in Didier Eribon, *Michel Foucault*, trans. Betsy Wing (Harvard University Press, 1991), 63. See also Philippe Sabot, "Entre psychologie et philosophie. Foucault à Lille, 1952–1955," in *Foucault à Münsterlingen. À l'origine de l'*Histoire de la folie, *avec des photographies de Jacqueline Verdeaux*, ed. Jean-François Bert and Elisabetta Basso (EHESS, 2015), 109.

5. Letter from Verdeaux to Binswanger dated 14 August 1954 (Binswanger Archives, Universitätsarchiv Tübingen, call number 443/60).

6. These notes can be consulted in Gérard Simon's archives, which are conserved in the Centre d'archives de philosophie, d'histoire et d'édition des sciences (Caphés), at the École normale supérieure, Paris (call number GS. 4.9).

7. See Eribon, *Michel Foucault*, 48.

8. This document is currently in the Roland Kuhn archives (Archives d'État du canton de Thurgovie, Frauenfeld, call number 9'40).

9. See David Macey, *The Lives of Michel Foucault* (Hutchinson, 1993), 58.

10. See on this topic excerpts of Foucault's correspondence with Jean-Paul Aron reproduced in "Archives. Vivre et enseigner à Lille," in Bert and Basso, eds., *Foucault à Münsterlingen*, 121–23. Moreover, we learn from Foucault's correspondence with André Ombredane that Foucault was counting on a psychology laboratory being set up at ENS so that he could lead a study "on the perception of forms from the perspective of information theory" (see on this topic the letter that Ombredane wrote to Jean Hyppolite,

who was then the director of ENS, on 22 February 1955). We also learn that this same lab would be supported by the work of a "seminar devoted to psychological research and study" (BNF, Fonds Michel Foucault, Box 5, folder 1, call number NAF 28803).

11. Michel Foucault, "La recherche scientifique et la psychologie" [1957], in *Dits et écrits*, vol. 1, *1954–1969*, ed. Daniel Defert and François Ewald, with the help of Jacques Lagrange (Gallimard, 1994), no. 3, 147.

12. Jean Piaget, *Insights and Illusions of Philosophy*, trans. Wolfe Mays (World Publishing, 1971), 25.

13. Georges Canguilhem, "What is Psychology?" trans. David M. Peña-Guzmán, *Foucault Studies* 21 (2016): 200–13.

14. Georges Canguilhem, "Naissance de la psychologie scientifique" [1960–1961], manuscript lecture, Caphés, Fonds Georges Canguilhem; quoted by Jean-François Braunstein in "Foucault, Canguilhem et l'histoire des sciences humaines," *Archives de philosophie* 79, no. 1 (2016): 17.

15. These lectures were published in the *Bulletin de psychologie* between 1949 and 1952, and by the Centre de documentation universitaire. See also Maurice Merleau-Ponty, *Merleau-Ponty à la Sorbonne. Résumé de cours, 1949–1952* (Cynara, 1988).

16. Maurice Merleau-Ponty, "Phenomenology and the Sciences of Man," trans. John Wild, in *The Primacy of Perception*, ed. James M. Edie (Northwestern University Press, 1964), 45.

17. Maurice Merleau-Ponty, *Phenomenology of Perception*, trans. Colin Smith (Routledge and Kegan Paul, 1962), 60.

18. BNF, Fonds Michel Foucault, Box 33a, folder 0 (call number: NAF 28730). We also find, in the same box, notes on Merleau-Ponty's seminar on "L'enfant et autrui."

19. BNF, Fonds Michel Foucault, Box 46, folder 4. Under the same call number, in Box 33a, folder 0, there are notes on a course by Foucault entitled "Husserl and Merleau-Ponty (psychology and phenomenology)," which seem to correspond to the manuscript fragment conserved in Box 46. These notes bear the date 23 November 1951, but it is impossible to identify the notetaker.

20. Letter from Foucault to Jean-Paul Aron dated 17 November [n.d.]. See "Archives. Vivre et enseigner à Lille," in Bert and Basso, eds., *Foucault à Münsterlingen*, 122. The article on Merleau-Ponty seems to correspond to

a 38-page typescript preserved in the BNF's Foucault archives (call number NAF 28803, Box 3, folder 7).

21. BNF, Fonds Michel Foucault, Box 33a, folder 0 (call number NAF 28730).

22. Eribon, *Michel Foucault*, 40.

23. Didier Eribon, *Michel Foucault et ses contemporains* (Fayard, 1994), 106.

24. Eribon, *Michel Foucault et ses contemporains*, 106.

25. See Sabot, "Vivre et enseigner à Lille," in Bert and Basso, eds., *Foucault à Münsterlingen*, 121.

26. BNF, Fonds Michel Foucault, Box 46, folder 4 (call number NAF 28730).

27. For the reading notes on Freud, see especially BNF, Fonds Michel Foucault, Box 39 (call number NAF 28730); for those on Husserl, see Box 42a, folder 3 (call number NAF 28730). Furthermore, we know from Foucault's correspondence with the German publisher Mohr (Paul Siebeck, Tübingen) that between 1952 and 1953 he intended to translate Husserl's article "Philosophy as Rigorous Science" into French (BNF, Fonds Michel Foucault, Box 5, folder 1, call number NAF 28803).

28. Eribon, *Michel Foucault et ses contemporains*, 112.

29. See in particular the reading notes held in Box 44 of the Fonds Michel Foucault, as well as the folders available under call number NAF 28803.

30. BNF, Fonds Michel Foucault, Box 37, folder 2 (call number NAF 28730).

31. BNF, Fonds Michel Foucault, Boxes 37, 38 and 44 (call number NAF 28730).

32. Martin Heidegger, "Anaximander's Saying," in *Off the Beaten Track*, ed. and trans. Julian Young and Kenneth Haynes (Cambridge University Press, 2002), 242–81.

33. Martin Heidegger, "Letter on "Humanism" [1947], in *Pathmarks*, ed. and trans. William McNeil (Cambridge University Press, 1998), 239–76.

34. Martin Heidegger, *Kant and the Problem of Metaphysics*, 5th ed., trans. Richard Taft (Indiana University Press, 1997) [1929]. See Foucault's reading notes held in Box 33a, folder 0 at the BNF (Fonds Michel Foucault, call number NAF 28730).

35. Michel Foucault, "The return of morality," trans. Thomas Levin and Isabelle Lorenz, in *Politics, Philosophy, Culture: Interviews and other Writings 1977–1984*, ed. Lawrence D. Kritzman (Routledge, 1990), 250. See also Maurice Pinguet's account, "Les années d'apprentissage," *Le Débat* 41, no. 4 (1986): 122–31.

36. See Eribon, *Michel Foucault et ses contemporains*, 319.

37. The folder concerning Jaspers can be found at the BNF, Fonds Michel Foucault, Box 42b, folder 1 (call number NAF 28730); as for Nietzsche, see Box 33a, folder 1 and Box 33b, folder 3 (call number NAF 28730).

38. Karl Jaspers, *Nietzsche: An Introduction to the Understanding of his Philosophical Activity*, trans. Charles F. Wallraff and Frederick J. Schmitz (Johns Hopkins University Press, 1997 [1936]); for the French translation, see Henri Niel, *Nietzsche. Introduction à sa philosophie*, letter-preface by Jean Wahl (Gallimard, 1950).

39. Jules Vuillemin, "Nietzsche aujourd'hui," *Les Temps modernes* 6, no. 67 (1951): 1921–54. Soon afterward a French translation of a 1922 book by Jaspers also appeared: *Strindberg et Van Gogh, Swedenborg, Hölderlin. Étude psychiatrique comparative*, trans. Hélène Naef, preceded by a study by Maurice Blanchot (Minuit, 1953).

40. See Jean Lacroix's letter to Foucault dated 25 February 1953 (BNF, Fonds Michel Foucault, Box 5, folder 1, call number NAF 28803; underlined in the original).

41. See on this topic Luca Paltrinieri, "De quelques sources de *Maladie mentale et Personnalité*. Réflexologie pavlovienne et critique sociale," in Bert and Basso, eds., *Foucault à Münsterlingen*, 197–219.

42. Michel Foucault, *Maladie mentale et personnalité* (PUF, 1954), 104.

43. Foucault, *Maladie mentale et personnalité*, 92.

44. Foucault, *Maladie mentale et personnalité*, 109n1. See also "Misère de la psychiatrie," ed. Albert Béguin, special issue, *Esprit* 197, no. 12 (1952).

45. Michel Foucault, "L'agressivité, l'angoisse et la magie," BNF, Fonds Michel Foucault, Box 46, folder 4, pp. 2–3 (call number NAF 28730).

46. In *L'Univers morbide de la faute* (PUF, 1949), for example, the psychoanalyst Angelo Hesnard drew on Georges Politzer's ideas to adopt a perspective combining a phenomenological orientation and a materialist approach, which he defined as "two sides of scientific observation" (461). This book, which featured a preface by Henri Wallon and commentary by

Daniel Lagache, attracted the young Foucault's attention, and he devoted a lengthy reading note to it (Fonds Michel Foucault, Box 42a, folder 3, call number NAF 28730; see also Box 33a, folder 0, call number NAF 28730).

47. Foucault, "L'agressivité, l'angoisse et la magie," p. 12.

48. Michel Foucault, "Dream, Imagination and Existence" trans. Forrest Williams, in *Dream and Existence*, ed. Keith Hoeller (Humanities Press, 1993), 31.

49. Foucault, *Maladie mentale et personnalité*, III. [This list is also reproduced at the end of *Mental Illness and Psychology*, trans. Alan Sheridan (University of California Press, 1987), 89–90—Trans.]

50. Henricus Cornelius Rümke, "Signification de la phénoménologie dans l'étude clinique des délirants," in *Congrès international de psychiatrie. Paris, 1950*, vol. I, *Psychopathologie générale. Psychopathologie des délires* (Hermann, 1950), 131.

51. Paul Guiraud, "Pathogénie et étiologie des délires," in *Psychiatrie générale* (Le François, 1950), 576–81.

52. Henri Ellenberger, "Analyse existentielle," in *Encyclopédie médico-chirurgicale. Traité de psychiatrie*, ed. Henri Ey (Éditions techniques, 1955), 1.

53. Angelo Hesnard and René Laforgue, "Avant-propos," *L'Évolution psychiatrique* 1 (1925): 8.

54. Hesnard and Laforgue, 7.

55. Eugène Minkowski, "La genèse de la notion de schizophrénie et ses caractères essentiels. Une page d'histoire contemporaine de la psychiatrie," *L'Évolution psychiatrique* 1 (1925): 193–236. Minkowski had first cited Binswanger's work in 1923 in "Étude psychologique et analyse phénoménologique d'un cas de mélancolie schizophrénique," *Journal de psychologie normale et pathologique* 20, no. 6 (1923), as an example of the way in which "phenomenology quickly found a vast scope of application in every scientific domain" (543). [This quotation does not appear in the English translation of this essay, which is based on the slightly condensed version of the article that appears in *Le Temps vécu* (D'Artrey, 1933); for the English translation, see *Lived Time: Phenomenological and Psychopathological Studies*, trans. Nancy Metzel (Northwestern University Press, 1970)—Trans.]

56. Ludwig Binswanger, "La conception de l'homme, chez Freud, à la lumière de l'anthropologie philosophique" [1936], trans. Hans Pollnow, *L'Évolution psychiatrique* 10, no. 1 (1938): 3–34; for the English translation,

see "Freud's Conception of Man in the Light of Anthropology," in *Being-in-the-World: Selected Papers of Ludwig Binswanger*, ed. and trans. Jacob Needleman (Basic Books, 1963), 149–81.

57. Jacques Lacan, "The Problem of Style and the Psychiatric Conception of Paranoiac Forms of Experience," trans. Jon Anderson, *Critical Texts* 5, no. 3 (1988): 4–6.

58. Letter from Maldiney to Kuhn dated 26 June 1953, in Henri Maldiney and Roland Kuhn, *Rencontre / Begegnung. Au péril d'exister, Briefwechsel / Correspondance, Français / Deutsch, 1953–2004*, ed. Liselotte Rutishauser and Robert Christe (Königshausen und Neumann, 2017), 26.

59. See Georges Gusdorf, "Georges Daumézon, l'homme," in *Regard, accueil et présence. Mélanges en l'honneur de Georges Daumézon, trente-deux études de psychiatrie et de psychopathologie* (Privat, 1980), 49.

60. Letter from Binswanger to the Russian philosopher Simon Frank dated 9 December 1950 (quoted by Max Herzog, *Weltenwürfe. Ludwig Binswangers phänomenologische Psychologie* (De Gruyter, 1994), 116–17).

61. Letter from Binswanger to Bachelard dated 5 October 1950 in "Correspondance Gaston Bachelard-Ludwig Binswanger, 1948–1955," trans. and ed. Elisabetta Basso and Emmanuel Delille, *Revue germanique internationale* 30 (2019): 195.

62. Ludwig Binswanger, "La Daseinsanalyse en psychiatrie," trans. Michel Gourevitch, *L'Encéphale* 40, no. 1 (1951): 108–13.

63. Gusdorf, "Georges Daumézon, l'homme," 48.

64. See the letter from Bachelard to Binswanger dated 9 January 1955: "Oh! How I would love to have human beings under my gaze like you! If nothing else, how you help the philosopher of books that I am by bringing me these direct testimonies of human life in its multiplicity!" (Basso and Delille, eds., "Correspondance Gaston Bachelard-Ludwig Binswanger, 1948–1955," 207).

65. The French version of the *Psychodiagnostik* [1921] was published in 1947: Hermann Rorschach, *Psychodiagnostic, méthodes et résultats d'une expérience diagnostique de perception*, trans. André Ombredane and Augustine Landau (PUF, 1947). In 1950, Georges and Jacqueline Verdeaux and André Ombredane participated in launching the "Groupement français du Rorschach," with Lagache as honorary president and Henri Piéron, Henri Wallon, and Merleau-Ponty among its members.

66. See "Correspondance Gaston Bachelard et Roland Kuhn. 1947–1957," trans. and ed. Elisabetta Basso, *Revue de synthèse* 137, nos. 1–2 (2016): 177–89.

67. Ludwig Binswanger, "The Existential Analysis School of Thought," trans. Ernest Angel, in *Existence: A New Dimension in Psychiatry and Psychology*, ed. Rollo May, Ernest Angel, and Henri F. Ellenberger (Basic Books, 1958), 211–12. On this subject, also see Elisabetta Basso, "'Une science de fous et de génies': la phénoménologie psychiatrique à la lumière de la correspondance échangée entre Gaston Bachelard, Roland Kuhn et Ludwig Binswanger," *Revue germanique internationale* 30 (2020): 131–50.

68. Foucault, "Dream, Imagination and Existence," 70.

69. Letter from Bachelard to Binswanger dated 15 April 1948, in Basso and Delille, eds., "Correspondance Gaston Bachelard-Ludwig Binswanger, 1948–1955," 188.

70. Letter from Bachelard to Binswanger dated 31 March 1951, in Basso and Delille, eds., "Correspondance Gaston Bachelard-Ludwig Binswanger, 1948–1955," 96.

71. Merleau-Ponty, "Phenomenology and the Sciences of Man," 47.

72. Eugène Minkowski, *La schizophrénie. Psychopathologie des schizoïdes et des schizophrènes*, new ed. (Desclée de Brouwer, 1953), 237.

73. Foucault, "Dream, Imagination and Existence," 31.

74. Letter from Foucault to Binswanger dated 27 April 1954, in "La correspondence entre Michel Foucault et Ludwig Binswanger, 1954–1956," ed. Elisabetta Basso, trans. René Wetzel, in Bert and Basso, eds., *Foucault à Münsterlingen*, 183.

75. See above, page 206.

76. Foucault, "Dream, Imagination and Existence," 33.

77. Foucault, "Dream, Imagination and Existence," 33 [in italics in the original].

78. For more information about Foucault's meeting with Binswanger and Kuhn, see Bert and Basso, eds., *Foucault à Münsterlingen*.

79. Letter from Foucault to Binswanger dated 21 May 1954, in Basso and Wetzel, ed. and trans., "La correspondence entre Michel Foucault et Ludwig Binswanger, 1954–1956," 193.

80. See above, page 207.

81. See above, page 32.

82. Foucault, "Dream, Imagination and Existence," 31.

83. This manuscript is incomplete and fragmentary (BNF, Fonds Michel Foucault, Box 4, call number NAF 28083).

84. Michel Foucault, "La recherche scientifique et la psychologie."

85. Michel Foucault, "Introduction générale," p. 4 (BNF, Fonds Michel Foucault, Box 46, folder 4, call number NAF 28730).

86. Foucault, "Introduction générale," p. 5.

87. Foucault, "Dream, Imagination and Existence," 31.

88. Foucault, "Introduction générale," p. 5.

89. Foucault, "Introduction générale," p. 5.

90. Foucault, "Introduction générale," p. 5.

91. Handwritten manuscript entitled "Introduction" (BNF, Fonds Michel Foucault, Box 46, folder 4, call number NAF 28730), pp. 2–4; the italics indicate material that is underlined in the manuscript.

92. Foucault, "Introduction," p. 3.

93. Foucault, "Introduction," p. 4.

94. Michel Foucault, "Preface to the *History of Sexuality*, Volume Two," trans. William Smock, in *The Essential Works of Foucault, 1954–1984*, vol. 1, *Ethics, Subjectivity and Truth*, ed. Paul Rabinow (The New Press, 1997), 200.

95. Michel Foucault and Charles Ruas, "An interview with Michel Foucault," in *Death and the Labyrinth: The World of Raymond Roussel*, trans. Charles Ruas (Continuum, 2004), 177. [In the original French interview, Foucault says "le problème"—the problem—rather than "the subject"—Trans.]

96. Letters from Verdeaux to Binswanger dated 1 July and 2 September 1954 (Binswanger Archives, Universitätsarchiv Tübingen, call number 443/60). Ludwig Binswanger, *Le Cas Suzanne Urban. Étude sur la schizophrénie*, trans. J. Verdeaux (Desclée de Brouwer, 1957; Alias, 2019).

97. Viktor von Weizsäcker, *Der Gestaltkreis. Theorie der Einheit von Wahrnehmen und Bewegen*, 4th ed. (Thieme, 1950). From Foucault's correspondence with the publisher Desclée de Brouwer, we learn that the philosopher had already completed the first part of his translation at the end of 1954 (BNF, Fonds Michel Foucault, Box 5, folder 1, call number NAF 28803).

98. Philippe Artières and Jean-François Bert, *Un succès philosophique. L'Histoire de la folie à l'âge classique de Michel Foucault* (Presses universitaires de Caen-IMEC Éd., 2011), 40–47.

99. Jakob Wyrsch, *La personne du schizophrène. Étude clinique, psychologique et anthropophénoménologique*, trans. J. Verdeaux (PUF, 1955 [1949]);

Roland Kuhn, *Phénoménologie du masque à travers le test de Rorschach*, trans. J. Verdeaux, pref. Gaston Bachelard (Desclée de Brouwer, 1957 [1944]).

100. Letter from Foucault to Verdeaux dated 29 December 1956 (Verdeaux family's private archives).

101. Michel Foucault, *Folie et déraison. Histoire de la folie à l'âge classique* (Plon, 1961). This description appears on the book's dust jacket and is not reproduced in the English translation.

102. This document is partly reproduced in Artières and Bert, *Un succès philosophique*, 94–95.

103. Artières and Bert, "Porter le livre chez les historiens: histoire et psychologie," in *Un succès philosophique*, 135–49.

104. Foucault, *Mental Illness and Psychology*, 84–85.

105. Foucault, "Preface to the *History of Sexuality*, Volume Two," 200.

106. Michel Foucault and Charles Ruas, "An interview with Michel Foucault," 176.

107. Michel Foucault, "Preface to the 1961 edition," in *History of Madness*, trans. Jonathan Murphy and Jean Khalfa (Routledge, 2006), xxvii.

108. Foucault, *Mental Illness and Psychology*, 74.

109. Foucault, *Mental Illness and Psychology*, 74.

110. Georges Canguilhem, "Report from Mr. Canguilhem on the Manuscript Filed by Mr. Michel Foucault, Director of the Institut Français of Hamburg, in Order to Obtain Permission to Print His Principal Thesis for the Doctor of Letters," trans. Ann Hobart, *Critical Inquiry* 21, no. 2 (1995): 281. See also Artières and Bert, *Un succès philosophique*, 93.

111. Pierre Macherey, "Aux sources de l'*Histoire de la folie*. Une rectification et ses limites," *Critique*, nos. 471–472 (1986): 770.

DETAILED CONTENTS

A Preface to Experience, by Bernard E. Harcourt vii
Foreword to the French Edition, by François Ewald xlix
Rules for Editing the Text, by Elisabetta Basso li
Translator's Note, by Marie Satya McDonough xlix

Binswanger and Existential Analysis

Introduction

I. Psychoanalysis and anthropology of life: 1. The vital and lived experience [le vital et le vécu]; *2. The return to lived experience: Freud and Husserl. II. Phenomenological psychology as an eidetic science: 1. The return to lived experience in eidetic phenomenology; 2. From the eidetics of lived experience to the genesis of constitutions. III. Phenomenological description and pathological experience: 1. "Lebenswelt"; 2. Negation and contradiction: psychopathology puts the phenomenological model in crisis. IV. The analysis of forms of existence as a radical surpassing of phenomenological analysis.*

Chapter One. The Ellen West Case

Theoretical construction and clinical observation in phenomenological psychopathology. I. The Ellen West case (Ludwig Binswanger):

1. The patient's history; 2. Comparison between the Ellen West case and the Nadia case (Pierre Janet); 3. The psychoanalytic interpretation of Ellen West; 4. The world of Ellen West; 5. The style of existence of Ellen West. II. Ontic and ontological.

Chapter Two. Space

I. Spatiality: 1. The originary lived experience of space: Husserl; 2. Spatiality founds itself on "being-in-the-world"; 3. Affective spatiality. II. The space of patients: 1. The Franz Weber case (Roland Kuhn): the "delusion of limits"; 2. The subject's mode of spatialization. III. The link between space and time: analyzing spatiality leads one to ask how existence is temporalized.

Chapter Three. Time

I. The problem of time: 1. Time in mental illness; 2. The common root of history and of temporality at the existential level. II. Analysis of two cases of schizophrenia: 1. The Georg case (Roland Kuhn); 2. One of Alfred Storch's analyses. III. Phenomenological description and existential analysis: 1. The morbid experience of time in the context of a purely phenomenological description; 2. The Rudolf R. case (Roland Kuhn); 3. Psychotherapy as a verification of the world-project.

Chapter Four. The experience of the other

I. Temporality and intersubjectivity: 1. The first explicit divergence between existential analysis and Heidegger's analytic of existence; 2. The experience of the other in the psychiatric tradition, in Freud and in Husserl. II. The figure of the Other in the morbid horizon: 1. The other in the phenomenological domain; 2. The totality of the other and sexual perversions. III. Clinical case studies: 1. The Konrad Schwing case (Medard Boss); 2. The Lola Voss case (Ludwig Binswanger). IV. Daseinsanalyse's distance from Husserl's phenomenology and

Heidegger's ontology: 1. The Jürg Zünd case (Ludwig Binswanger); 2. The anthropological primacy of love.

Chapter Five. Existential Anthropology

Daseinsanalyse *in relation to phenomenological psychology and to Sartre's existential psychoanalysis: 1. The reflection on existence; 2. The patient and the forms of his freedom. II. Daseinsanalyse's therapeutic vocation: the physician-patient relationship. III. Signification and expression: 1. "Existenzerhellung"; 2. The Lina case (Roland Kuhn). IV. Daseinsanalyse between metaphysics and objective analysis.*

Manuscript Context

The Research Projects of the 1950s: Between Philosophy and Psychology, by Elisabetta Basso

Index of Notions   265
Index of Names   271

SUBJECT INDEX

abreaction, 181*nx*, 196
abstraction, 14, 96, 110, 171–72, 176, 180, 186, 197, 201
adaptation, 7–8, 35, 188
affectivity/affective/affection, 38, 40, 48, 56, 58, 60, 83, 88–89, 109, 138–39, 146, 183, 198, 204
aggressivity/aggressive/aggression, 139, 157, 160, 162, 208
alienation (*Entfremdung*), xxi–xxiii, xxiv, xxxi, xxxiii, 28–30, 131*n*1, 161, 175, 234–35
analyst/psychoanalyst, xxvi, 51, 53, 72, 75, 124, 187, 195–96, 203–4, 237, 254
animal/animality, 73, 104, 144–45, 173–74, 232
anorexia, 55
anthropology/anthropological, x, xvii, xviii, 5*n*b–6*n*b, 6–8, 32, 37*n*7, 41*n*11, 73, 81*n*17, 96*n*2, 98*n*5, 143, 156, 162–64, 169–207, 210*n*5, 211*n*8, 212*n*10, 213*n*13, 219*n*21, 233, 235–37, 240–47, 250
anxiety, 35, 46, 48, 64–65, 67–68, 75, 77, 79, 87, 103–5, 107, 109, 117–18, 120, 122, 146–47, 150, 152, 158–59, 163, 192, 194, 196–200; *Angsterleben* (lived anxiety), 131*n*1
aphasia/aphasiac, 71, 86–87, 99*n*6, 99*n*7, 100*n*9, 216*n*18
a priori, 79, 147, 153, 248
Arztsein (being a physician), 217*n*19
asomatognosia, 86, 86*n*f
associationism, 36*n*7
authenticity/authentic, xxviii, xxix, xxx–xxxi, 30, 63, 67, 71, 79*n*13, 94, 108, 111, 129, 136, 146, 156, 167*n*11, 199–200, 207
autism/autistic, 76*n*8, 91, 138, 165*n*4

behavior/conduct, xvi, xxvii–xxviii, liv, 7–9, 10, 26, 56–57, 61*n*uu, 67–68, 121, 124–25, 137, 139, 143, 145, 148, 152–53, 173–74, 176, 185–86, 208*n*1, 216, 235
being (*Sein*), x, xvi–xvii, xxiv, xxvi, xxviii, xxix, xxx–xxxii, xlv*n*86, 63, 136, 177, 210*n*5, 216*n*17; *auseinandersein* (being one outside the other), 189; *Hineingeworfensein* (being-thrown-in), 222*n*26; *-In-der-Welt-sein* (being in

being (*Sein*) (*continued*)
the world), 31, 43n20, 156, 167n11, 210n12; *-In-der-Welt-über-die-Welt-hinaus-sein* (Being-in-the-world-beyond-and-above-the-world), 156, 167n11, 205; *Leersein* (being-empty), 69; *Menschsein* (being-human), 167n11, 172, 210n5; *miteinandersein* (being one with the other), 189, 223n27; *Mitmenschensein/Mitsein* (being-with), 189, 202, 217n19; *mitmenschlich* (interhuman relationship), 189; *Möglichsein* (possible being), 164n1; *Objektsein* (object being), 218n21; *Seindürfen* (being-allowed-to-be), 167n11, 206; *Seinkönnen* (being-able-to-be), 167n11, 206, 208n1; *Seinslehre* (doctrine of being), 223n28; *Seinsmodus* (mode of being), 161, 221n26; *Seinsproblem* (problem of being), 177, 212n11; *Seinsverbundenheit* (connectedness of being), 221n26; *Selbstsein* (being oneself), 163, 167n11, 208n1; *Wirsein* (being-we), 163, 167n11, 205; *Zu sich selber Sein* (being beside oneself), 223n27. *See also Arztsein*; *Dasein*

Bergsonism, 12–13, 37n9, 108

Beruf (occupation, vocation), 182, 182ny

biography/biographical, xxxiii, 5, 26, 103, 110–12, 128, 202, 204, 213n12

body, xv, xxviii, 4–5, 5nb, 7, 18–19, 21, 49, 55–56, 59–60, 67–70, 83, 85–86, 88, 91, 97n3, 107, 110, 121–24, 126, 128, 142–46, 153, 162, 165n5, 192, 221n26

care, ix, xxvii, xxxi, xlivn58, 93, 144, 150, 152, 157, 221–21n26

category/categorical, 46, 86–87, 100n9, 174, 177, 208n1

causal/causality, 9–11, 18, 27–30, 142, 228

choice/to choose, lv, 27, 54, 172, 176, 205, 207, 208n2, 221, 231

clinic, 42, 47, 51, 53, 57, 74n1, 75n3, 76n8, 99n7, 101n11, 131n6, 239

concrete, xviii, xxii, xxxii, 12–13, 20, 31, 34, 37, 90, 98n5, 108, 125, 137, 140, 144, 147, 153, 170–72, 176, 178, 183–84, 188–89, 200–201, 203–4, 206–8, 222n26, 232–36, 240, 242, 247, 248

conduct. *See* behavior/conduct

conflict, xix–xxii, xxvi, 35, 50, 53, 66, 160, 165, 189, 220, 234

contradiction, xxi–xxii, 3, 23–25, 30–31, 35, 48, 61, 64–65, 67, 69–70, 93, 108, 121, 128, 130, 139–40, 160, 165, 184, 198

cure. *See* healing

Dasein (being-in-the-world; being-there; existence), xvii, xxviii, 71, 76n10, 79n13, 96, 132, 167n11, 176–78, 205, 208n1, 210n5, 212n10, 212n11, 218n21, 221–22n26, 223n7; *Daseinsanalyse* (existential analysis), viii–ix, xi, xv, xviii, xxix, xxxviii, 32, 41n15, 72–73, 132n8, 155, 169–70, 172, 177–78, 182, 205, 207, 208n1, 210n8, 212–13n12, 218–19n21, 223n28, 237–43, 245–48; *Daseinsanalytik* (analytic of existence), 78, 94, 101, 135–36; *Daseinsformen* (forms of being-in-the-world),

SUBJECT INDEX 267

xvii, 32, 84, 84*n*c, 173, 205, 213*n*12; *Daseinsgrund* (raison d'être), 77*n*2; *Daseinsmodus* (mode of being-in-the-world), 223*n*27; *Daseinsverlauf* (existential trajectory), 213*n*12; *Daseinsweisen räumlichen* (spatial and temporal modes of being), 223*n*27; *Dasein überhaupt* (in general), 212*n*10
daydream, 48, 198
death (*Tod*), 49*n*m
deficit, 4, 9, 34*n*3, 99*n*6, 184–85
delusion (*Wahn*), 23, 25, 41*n*15, 42*n*17, 89, 91–94, 101*n*12, 107, 110–12, 118–19, 138–39, 148, 151, 153, 160, 228; *Weltuntergangswahn* (delusion of the end of the world), 23
depression/depressive, xvii, 46–49, 53–54, 74*n*2, 89, 114, 180
derealization, 72, 148, 166*n*9
desire, xxiv, xxviii, xxx–xxxi, xxxvii, 5, 49–53, 56, 60, 64, 66, 70, 111, 114, 117, 143, 161, 166*n*7. *See also Neigung*; *Wunsch*
destiny, 62, 67, 105, 110, 112, 120, 125, 129–30*n*1, 138
dialectic, 24, 30–32, 35, 84, 108, 125, 140, 154, 166*n*5, 189–90, 208*n*1, 217*n*19, 222*n*26
disorder, 4, 6, 9, 76*n*7, 86, 99*n*6, 106, 120, 138, 154, 180, 209*n*4
dream, xvi, xvii–xviii, xxi, xxv, 42, 48, 59–61, 63–65, 67, 70, 78–79*n*12, 89, 114, 125–26, 145, 162, 165*n*4, 192–95, 198–201, 220*n*24, 241

eidetic/eidetics, 3, 10, 12–19, 36*n*6, 84, 120, 147–48, 179, 243

electroencephalography/electroencephalogram (EEG), xiv, 228
electroshock/electroconvulsive therapy (ECT), 158, 180
Empfindlichkeit (sensitivity), 129
Entschlossenheit (resolution), 167
epileptic/epilepsy, 180–81
Eros/eroticism/erotic, 4, 35, 60, 143–46, 166*n*7, 198
essence (*Wesen*), xxvi, xlvi*n*93, 12–16, 18–20, 25, 31, 39*n*10, 47, 63, 125, 128, 138, 140–42, 147, 171, 173, 177, 184, 190, 217*n*19, 235–36, 245–46
evolutionism/evolutionist, 5–6*n*b, 7, 9–10, 28, 35*n*4, 35*n*5, 139, 165*n*5, 183, 186, 234
existence/existential: coexistence, xxvii, 14–15, 77, 136, 139–41, 155, 160; *Existenzerhellung* (existential elucidation), 169, 191, 217*n*19, 218–19*n*21; *Existenzhortung* (existential "hoard"), 93. *See also Dasein*
existentialism, xlvi, 208*n*2
Existentialität (existentiality), 210*n*5
experience: *Erfahrungsweise* (forms of experience), ix, x, 213*n*12, 234; *Erfahrungswissenschaften* (sciences of experience), 178; *le vécu/Erlebnis* (lived experience), xxxiii, xxxvi, 3, 5, 5–6*n*b, 7–12, 16–20, 25–31, 58, 83, 88, 128, 190; *le vital* (vital), 3, 5, 5–6*n*b, 7–11
expression, xxi, xxiv, xxvi, xxvii, xxx–xxxi, 16, 25, 30, 36, 59–61, 70, 81, 86, 88, 111, 118, 130, 154, 167, 190–91, 205–7, 217, 220, 222, 232, 234, 241, 247

feeling, xxx–xxxi, 16–17, 53, 56–57, 67, 69, 76–77, 109, 114, 130, 144, 156–57, 159, 166, 192, 196–97, 199
fetishism, 142–46, 166
freedom/liberty, xvii, 30, 71, 73, 79, 89, 112, 136, 148*n*u, 172, 174–77, 208–9, 246
function/functional, 4–7, 16, 33, 40, 56, 87, 112, 132, 154–55, 165–66, 173–74, 180, 185, 189, 216, 220. *See also* life/vital

Geborgenheit (protection, secrecy, security), 129
genesis, 5–6*n*b, 7, 9–10, 14, 17–24, 26–28, 31, 35–36, 83–85, 120, 125, 140, 148, 155, 248
Gestalt (form), 125
Geworfenheit (thrownness), 207–8*n*1; *Zurückgeworfensein* (being-thrown-back), 221–22*n*26
guilt (*Schuld*), 117–18, 120, 144, 156, 192, 199; *Scham-und-Schuld-Gefühl* (feeling of shame and guilt), 76–77*n*10

hate/hatred, 17, 26, 50*n*p, 69, 122, 124, 143*n*i, 194, 202–3
healing/cure, xxii, 54, 118, 157, 179, 181–82, 193, 196, 200, 202, 204, 214, 220
health (*Gesundheit*), xx, 50, 159, 180, 188, 218
history, ix, x, xv, xxiii, xxv, xxxv–xxxvi, xliii*n*40, 3, 5–6*n*b, 7–8, 11, 46–73, 79*n*13, 81*n*17, 84, 103–6, 108–9, 112–13, 116, 118, 120–21, 128, 167, 189–90, 195, 204, 207, 229, 230, 236, 244, 247–50

humanism, xxiii, 9, 28
humanitarianism, 183
hysteria/hysteric, 3–5, 9

Ideenflucht (flight of ideas), 172, 178, 210
illness, ix, xix, xx–xxiii, xxxii, 4–5, 26, 28–29, 31, 34, 43, 52–54, 57–58, 61, 61*n*uu, 71–73, 87, 90–91, 96, 98, 101, 103–4, 106, 113–14, 138, 152, 156, 159, 171, 174, 179–82, 184–86, 188, 196–97, 203, 205, 209, 214–15, 233–34, 243, 248–50
image, xvi, xvii, 22, 42, 58, 69, 77–79, 90, 94, 96–97*n*2, 110, 129*n*1, 153, 172, 200, 221–22*n*26
imaginary, 12–13, 60, 104, 126, 139–40, 200, 203, 215*n*2
imagination, xiii, 64, 126, 144–45, 239, 241
imago, 138–39, 187, 195
individual (*Einzelne*). *See* space
individuality, 47, 92, 112, 138, 159–60
individuation, 12
instant/moment, xvii, xxiv, xlvi*n*93, 10–12, 17–18, 22, 23, 24, 26, 29–31, 53, 64, 69, 77–78*n*11, 86, 88–89, 106, 111, 115–16, 118–20, 137–40, 143, 147–48, 155–56, 159, 165–66*n*5, 171, 174, 176, 185, 193–94, 197, 200, 205, 206, 241
instinct, xxvi, xxxi, 60, 65, 67–68, 106, 108, 143, 143*n*i, 248
intentionality, lv, 221–22
interpretation, xxv, xxviii, xxxiii, xxxiv, xxxv–xxxvi, 42*n*16, 46, 58–60, 61*n*uu, 73, 78, 107–8; *philosophische Deutung*

SUBJECT INDEX 269

(philosophical interpretation), 45, 75*n*4
intuition, 14, 16, 39, 46, 218–19*n*21

Jacksonism, 5–6*n*b, 8

knowledge, 36, 38–39*n*10, 93, 115, 117, 186, 212–13*n*12, 217*n*19, 246

language, xvii, xxxi, liii, liv, 71–72, 77–78*n*11, 91, 100*n*9, 110, 137–38, 140, 155, 205–6, 232
liberty. *See* freedom
libido/libidinal, 5–6*n*b, 8, 35*n*4, 124, 139, 200
life/vital, vii–ix, xxv–xxvi, xxxiii, xxxvi–xxxvii, xlvi*n*93, liv, 5, 5–6*n*b, 7–11, 20, 23, 27, 29, 29*n*mm, 35–36*n*5, 36–37*n*7, 42*n*16, 48–49, 51–54, 58–60, 62–65, 67–68, 70, 73, 75–76*n*6, 78–79*n*12, 86, 106, 108–9, 112–14, 109, 116–18, 123–24, 126–30, 150–51, 155, 156–57, 184, 189, 197, 200–201, 247; *Binnenleben* (inner life), 164–65*n*4; *Lebensfunktion* (vital function), 189–90, 213*n*14, 217–18*n*19; *Lebensgeschichte* (lived history), 5, 189–90, 217–18*n*19. *See also* movement; world (*Welt*)
love (*Liebe*)/romantic, ix–x, xxvii, xxxi, 17, 42*n*17, 48–49, 63, 64, 69, 71, 76–77*n*10, 110–11, 122, 126, 136, 145–46, 148*n*u, 162–63, 167*n*11, 193–94, 198–99, 205, 207–8, 215–16*n*16, 221–22*n*26, 242; *liebende Begegnung* (encounter in love), 163; *liebenden Seinsicherheit* (security of being in love),

221–22*n*26; *Menschenliebe* (love for humans), 215–16*n*16; *Selbst-Liebe* (self-love), 76–77*n*10

madness/mad/demented, vii, xvi, xxi, xxi, xxiii, 27–28, 124, 175, 176, 184, 238, 249, 250
man (*Mensch*), xvii, xviii, xxii, xxiii, liv, 5–6*n*b, 7–8, 30, 43*n*19, 46–48, 57, 60, 63, 68, 72–73, 90, 93, 106, 108, 112, 115, 117, 122, 138, 149, 170–74, 176, 177, 180, 182–84, 189, 193–94, 198–202, 205–6, 208–9*n*2, 210*n*5, 218–19*n*21, 232–36, 244–46, 250; *Menschenwesen* (being of man), 217–18*n*19. *See also Menschenliebe*; *Menschsein*
mania/manic, 47, 54, 73, 180, 209*n*4
materialism/materialist, xi, xix, xx, xxii, xxiv, xxxiii, 5–6*n*b, 7, 234–35, 246–47, 254*n*46
meaning, xi, xvii, xxi, xxvi, xxvii, xxx, xxxvi, liv–lv, 3–5, 5–6*n*b, 7, 9, 13, 16, 19, 21–24, 26–31, 35–36, 39, 42*n*16, 46, 58, 60–62, 65–66, 68–70, 72, 77–78*n*11, 78*n*12, 81*n*17, 84–85, 87, 93–94, 101*n*12, 107, 113, 117, 119–20, 126–28, 135–41, 144, 147–48, 152, 154–55, 160, 162–64, 169, 171, 174, 179, 184–86, 189, 191, 197, 199–200, 205, 206, 209*n*3, 221*n*26, 246, 250
medicine, xx, 42, 74*n*2, 75*n*3, 101, 188*n*ff
memory, 5, 47, 69, 111, 125, 128, 150, 195–96, 199, 219–20*n*23
metaphysics/metaphysical, ix, xxxi, 4, 5–6*n*b, 106, 108, 171, 176–77, 205–7, 221*n*25, 242
motricity/motor, 5, 21, 86–87

270 SUBJECT INDEX

mourning/work of mourning (*Trauerarbeit*), 124–25, 200
movement: *Kreisbewegung* (circular movement), 79; *Lebensbewegung* (life movement), 130
myth/mythic, 4, 11, 36–37n7, 60, 110, 111, 112, 117, 120, 140, 172

Neigung (inclination, desire), 50
neo-Jacksonism, 5–6nb, 33–35n3
neurology/neurologist, 75n3, 97–98n5, 132n8
neurosis/neurotic, 8, 54, 68, 105–6, 187, 191, 219–20n23; *Zwangsneurose* (obsessional neurosis), 59n00
nihilism, 47, 63
norm, 5–6nb, 7, 148nu, 174, 184, 185, 217
normal/abnormal, xx, xxviii, xxviii, xxix, xxxiii, 8–9, 22, 28, 68, 72, 142, 148, 153, 164, 184, 229
normativity/normative, 120, 164, 186

obsession/obsessional, 3, 54, 55–56, 65, 66–67, 68, 73, 151
Oedipus complex, 138
ontic, xxxii, 73, 178
ontology/ontological, ix, x, xviii, xxxii, xlvin93, 32, 73, 94, 135–36, 155, 177–78, 186, 205–6, 210, 212–13, 223, 241, 248, 250
organism, 10, 143, 173–74, 185–86
organo-dynamism, 33n3, 237
other/Other (*autrui/Autre*), 135–64, 170ne, 184, 197–98

passion, 69, 140, 175, 188, 190
pathology/pathological, xxix, xxxiii, 8–9, 20–24, 26, 28, 31–32, 33–35n3,

46, 57, 65, 72, 74–75n2, 95–97n2, 107, 114–15, 120–21, 138, 141, 148, 154–55, 163–65, 174–75, 176, 180, 184, 200, 209n3, 216–17n18, 243–44
patient, ix, xxii, xxvi–xxx, xxxiii, 10, 46–73, 91, 93–94, 107, 110–11, 114–20, 131–32n6, 138, 153, 159–60, 162, 175, 181–89, 194–97, 199–204, 206, 215–16n16, 219–20n23
perception, xxviii, 39, 78, 137, 239, 251
person, xxi, xxvi, xxvii, xxix, xxx, xxxi, xxxii, xxxiii, liv, 16–17, 30–31, 61, 73, 92, 125, 141–42, 161, 171, 174, 180, 187, 198, 200, 214n15, 217n19, 221n26, 234
personality, 26, 30, 34, 114, 130, 143, 199, 208, 217
perversion, 142–43
phenomenology/phenomenological, x, xi, xiii, xv–xvii, xix, xxiii–xxvii, xxx, xxxii, xxxiv, xxxviii, xxxixn9, xlivn65, xlvn86, xlvin93, liii, lv, 12–13, 19, 22, 25, 31, 38–39n10, 45, 80n16, 84–85, 108, 120, 140, 155, 230, 232, 236, 238, 240–41, 243–47, 249, 255n55
philosophy/philosophical, vii–xv, xviii, xix, xxi–xxiv, xxxii–xxxiii, xxxvii, xxxviii, xlvin93, xlix, 9, 11, 37n9, 43n19, 58, 74n2, 81n17, 97n4, 132n8, 137, 172, 175–76, 178, 188, 207, 208n2, 210n8, 211–12n9, 218–19n21, 223–24n28, 227–50
phobia/phobic, 22, 103, 104, 105, 129–31n1, 131n2, 139, 151; agoraphobe, 104
physician, 10–11, 53, 61nuu, 75n3, 78–79n12, 110, 114, 149, 151, 157–58, 182–90, 193, 201–4, 206, 217–18n19
process, vii, xx, xxiv, liii, 4, 6nb, 7–9, 11, 13, 15, 26–28, 30, 58–59, 72–73,

SUBJECT INDEX   271

90, 94, 118, 123, 129n1, 142, 166n5, 179–81, 181nx, 185, 186, 189, 202; *Naturprozess* (natural process), 215n16

project, ix, xxviii, xxx, xxxvii, l, lv, 11, 36n7, 57, 70, 73, 89, 108, 121, 128, 155, 160, 162–63, 170, 170ne, 174, 208n1, 209n2, 223n27, 223n28, 228, 229, 236, 241, 242, 243, 245, 247, 249, 250. *See also* world (*Welt*)

psyche, 25, 35n4, 38–39n10, 186, 189, 217n19

psychiatrist, viii, xvi, xxix, 42n18, 54, 65, 72, 74n2, 76n8, 80n15, 97n3, 98n5, 99n9, 100n10, 101n11, 157, 180, 189, 195, 202, 217n19, 233, 237–40, 242

psychiatry/psychiatric, viii, ix, x, xi, xii, xiii, xv–xviii, xx, xxiv–xxviii, xlivn58, liii, 3, 5nb, 37n7, 39n10, 42n18, 61nuu, 74n2, 75n3, 76n8, 97n3, 98n5, 100, 100n10, 132n8, 148, 170, 175–76, 178, 190, 221n25, 229, 235, 236–37

psychoanalysis/psychoanalytic, viii, xi, xvi, xvii, xx, xxii, xxv, xxvi, xxvii, xxix, xln16, 3–4, 10, 35n4, 42n16, 46–47, 50–52, 58–61, 70, 78n12, 103, 124naa, 132n8, 140, 145, 157, 166n5, 166n6, 169, 187, 189, 190, 196, 197, 201, 203–4, 209n2, 217n19, 219n22, 220n23, 231, 232

psychodiagnostic test/Rorschach test, 101n11, 228, 239, 248

psychology/psychological, xi, xii–xv, xviii–xxiv, xln16, xlin18, xlin20, xlin24, xlix, 4, 8–12, 12nh, 14–16, 19, 25, 29nmm, 30, 34n3, 35n4, 35n5, 36n6, 36–37n7, 38–39n10, 41n14, 42–43n18, 43n19, 43n20, 45,

57, 62, 68, 74n2, 75n3, 75n4, 76n7, 79n13, 81n17, 97n4, 99n6, 99n7, 108, 131n3, 138–40, 164n1, 164n2, 165–66n5, 169–72, 175, 175nk, 179, 181, 189, 190, 208–9n2, 211–12n9, 213n12, 217n19, 223n28, 227–39, 243–50

psychopathology/psychopathological, xiv, xix, xx, 12nh, 24–25, 28, 30, 40, 45, 74n2, 75n4, 97, 132, 163, 169, 174–77, 208n1, 209n2, 215n16, 223–24n28, 228, 231, 240

psychosis/psychotic, xxvi, 43n18, 54, 58, 61, 118, 209n4

real/reality, vii, viii, xi, xx, xxi, xxii, xxiv, xxv, xxvi, xxviii, xxix, xxx, xxxii, xxxiii, xxxv, xxxvii, xxxviii, lii, 4, 7, 13–14, 16, 22, 24, 30–31, 37, 38n10, 40, 43, 50, 57, 63–64, 67, 70, 79, 103–4, 108, 110, 112, 116, 117, 118, 124–25, 127–28, 139, 142, 151, 154, 159, 165, 169–71, 173, 175, 176–78, 179, 180, 183–84, 187–88, 196, 198–204, 205, 206, 208n1, 209n3, 214–16, 218, 238, 247

recognition/recognize, xxii, xxxi, 11, 25, 27, 37, 64, 87, 111, 142, 148, 161, 174, 205, 218–19n21

repression, 3, 58, 59, 138, 188

ressentiment/resentment, 17, 26, 37n7, 41n12

sadness, 12, 15–16

schizophrenia/schizophrenic, xxix, 3, 12nh, 23, 28, 38n10, 42n15, 43n18, 46, 54, 71–73, 76, 91, 109, 109nh, 117, 131n5, 138, 164n4, 167n9, 180, 207–8n1, 237

science (*Wissenschaft*)/scientific, vii,
xiii, xx, xliii*n*48, xliv*n*57, xlv*n*81,
10, 13*nj*, 14–15, 35*n*4, 36, 76*n*9, 157,
172–73, 178, 178*nt*, 179, 182, 182*ny*,
186, 197, 208*n*1, 210*n*5, 211*n*9,
221*n*25, 229–30, 235, 244, 245, 249,
255*n*55
security, 63, 92, 107, 111, 118–19,
129*n*1, 161, 163, 184, 186, 219*n*21;
Sekuritätsbedürfnis (need
for security), 219*n*21. *See also*
Geborgenheit
self (*Selbst*), 49, 70, 77, 208, 219;
inneres Selbst (inner self),
49; *Selbstauslöschung* (self-
effacement), 130; *Selbsteinfaltung*
(withdrawal of the self), 130;
Selbsteinsargung (burying of the
self), 130; *Selbstheit* (selfhood),
96; *Selbst-Liebe* (*See* love *(Liebe)*/
romantic); *Selbstsein* (*See*
being *(Sein)*); *Selbsteinkönnen*
(power to be oneself), 208*n*1;
Selbstwerden (becoming oneself),
79
separation (*Loslösung*), 59, 127, 165
sexuality, vii, viii, ix, xxv, xxviii, 41*n*11,
63, 70, 127, 142, 144, 161, 166*n*5
society/social, xii, xiii, xix, xx, xxi,
xxii, xxv, xxviii, xxxvii, 48, 56,
62–63, 70–71, 77, 77*n*10, 90, 92,
97, 97*n*4, 111, 112, 137–38, 144,
156, 158, 160–61, 188, 232, 234–35;
Gesellschaft, 112
soul, xv, 4–5, 5–6*n*b, 7, 18, 48, 52, 63,
142, 193
space (*Raum*)/spatiality, 83–95,
99*n*6, 99–100*n*7; *Eigenraum*
(individual space), 86–87,
90, 138; *Fremdraum* (foreign
space), 87; *gestimmter Raum*
(emotive or affective space), 40;
Leibraum (space of the body),
85–86, 91; *Umraum* (space of the
milieu), 85; *Zweckraum* (finalized
space), 86
spirit (*Geist*), xlvi, 14, 19, 22, 31, 41*n*11,
69, 115, 173, 179
strangeness, 68, 166–67*n*9
structure, 6*n*b, 7, 13, 16, 31, 34*n*3, 37*n*8,
43*n*30, 58, 73, 83, 92, 104, 109, 116,
118, 120, 147, 155, 163, 182, 190,
210*n*4, 220*n*24, 222*n*26, 227
style, liii, lv, 6*n*b, 9–12, 14, 17–19, 22,
28, 30–31, 48, 63, 79, 81, 105, 109,
113, 137, 155, 173, 178, 185, 206
subject, x, xvii, xxiii, xxvii, xxviii, xxx,
xxxi, xxxiii, xxxv, xxxviii, xlix, 10,
27, 29*n*11, 29–31, 34*n*3, 40*n*11, 59,
62, 64, 68, 76*n*10, 79*n*13, 88, 99*n*6,
100*n*9, 105, 118–19, 141, 154, 162,
171, 174, 176, 178, 179, 233, 235, 237,
243, 247
subjectivity/subjective, 18–19, 28, 38;
intersubjectivity, 135, 141
symbol/symbolic/symbolism, xvi,
xxvi, xxx, xxxiii, 3, 9, 25, 58–61,
68, 77–78*n*11, 87–88, 103–5,
124, 130, 145–46, 148, 150–52,
166–67*n*9, 195
synthesis, 79

tendency, 66, 106, 124; *Lebenstendenz*
(vital tendency), 130
tension (psychic tension), xxxii,
xlv*n*86, 57, 110, 113, 137, 139
therapeutics/self-therapy/
psychotherapy, 131*n*6, 181*nx*, 182,

SUBJECT INDEX   273

185, 186, 187, 189–90, 193, 198, 199–202, 205, 207, 217*n*19
time/temporality/temporalization/temporal, xxv, xxix, xxix, xxx, xlv, 32, 71, 72, 73, 74, 75, 79, 83–84, 93–94, 103–29, 132*n*6, 133, 135–36, 144, 152, 154–55, 162–63, 167*n*11, 199, 200, 205, 221, 223
totality, 10, 18, 21, 34, 43, 94, 98, 116, 121, 135, 137, 140–41, 142–43, 146–48, 154, 170–72, 174, 185, 209*n*3, 210*n*5, 222*n*26, 223*n*28, 235
transcendence/transcendent, 32, 136, 153, 155, 187, 190, 207, 242
transcendental, 19–20, 38, 141, 155, 176, 213, 219, 232, 243–44
transfer, xxx, xxxiii, 10, 54, 150, 166, 187, 196–97, 201–2, 220
traumatism/traumatic, 4, 78, 103
truth, xxvi, xxxiii, xxxiv, xxxv, xlvi, liv, 6, 6*n*b, 13*n*j, 31, 52, 61, 61*n*uu, 105, 112, 125, 127, 129, 136, 164*n*1, 174, 175–76, 180, 182, 186, 196–97, 214, 215, 243–44, 249–50

unconscious, xxvi, xxvii, xxxiii, 3, 4, 10, 27, 59, 61, 61*n*uu, 78, 103, 186, 196–97, 220
understanding (*Verstehen*)/understand, ix, xvi, xvii, xix, xx, xxiii, xxiv, xxvi–xxviii, xxix, xxx, xxxiii, xxxiv, 1, 10–11, 16, 21, 24–28, 31, 36, 38, 42, 46, 59, 61, 69, 73, 80, 87, 96, 98, 113, 126, 136*n*c, 137, 156, 158, 163, 165, 171, 173–74, 177, 179–80, 184, 189, 199, 205, 210–11, 213, 217, 221, 223, 241, 244–45
unreason, 188, 249

Verlorenheit (forlornness), 131
Verweltlichung (mundanization), 169*n*b, 207–8*n*1
violence (*Gewalt*)/violent, 49, 77, 115, 123, 130, 160, 194–95, 202, 203
vital. *See* life/vital
Vorahandenen (presence-at-hand), 102

Weite (expanse), 129–31
Werden (becoming): *Entwerden* (unbecoming), 79, 129–30; *Werdenshemmung* (inhibition of becoming), 130–31; *Werdensrichtung* (direction of becoming), 130
will/voluntary, 6*n*b, 7, 33, 50
Wirklichkeit (reality), vii, viii, xi, xxiv, xxiv, xxv, xxvi, xxviii, xxix, xxx, xxxiii, xxxv, xxxvii, xxxviii, 7, 16, 22, 30–31, 37, 40, 43, 57, 79, 110, 112, 116, 124–25, 127–28, 139, 142, 154, 165, 169–71, 173, 176–78, 184, 187, 196, 199, 201–3, 205, 207, 208*n*1, 209*n*3, 214–16, 218, 238, 247
wish (*Wunsch*), 34, 47, 50, 60, 94, 114, 130, 209*n*3, 229, 233, 250
world (*Welt*): *Eigenwelt* (world of the self), 62, 65, 66; *Gegenwelt* (world across), 160, 160*n*tt, 161; *Lebenswelt* (world of life), 3, 20, 67, 73, 261; *Mitwelt* (social milieu), xxii, 62, 77, 145, 160–61, 182; *Nahwelt* (vicinity), 129; *Umwelt* (material milieu), 62, 73, 80, 130, 173, 210, 216; *Weltanschauung* (vision of the world), 217–19; *Weltarbeit*

world (*Welt*) (*continued*)
(work of the world), 222;
Weltentwurf (world project),
96, 208n1; *Weltlichkeit*
(worldhood, worldliness), 96;
Weltregierung (government of the
world), 118, 118nv; *Weltuntergang*
(end of the world), 115, 115n1,
118; *Weltuntergangswahn* (See
delusion (*Wahn*)). *See also*
being (*Sein*); *Verweltlichung*

Wunsch (wish), 34, 47, 50, 60, 94, 114,
130, 209n3, 229, 233, 250

Zuhandenen (readiness-to-hand), 80,
85, 93, 95, 102

NAME INDEX

Abraham, Karl, 76
Ajuriaguerra, Julian de, 98
Alembert, d', 175nl
Alexander, Franz G., 204, 219–20
Allendy, René, 237
Althusser, Louis, xix, xxiii, xxxvi, xlii, xlvi, 228, 234, 238
Andersen, Wilhelm, 219
Aron, Jean-Paul, 231, 251–52*n*10, 252–53*n*20
Artières, Philippe, 258–59

Babinski, Joseph, 181
Bachelard, Gaston, 233, 239, 248, 256*n*61, 256*n*64, 257*n*66, 257*n*67, 257*n*69, 257*n*70, 259*n*99
Bachelard, Suzanne, 13*n*l
Basso, Elisabetta, viii, xii, xviii, xxxviii, xxxix*n*2, xxxix*n*10, xl*n*13, xl*n*15, xlii*n*25, xlii*n*36, xlvi*n*92, xlvi*n*95, l, liv, lv, 37, 80, 101, 251*n*1, 251*n*4
Bastide, Georges, 233
Baudelaire, Charles, 208–9*n*2
Bayle, Pierre, 231, 237
Becker, Oskar, 83*n*a
Béguin, Albert, 235, 254*n*44
Bergson, Henri, xv, 11*n*g, 37, 38, 99, 231

Bert, Jean-François, 101, 213, 251*n*4, 252*n*14, 258*n*98
Bianco, Giuseppe, 37
Biemel, Walter, 132*n*7, 233
Bilz, Rudolph, 41
Binswanger, Ludwig, viii–xii, xv–xviii, xxi, xxiv–xxv, xxvii, xxix, xxx–xxxii, xxxiv, xxxviii, xxxix*n*2, xxxix*n*4, xl*n*14, xl*n*15, xlii*n*31, xlii*n*37, xlii*n*38, xlii*n*39, xliii*n*49, xlv*n*81, xlv*n*86, xlv*n*92, xlvi*n*93, li, liii, liv, 16, 16*n*q, 16*n*r, 30*n*oo, 30*n*pp, 32*n*rr, 33*n*2, 35–36*n*5, 39–41*n*11, 43*n*20, 45–46, 46*n*d, 47*n*e, 47*n*f, 49*n*m, 50*n*p, 54–55, 60*n*qq, 62–63, 68, 69*n*ggg, 74–75*n*2, 75*n*3, 75*n*5, 76*n*8, 78–79*n*12, 79*n*13, 80*n*15, 80*n*16, 81*n*17, 86*n*g, 87*n*h, 87–88, 88*n*j, 89, 89*n*l, 94, 94*n*u, 95–97*n*2, 99–100*n*7, 101*n*11, 117–18*n*2, 119*n*4, 125*n*bb, 132*n*8, 135, 148*n*v, 148–51, 151*n*aa, 151*n*z, 152*n*bb, 156, 156*n*ii, 156*n*ff, 156*n*gg, 156*n*hh, 157*n*mm, 157*n*jj, 158*n*oo, 160*n*rr, 161*n*uu, 162*n*vv, 163, 163*n*xx, 163*n*ww, 163*n*yy, 165, 167*n*11, 169, 169*n*b,

NAME INDEX

Binswanger (*continued*)
170–78, 171*n*f, 172*n*g, 178*n*r, 178*n*t, 179, 182, 183*n*aa, 183*n*z, 183–86, 184*n*cc, 185*n*dd, 187*n*ee, 188*n*gg, 188*n*hh, 189–91, 190*n*kk, 200, 200*n*rr, 202, 202*n*ss, 203, 205*n*vv, 206*n*yy, 207, 207–8*n*1, 209–10*n*4, 210*n*5, 210*n*7, 210–11*n*8, 212*n*10, 212–13*n*12, 213*n*14, 215–16*n*16, 217–18*n*19, 221–22*n*26, 222–23*n*27, 223–24*n*28, 227–28, 236–44, 246–47, 250, 251*n*5, 255*n*55, 255–56*n*55, 256*n*60, 256*n*61, 256*n*62, 256*n*64, 257*n*67, 257*n*69, 257*n*70, 257*n*74, 257*n*78, 257*n*79, 258*n*96, 261–63
Blanchot, Maurice, x, xxxiv, 254*n*67
Bleuler, Eugen, xxviii, 42, 71*n*iii, 76*n*8, 164–65*n*4, 237
Bleuler, Manfred, xxviii, 30*n*25, 42–43*m*8
Blondel, Charles, 3–4*m*1, 5, 33*n*1, 138, 164*n*3
Bonnafé, Lucien, 235
Bonnefoy, Yves, 129*n*gg
Borges, Jorge Luis, 100
Boss, Medard, 96, 135, 143*n*k, 144, 144*n*m, 144*n*o, 144*n*p, 144*n*q, 144*n*r, 144*n*1, 144*n*n, 146, 146*n*s, 146*n*t, 146*n*122, 166*n*8, 262
Braunstein, Jean-François, 252*n*14
Breton, André, 184, 184*n*bb
Bruyeron, Roger, 37*n*9
Bühler, Karl, 38–39*n*10
Burckhardt, E., 97–99*n*5
Buytendijk, Frederik Jacobus Johannes, 95–97*n*2

Cabanis, Pierre Jean Georges, 228
Canguilhem, Georges, 33–35*n*3, 37*n*9, 97–99*n*5, 230, 247, 249, 252*n*13, 252*n*14, 259*n*110
Cassirer, Ernst, 87, 90*n*m, 99*n*6

Christe, Robert, 256*n*58
Corbin, Henry, 164*n*1

Dammann, Gerhard, 131
Darwin, Charles, 11, 35, 75
Daumézon, Georges, 235, 238, 256*n*59, 256*n*63
Defert, Daniel, xix, xxiv, xl, xli*n*21, xli*n*24, xlii*n*27, xlii*n*39, xlii*n*40, xlii*n*41, xlii*n*42, xliv*n*61, xlvii*n*112, l, 35, 81, 251*n*2, 252*n*11
Delay, Jean, xiv, 179*n*u, 180*n*v, 221*n*25
Deleuze, Gilles, 37*n*9
Delille, Emmanuel, 33–35*n*3, 256*n*61, 256*n*64, 257*n*69, 257*n*70
De Rosa, Renato, 132*n*8, 223–24*n*28
Derrida, Jacques, 132–33*n*9
De Waelhens, Alphonse, 233
Diderot, Denis, 175*n*l
Dilthey, Wilhelm, 38–39*n*10, 179, 211–12*n*9
Dora (case), 9, 9*n*d
Duhem, Pierre, 12, 37*n*8
Dumas, Georges, 229
Dumézil, Georges, 232, 236
Durand, Charles, 96

Edinger, Ludwig, 97–98*n*5
Elfriede, 110
Ellenberger, Henri Frédéric, 32*n*rr, 42–43*n*18, 46*n*d, 80*n*16, 95–97*n*2, 101*n*11, 107*n*e, 121*n*x, 156*n*ee, 166*n*8, 167*n*11, 171*n*f, 206*n*yy, 222–23*n*27, 237, 255*n*52, 257*n*67
Eribon, Didier, xlii*n*42, xlii*n*43, xliv*n*62, 251*n*4, 251*n*7, 253*n*22, 253*n*23, 253*n*24, 253*n*28, 254*n*36
Ewald, François, l, 35–36*n*5, 81*m*17, 252*n*11, 261
Ey, Henri, 33–35*n*3, 85*n*d, 95–97*n*2, 235, 237, 240, 255*n*52

NAME INDEX 277

Ferenczi, Sándor, 219–20*n*23
Fischer, Franz, 39–41*n*11, 80*n*16, 119*n*w, 119*n*4
Folch, Pedro, 95–97*n*2
Forel, Auguste, 76*n*8
Frank, Simon, 256*n*60
Freud, Sigmund, viii, xi, xvi, xxv, xxvi, xxxvi, 3–4, 8–10, 9*n*d, 35–36*n*5, 36*n*6, 42*n*16, 62*n*vv, 76*n*8, 77–78*n*11, 105, 106, 108, 124*n*aa, 135, 138, 142, 143*n*i, 165–66*n*5, 184*n*bb, 187, 195–96, 200, 211–12*n*9, 228, 232, 237, 253*n*27, 255–56*n*56, 261–62
Frings, Manfred S., 38–39*n*10, 39–41*n*11

Gadamer, Hans-Georg, 81*n*17
Galileo, 84
Gebsattel, Viktor Emil von, 45, 45*n*c, 74–75*n*2, 75*n*3, 75*n*4, 79*n*13, 104*n*a, 129–31*n*1, 143, 143*n*j, 143*n*k, 166*n*7, 166*n*8
Gelb, Adhémar, 29*n*mm, 86, 97*n*4, 97–99*n*4, 100*n*9
Georg (case), 103, 109–12, 262
Gerhardt, Carl I., 79–80*n*14
Goethe, Johann Wolfgang von, 54, 62*n*vv
Goldstein, Kurt, 29*n*mm, 33–35*n*3, 86–87, 97*n*4, 97–99*n*5, 100*n*9, 185*n*dd, 186, 209*n*3, 216*n*17, 216–17*n*18
Gouhier, Henri, 231
Gros, Frédéric, xl*n*12, l, 251*n*2
Gruevska, Julia, 95–97*n*2
Grünbaum, Abraham Anton, 86, 86*n*g, 99–100*n*7
Guillaume, Paul, 229
Guiraud, Paul, 237, 238, 255*n*51
Gurwitsch, Aron, 97–99*n*5
Gusdorf, Georges, 238–39, 256*n*59, 256*n*63

Häberlin, Paul, 81*n*17, 174, 210–11*n*8, 211–12*n*9, 221–22*n*26
Halbwachs, Maurice, 71, 71*n*jjj
Head, Henry, 216–17*n*18
Hécaen, Henri, 97–99*n*5
Hegel, Georg Wilhelm Friedrich, xi, xx, 63*n*ww, 78–79*n*12, 125, 125*n*ee, 183*n*, 221–22*n*26, 233
Heidegger, Martin, viii, ix–xi, xvii, xxiv, xxvi, xxvii, xxxi, xxxviii, xlv*n*86, xlvi*n*93, 73, 80*n*16, 84*n*c, 85, 93, 95*n*1, 95–97*n*2, 101–2*n*13, 116*n*t, 132–33*n*9, 135–37, 136*n*c, 155, 163, 164*n*1, 174, 174*n*j, 177, 177*n*m, 177*n*o, 177*n*n, 178, 205–6, 207–8*n*1, 212*n*10, 222–23*n*27, 233, 241, 244, 253*n*32, 253*n*33, 253*n*34, 262–63
Heimsoeth, Heinz, 218–19*n*21
Herzog, Max, 172*n*g, 216*n*17, 256*n*60
Hesnard, Angelo Louis Marie, 237, 254–55*n*46, 255*n*53, 255*n*54
Horney, Karen, 204, 204*n*tt, 219*n*22, 219–20*n*23
Husserl, Edmund, viii, ix, xi, xxiv, xxv–xxvii, xxxii, xxxviii, xlv, 3, 10, 10*n*e, 12*n*i, 13*n*l, 13*n*j, 13*n*k, 14*n*m, 15*n*o, 15*n*n, 16*n*p, 18*n*w, 18–23, 19*n*x, 19*n*y, 19*n*z, 21*n*aa, 21*n*bb, 23*n*ff, 35–36*n*5, 36*n*6, 38–39*n*10, 41*n*13, 83–84, 84*n*b, 113*n*n, 114*n*o, 116, 116*n*t, 120, 132*n*7, 132–33*n*9, 135, 140, 141*n*d, 141*n*e, 141*n*f, 142, 142*n*h, 155, 179, 211, 228, 231–32, 236, 241, 243–44, 252*n*19, 253*n*27, 261–62
Hyppolite, Jean, 63*n*ww, 251–52*n*10

Iphigenia, 110–12

278 NAME INDEX

Jackson, John Hughlings, 5–6nb, 8, 33–35n3, 185, 216–17n18
Jaensch, Erich Rudolf Ferdinand, 38–39n10
James, William, 38–39n10
Janet, Pierre, 4, 5–6nb, 8, 16, 45, 55, 55$n$ii, 55$n$gg, 55$n$hh, 55$n$jj, 55$n$kk, 57, 61$n$uu, 69, 76n9, 137, 151, 164n2, 229, 262
Jaspers, Karl, xl$n$16, 25, 25$n$hh, 26$n$ii, 26$n$kk, 27–28, 28$n$ll, 33–35n3, 38–39n10, 42n16, 42n17, 81n17, 170, 182–83, 183$n$aa, 183nz, 188, 188$n$gg, 188$n$hh, 190, 211–12n9, 215–16n16, 217–18n19, 218–19n21, 221–22n26, 223–24n28
Jung, Carl G., 76n8

Kardiner, Abram, 179, 213n13
Katz, David, 38–39n10
Keller, Gottfried, 89
Kierkegaard, Søren, 80n15
Klein, Melanie, 139, 166n6
Kleist, Heinrich von, 112, 112$n$nl
Klossowski, Pierre, 39–41n11
Köhler, Wolfgang, 38–39n10
Kojève, Alexandre, 238
Kraepelin, Emil, 74n1, 75n3, 237
Krüger, Felix, 38–39n10
Kuhn, Roland, xvi, xlv$n$81, 83, 91, 91no, 91nn, 92nq, 92nr, 93ns, 101$n$ii, 101n12, 103, 109, 109ng, 111nj, 111nk, 112nm, 118, 121, 121nx, 122ny, 125$n$bb, 131n5, 131–32n6, 133n10, 166n8, 169, 189, 191, 191$n$ll, 191$n$mm, 192$n$oo, 192$n$pp, 192$n$qq, 192$n$nn, 195, 197, 203, 216n17, 222–23n27, 238, 239, 248, 250, 251n8, 256n58, 257n66, 257n67, 257n78, 259n99, 262–63

Kulenkampff, Caspar, 41–42n15
Kuntz, Jean, 97–99n5
Kunz, Hans, 39–41n11, 43n20, 73, 73$n$mmm, 75n4, 80n15, 81n17, 218–19n21

Lacan, Jacques, 36–37n7, 165–66n5, 209–10n4, 238, 256n57
Lacroix, Jean, 233, 254n40
Laforgue, René Joseph, 237, 255n53, 255n54
Lagache, Daniel, xl, 26$n$jj, 36–37n7, 42n17, 124$n$aa, 148nu, 166n6, 229, 254–55n46, 256n65
Lagrange, Jacques, 35–36n5, 39–41n11, 81n17, 252n11
Lalande, André, 11nf
La Mettrie, Julien Offray de, 228
Lantéri-Laura, Georges, 97–99n5
Lavelle, Louis, 39–41n11
Le Guillant, Louis, 235
Leibniz, Gottfried Wilhelm, 68, 79–80n14, 228
Le Senne, René, 39–41n11
Lina (case), xliv$n$68, 169, 191–92, 194, 197, 199–201, 263
Löwith, Karl, 81n17
Luchsinger, Katrin, 131–32n6
Luczak, Jeannine, 210–11n8
Lyhne, Niels, 47, 75–76n6

Macey, David, 251n9
Macherey, Pierre, xliv$n$65, 250, 259n111
Maine de Biran, François-Pierre, xv, 231
Maldiney, Henri, 238, 256n58
Malebranche, Nicolas, xv, 231
Martineau, Emmanuel, 80n1, 101–2n13

NAME INDEX 279

Mead, Margaret, 179, 213*n*13
Merleau-Ponty, Maurice, xiii, xiv, xv, xxxviii, xli*n*17, xli*n*20, 29*n*mm, 33–35*n*3, 36–37*n*7, 37*n*9, 41*n*12, 96, 98, 99*n*6, 99–100*n*7, 100*n*8, 100*n*9, 165–66*n*5, 210–11*n*8, 228–31, 237–39, 245, 252*n*15, 252*n*16, 252*n*17, 252*n*19, 252–53*n*20, 256*n*65, 257*n*71
Messer, August Wilhelm, 38–39*n*10
Meyerson, Ignace, 99*n*6
Minkowska, Françoise, 181*n*w
Minkowski, Eugène, 12*n*h, 36–37*n*7, 74–75*n*2, 76*n*8, 95–97*n*2, 106, 107*n*e, 108, 116, 131*n*3, 165–66*n*5, 209–10*n*4, 237–38, 240, 255*n*55, 257*n*72
Monakow, Constantin von, 216–17*n*18
Mounier, Emmanuel, 36–37*n*7
Müldner, Heinrich G., 216*n*17

Nadia (case), 45, 55–56, 76–77*n*10, 262
Napoleon I, 62*n*vv
Natorp, Paul Gerhard, 38–39*n*10, 211–12*n*9
Nietzsche, Friedrich Wilhelm, x–xi, xix, xxiv, xxxiv, xxxvi, xxxviii, xxxix*n*11, xlvi*n*93, xlvii*n*97, xlvii*n*114, 9, 17, 17*n*t, 18*n*u, 37, 47, 233, 254*n*37, 254*n*38, 254*n*39
Nohl, Herman, 63*n*ww

Ombredane, André, 99*n*6, 99–100*n*7, 101*n*11, 228, 251–52*n*10, 256*n*65
Orpheus, 90

Paltrinieri, Luca, 254*n*41
Pavlov, Ivan Petrovič, xix, 234, 237, 242, 254*n*41
Piaget, Jean, 229–30, 252*n*12
Picard, Yvonne, 132–33*n*9

Pichot, Pierre, 99*n*6
Piéron, Henri, 229, 256*n*65
Pinel, Philippe, 236
Pinguet, Maurice, xix, xlii*n*43, 254*n*35
Plato, 188*n*ff, 205
Plessner, Helmuth, 80*n*16
Polin, Raymond, 231
Politzer, Georges, 36–37*n*7, 37*n*9, 165–66*n*5, 171, 235, 254–55*n*45

Rank, Otto, 219–20*n*23
Ribot, Théodule-Armand, 229
Ricoeur, Paul, 12*n*i, 19, 19*n*y, 210–11*n*8, 233
Rilke, Rainer Maria, 54
Rocher, Daniel, 85*n*d
Roggenbau, Christel Heinrich, 45*n*c
Rorschach, Hermann, 76*n*8, 101*n*11, 228, 239, 248, 256*n*65
Rouart, Julien, 33–35*n*3
Rudolf R. (case), 41–42*n*15, 101*n*12, 103, 121–27, 166*n*8, 262
Rümke, Henricus Cornelius, 224, 237, 255*n*50
Rutishauser, Liselotte, 101*n*11, 250, 256*n*58

Sabot, Philippe, xxxviii, xxxix*n*10, xl*n*12, xl*n*13, xl*n*14, xli*n*23, xli*n*24, xli*n*26, l, 236, 251*n*4, 253*n*25
Sade, Donatien Alphonse François de, 184*n*bb
Sartre, Jean-Paul, xiii, xl*n*16, xlvi*n*93, 17, 17*n*s, 36–37*n*7, 37*n*9, 125*n*ee, 165–66*n*5, 169, 169*n*c, 170, 170*n*d, 170*n*e, 171–72, 208–9*n*2, 237–38, 244, 263
Scheid, Karl Friedrich, 223–24*n*28
Scheler, Max, 17, 36–37*n*7, 38–39*n*10, 39–41*n*11, 41*n*12, 80*n*16, 233, 244

Schilder, Paul, 86, 97*n*3
Schneider, Carl, 87, 87*n*i, 88*n*j, 100*n*10
Schneider, Kurt, 45, 45*n*a, 74*n*1, 75*n*4
Schreber, Daniel Paul, 9*n*d, 140
Schwing, Konrad (case), 135, 144, 166*n*8, 262
Shaw, George Bernard, 54
Simon, Gérard, 228, 251*n*6, 256*n*60
Specht, Wilhelm, 39
Spranger, Eduard Franz Ernst, 211–12*n*9
Stewart, Jon, 80*n*15
Storch, Alfred, 41–42*n*15, 103, 114, 114*n*p, 117–18*n*2, 118–19*n*3, 119*n*4, 120, 132*n*8, 262
Strasser, Stephan, 38–39*n*10
Straus, Erwin, 45, 74–75*n*2, 75*n*4, 86, 86*n*e, 88*n*k, 105, 105*n*b, 114*n*o, 119*n*w
Stumpf, Carl, 39, 97*n*4
Szilasi, Wilhelm, 212–13*n*12

Tennyson, Alfred, 54
Theseus, 90
Thévenaz, Pierre, 210–11*n*8
Tosquelles, François, 41–42*n*15, 235
Trân Duc Thao, xi, xxxviii, xxxix*n*9, 233

Uexküll, Jakob von, 73, 80*n*16, 95–97*n*2, 173, 210*n*6
Urban, Suzanne (case), 247, 258*n*96

Valéry, Paul, 68, 69*n*ggg
Van Breda, Herman Leo, 38–39*n*10, 210–11*n*8
Van Gogh, Vincent, 16, 254*n*39
Verdeaux, Georges, xiv, 101*n*11, 228–29, 256*n*65
Verdeaux, Jacqueline, xiv–xvi, 89*n*1, 101*n*11, 228–29, 239, 241–42,
247–48, 250, 251*n*4, 251*n*5, 256*n*65, 258*n*96, 259*n*99, 259*n*100
Veysset, Philippe, 49*n*m
Voss, Lola (case), 80*n*15, 135, 148*n*v, 148–49, 151, 151*n*aa, 151*n*z, 167*n*10, 207–8*n*1, 262
Vuillemin, Jules, 233, 254*n*39

Wahl, Jean, 21*n*aa, 210–11*n*8, 238, 254*n*38
Wallon, Henri, 234, 254–55*n*46, 256*n*65
Weber, Franz (case), 83, 91, 101*n*12, 101–2*n*13, 118–19*n*3, 262
Weber, Max, xxix, 182, 182*n*y
Weizsäcker, Viktor von, xxxix*n*4, 85, 85*n*d, 95–97*n*2, 216*n*17, 247, 258*n*97
Wernicke, Carl, 97–99*n*5
Wertheimer, Max, 97*n*4
West, Ellen (case), xxv, xxvi, xxviii, xxxi, xliii*n*49, 39–41*n*11, 45–47, 46*n*d, 47*n*e, 47*n*f, 47*n*g, 48*n*i, 48*n*h, 48*n*j, 48*n*k, 49*n*l, 49*n*m, 49*n*n, 50, 50*n*p, 50*n*q, 50*n*r, 51*n*s, 51*n*t, 51*n*u, 52*n*v, 52*n*x, 52*n*aa, 52*n*w, 52*n*y, 52*n*z, 53*n*cc, 53*n*dd, 53*n*bb, 53*n*ee, 54*n*ff, 55–56, 58–59, 59*n*pp, 60*n*rr, 60*n*ss, 61, 61*n*tt, 63*n*xx, 63*n*yy, 63*n*zz, 63–65, 64*n*ccc, 64*n*aaa, 64*n*bbb, 67*n*eee, 67–69, 68*n*fff, 69*n*ggg, 71–72, 75*n*5, 76–77*n*10, 79*n*13, 80*n*15, 89, 156*n*ff, 167*n*11, 206*n*yy, 261–62
Woerkom, Willem Van, 86, 99*n*6
Wyrsch, Jakob, 248, 259*n*99

Zünd, Jürg (case), 76–77*n*10, 80*n*15, 119*n*4, 135, 156, 156*n*ii, 156*n*gg, 156*n*hh, 157*n*mm, 157*n*jj, 158*n*oo, 160*n*rr, 161, 161*n*uu, 162*n*vv, 207–8*n*1, 263

GPSR Authorized Representative: Easy Access System Europe, Mustamäe tee 50, 10621 Tallinn, Estonia, gpsr.requests@easproject.com

www.ingramcontent.com/pod-product-compliance
Lightning Source LLC
Chambersburg PA
CBHW022031290426
44109CB00014B/817